Feminist Literacies, 1968–75

Feminist Literacies, 1968–75

KATHRYN THOMS FLANNERY

UNIVERSITY OF ILLINOIS PRESS
Urbana and Chicago

Manufactured in the United States of America
C 5 4 3 2 1

∞ This book is printed on acid-free paper.

Library of Congress Cataloging-in-Publication Data

Flannery, Kathryn T.
Feminist literacies, 1968–75 / Kathryn Thoms Flannery.
p. cm.
Includes bibliographical references and index.
ISBN 0-252-02961-5 (cloth : alk. paper)
1. American literature—Women authors—History and criticism.
2. Feminism and literature—United States—History—20th century.
3. Women—Books and reading—United States—History—20th century. 4. Women and literature—United States—History—20th century. 5. Feminism—United States—History—20th century.
6. Women—United States—Intellectual life. I. Title.
PS228.F45F58 2004
810.9'9287'09046—dc22 2004015291

In memory of my great aunt,
Alvina Thoms, suffragist

Contents

Illustrations

Preface

> The difficulty of learning about the history of women in America is that, for the most part, it is an unwritten history of millions of private lives, whose voices, those that were recorded at all, are scattered and buried.... Women did write novels, essays, poems, magazine articles, but most of these are long out of print, and the task of digging up those old sources is still ahead of us.
>
> —Connie Brown and Jane Seitz, "'You've Come a Long Way, Baby'"

I HAVE BEFORE ME two versions of a flyer containing a list of demands titled "Workshop #13: Politics of Inclusion." One appears to be a draft, written in green ink. The other is a mimeographed sheet with strike-outs, typeovers, and handwritten corrections suggesting that it was hastily made (see figure 1). Neither text by itself reveals much more about the circumstances in which it was produced or the precise purposes to which it was put. Neither identifies an author or authors. Neither is dated. Like other ephemera of the women's movement, these copies just happen to have been saved. Found in a folder with other, mostly raggedly dittoed materials—a program for the New York State Women's Political Caucus, a list of Black Student Action Association demands, a statement on "campus complicity" in the Vietnam War, a schedule of Student Mobilization Committee Strike events, the Ohio Socialist Campaign Committee's statement on women's liberation, and a schedule of Free University workshops for International Women's Day—this flyer can be read as representative of the written work that helped spread social activism in the late sixties and early seventies. In particular, it was part of a remarkable but largely unremarked print explosion that fueled the mid-twentieth-century resurgence of feminism, produced not out of one unified, hierarchical organization but as part of a loose coalition of groups that constituted the highly decentralized and widespread

Workshop # 13
Politics of Inclusion

The women's political caucus will address itself to the problems of all women. We are particularly concerned with the problem of getting people to come and participate.
Most important is to have a relevant program
1. avoid unnecessary rhetoric,
2. know local issues and devise programs to deal with local problems--let people know what you can do for them, and what you can do together
Specific issues to be concerned about include:
Quality education--make sure schools teach the authentic history of the American peoples and recognize and expose the roots of white racism
Support and participate in the Children's March for Survival on March 24 and 25. Contact your local Welfare Rights for further info.
Women should be guarenteed the right of self determination and economically sustained to implement this goal.
We oppose the Nixon-Mills HR I plan for so called Welfare Reform as a measure that violates women's right to self determination.
We will support all women, this includes Gay Women, the Aged, Women in Prison, Single Parents, ethnic groups, the young, ALL WOMEN
Woman will no longer accept anyone else's definition of thier self value and the value of their work
The women's causus must address itself to the working poor--to recognize their commonality with other oppressed people
We must work for economic justice for all.
We shall educate ourselves and others to the fact that we all are dependent on the governments assistance in some way and therefore, are all, in effect on welfare.
3. Use neighborhood communications--contact organziations such as the Golden Agers, Welfare Rights, NAACP, grass roots poverty organizations. Organize voter registration, use the media--multi language radio, underground papers, people's papers--go knocking door to door and talk and listen.
4. The structure of the caucus must allow all women to speak for themselves.
5. Eliminate economic barriers to membership. There should be no membership dues. Each should contribute according to her means. Provide funds for low income women to attend meetings, provide transportation.
6. Recognize the mechanics--the system and tactics that keep us all divided and that encourage oppressed people to fight each other

SOCIETY SHOULD TAKE CARE OF US BECAUSE WE ARE SOCIETY

Figure 1. Workshop 13 Flyer: Politics of Inclusion, 1973 New York Women's Political Caucus (*source:* author's collection).

women's movement. Much of this material is of the moment, produced for a particular occasion, intended to incite others to action, and much of it was collectively composed.

What can such materials tell us? In what sense is such a document as the workshop 13 flyer readable? Coming to the flyer cold, without the other papers in the folder, we might well be at a loss. The title, "women's political caucus," appears in the first line but is not capitalized, as if it does not signal a specific organizational entity. We might do some digging and learn about the 1971 Nixon-Mills Welfare Reform bill or the 1972 Children's March for Survival, organized to protest cuts in welfare benefits effected by the Nixon-Mills bill (both events mentioned in the flyer), but beyond that, we would be hard-pressed to make much headway with this document. With the Women's Political Caucus Program (see figure 2) to provide some greater sense of the historical and rhetorical context, however, we can begin to make some headway, but there are still a number of pitfalls.

The three women listed on the program for workshop 13 did not compose the flyer. They were conveners who served as resources for the workshop participants. It was the members of the anonymous workshop who did the talking and writing that produced the flyer. I cannot say that they "earn[ed] rhetorical authority by... stating explicitly their identities, positions or locations," to use Nedra Reynolds's formulation of a distinctly feminist rhetoric (330), nor is it clear what might be their "personal" or "individual" relationships to the political assertions that make up the bulk of the flyer. What is their investment in the issues they raise? Who is this "we"? The piece of paper does not speak its own context, any more than any piece of writing can. In fact the anonymous text is not so unlike a text with an author's name attached: no text is ever readable independent of a complex rhetorical matrix, either in terms of the context from which it was produced or those from which it is read, nor is its meaning simply determined (or limited to) its contexts of production and reception or appropriation. The author's name itself signals an outside, a body that stands prior to the written text, carrying with it a history that is more or less available to us as readers, however explicitly the writer names herself. Like much of the ephemera of activism, this flyer assumes an immediacy of context, presuming a close proximity between the bodies that made it and the bodies that received it. In this case, the flyer was read to an assembled plenary session, with television cameras rolling. While a written text, it nonetheless worked initially—for its first audience—as oratory, and the body of the woman who read the flyer to the assembled caucus served in new york state WOMEN'S POLITICAL CAUCUS

PROGRAM

March 4, 1972

Saturday

8:00 A.M. - 10:00 A.M. Registration — Lobby

10:00 A.M. Plenary Session — Lower Lobby

Welcome: Linda Lamel - Conference Coordinator

Greetings: Constance Cook - New York State Assemblywoman (R-125 A.D.)

Speakers: Liz Carpenter - former Press Secretary and Special Assistant to Mrs. Lyndon Johnson

Barbara G. Kilberg - Former member President Nixon's White House Staff; Member, Board of Directors, Common Cause

Laurie Beers - Co-chairwoman, National Youth Caucus

Jonnie Jones - Coordinating Committee, Manhatten Women's Political Caucus

Amy Betanzos - New York City Commissioner of Housing Relocation

Barbara Smith - Coordinator, Saratoga County Women's Political Caucus

12:30 P.M. Box Lunch — Lobby

1:30 - 5:30 Workshops -

1. State Structure — Starlight Room
   Evaluation of proposals for temporary state structure
   Resource people:
   Anne Cohan - Co-chairwoman, State Structure committee
   Joyce Ahrens - Co-chairwoman, State Structure committee
   Ronnie Feit - National Policy Council, National Woman's Political Caucus; member, State Structure committee
2. Priorities — Lower Level #4
   Formulation of goals and political targets for New York State Women's Political Caucus
   Resource people:
   Representatives from local caucuses
3. Party Rules and Their Reform — Room 331
   The rules by which the parties operate and how they should be changed so that they no longer systematically exclude women from decision-making
   Resource people:
   Nancy Dubner - member, Democratic State Committee (Rochester)
   Sarah Liebshutz - Professor, Political Science, S.U.N.Y. Brockport
4. Delegate Selection and National Party Conventions — Lower Level #3A
   How are delegates to the national conventions chosen; how to become a candidate for delegate; what role you can play at the convention

Figure 2. 1973 New York State Women's Political Caucus Program (*source:* author's collection).

Resource people:
Jane Selman - Former Democratic candidate, Monroe County Legislature
Jo Lombardo - Prominent Monroe County Republican
Danielle Sandow - Delegate Selection Committee, Manhatten Women's Political Caucus
Tanya Melich - member of national board, Ripon Society; political writer
Brenda Fasteau

√ 5. Techniques of Local Organizing — Lower Level #1
How to begin a caucus and build it as a broadly based multi-partisan group
Resource people:
Cathy Samuels - Coordinating committee, Manhatten Women's Political Caucus
Joyce Svilokos - Erie County Women's Political Caucus
Barbara Smith - Saratoga County Women's Political Caucus
Crystal Hegarty - Assistant Secretary, Metropolitan Club; Co-campaign manager for Peter Sprague

6. Campaigning — Lower Level #3B
How to win!
Resource people:
Mary Anne Krupsak - New York State Assemblywoman (D-104 A.D.)
Sherry Carr - Assistant to Assemblywoman Cook

7. Political Fund-Raising — Room 204
Political action costs money. Can you pay the bills?
Resource people:
Ellie Guggenheimer - Day care organizer
Mary Jean Tully - Chairwoman, conference fund-raising committee, New York State Women's Political Caucus
Lee Gochburg - Chairwoman, Junior Division, Women's National Republican Club

8. Party Structure — Room 304
Structure of political parties, how they function and how to operate within them
Resource people:
~~Mary Ann Knauss~~ Jo Lombardo - Executive Assistant to Republican State Chairman
Ronnie Eldridge - former special assistant to Mayor, New York City; national campaign coordinator of major presidential candidate

9. Local Action Programs — Room 547
Activities such as electoral analysis, voter registration, delegate selection, watchdog committees, candidates search and recruitment, local elections

Resource people:
Esther Lewis - former chairwoman, Legislative Action Committee, New York State League of Women Voters
Judith Glazer - Director of Special Projects, S.U.N.Y. Purchase; President of Board of Education, Rye
Yolanda Quitman - founder of Pulse of Women (P.O.W.)

10. Public Relations — Room 549
Image-building and use of the media
Resource people:
Letty Pogrebin - Editor of Ms magazine; former publicist for major publishing firm
Ellen Lochoya - Public relations director for successful candidate for Albany County District Attorney

11. Candidates — Room 548
How to become a candidate and who should be one
Resource people:
Karen Burstein - former Democratic candidate for 4th Congressional district
Janice Dooley - former Democratic candidate for Albany County Legislature
Liz Lynch - former candidate Schenectady County Board
Mary Ella Reutershan - former candidate East Hampton town board; Legislative Chairwoman, American Association of University Women

12. Analyzing Incumbents — Room 546
Finding the weak ones: what information to get, where to get it and how to use it
Resource people:
Joanna Banthin-Stelzer - Political scientist
Cornelia Netter - Planning associate, New York State Office of Planning Services; paid campaign organiser and manager
Linda Davidoff - Urban planner; Author, The Suburbs Must Open Their Gates

13. The Politics of Inclusion — Lower Level #2
How to reach the unaffiliated, the poor, the aged, the young, the minority women and why it is essential to do so
Resource people:
Althea Simmons - Secretary for Training, National Association for the Advancement of Colored People
Irma Santaella - Eastern Regional Chairwoman National Caucus of Spanish Speaking Women
Jeanette Washington - Welfare Mothers Organizer

6:45 P.M.	Buffet Dinner	Lobby and Starlight Room
8:00 P.M.	Plenary Session Speaker: Bella Abzug - Congresswoman (D-19th Congressional District) Some Workshop reports if ready	Lower Level
9:30 P.M.	County Caucus Meetings	(Rooms to be announced)

<u>Sunday</u>

9:00 A.M.	Plenary Session Greetings: Mary Anne Krupsak - New York State Assemblywoman (D-104 A.D.) Speaker: Betty Friedan - Founder of National Organization for Women (N.O.W.); Convener, National Women's Political Caucus	Lower Level
10:00 A.M.	Resolutions and Voting	Lower Level
11:30 A.M.	Nominations and Elections	Lower Level
12:00 Noon	Box Lunch	Lobby
1:30 P.M.	Election Results, Remaining Workshop Reports, Wrap-up	Lower Level

Helaine Waldman
Box 159 Indian Quad
SUNY Albany
Albany NY
12222

complex ways as guarantor of a certain kind of seriousness, physically investing the text with an authority the words themselves do not command.[1]

But how do I know that, and what kind of authority can I claim to support my reading of this document? On the one hand, I was there. I was a participant in workshop 13. Like much activist print production, this flyer exists because ordinary people like me saved such materials—sometimes donating them to college libraries, sometimes packing them away in files. But the experiential knowledge for which the flyer serves as mnemonic prompt—powerful as it is for me—is not by itself sufficient. Judith Roof and Robyn Wiegman reflect on this kind of authority in useful ways:

> If authority is claimed on the basis of personal experience, then authority becomes a matter of interpreting one's life, often without reference to the assumptions, beliefs, or methods by which that interpretation is accomplished. When personal experience is the basis for critical knowledge, such knowledge may be premised on a fairly unexamined opinion, whose rhetorical force comes from its appeal to the "authentic." When opinion claims to be unassailable because it is based on experience, authority becomes tautological—it *is* because I say it is and who are you to question my life? (93)

I can claim a certain kind of authority to write about the workshop flyer based on personal experience, but I am also at more than thirty-years remove from that time and place. I have ways of making sense of that event now that I did not have available to me then, and yet of course I cannot reproduce the moment as lived nor can I speak for all those other participants. Here in capsule is the paradoxical rhetorical move that Adrienne Rich identifies in her essay "Notes toward a Politics of Location": as the writer delimits her range of vision to make clear that she cannot speak for everyone, for all time, and across all difference, she at the same time claims to speak out of a particular body, place, and historical and cultural moment. The very limitation of vision is offered as a kind of authorizing. Thus, I announce—as *caveat emptor*—that I have special and necessarily limited experiential knowledge in order to claim authority to speak, knowing that the authority is at best provisional and that my experiential knowledge cannot by itself be sufficient. But while I have to bring other knowledges to bear in order to frame my experience for purposes of critical analysis, I also have to keep those knowledges in some degree of critical tension with the lived experience.[2]

I participated in the caucus as part of a Welfare Rights delegation from the western part of upstate New York. Welfare Rights organizations were grassroots efforts aimed at radically transforming the welfare system. The heavily bureaucratized welfare system seemed designed to punish recipients for their poverty rather than to enable individuals and families to maintain a sense of human dignity as they worked to become self-supporting. I was a VISTA volunteer working for a migrant housing project in the "stoop fruit"–producing mucklands of New York.[3] Part of my role was to serve as advocate for clients of the welfare system, primarily migrant workers, and to witness as they negotiated the complicated welfare bureaucracy or tried to ensure that the public schools provided a decent education for their children. Most of the migrant workers were African Americans in the Florida to New York "stream"—picking citrus in Florida and tomatoes, onions, cabbages, and other fruits and vegetables in New York. The local Welfare Rights organizer had asked me to drive a group of local women to attend the caucus in Albany. The organizer, a white woman who was not a migrant worker but who had grown up in the area, was herself on welfare, living with her nine children in a house without running water or indoor plumbing. She would now be categorized as part of the invisible rural poor, but she was hardly invisible. She was instead a vibrant part of a local antipoverty network. Once in Albany, we met with women from around the state, most of whom were representing other Welfare Rights groups. I served as recorder for the workshop and helped put in final form the report to the plenary session.

I have kept a file from the caucus, with various flyers, a bibliography on voting and political involvement, a list of pending legislation concerning women's issues, an outline of the steps for becoming a committeewoman (for whatever political party), and the like. In addition, the folder includes a set of notes from the Inclusion Workshop, the minutes and the drafts of the workshop report, and the mimeographed flyer distributed in the plenary session. Although the participants in workshop 13 were a racially and ethnically diverse group, I was the only middle-class, college-educated white woman. I thus occupied a position just this side of male: presumably I could know more than a man could know about "women's experience," but I couldn't know from the inside what it means to be a poor woman on welfare with limited access to schooling and jobs. My role as recorder may have made it easier on some level for other participants to teach me what I could not know firsthand: they could direct their comments to me, facing me with criticisms of the class and racial bias of the larger political caucus organization, to make sure I *got it* in the sense of getting it down on paper but also hoping I *got it* on a deeper level. I was an individual who happened to be recorder, but I also felt myself to be both a surrogate for that group of prominent women—the headliners—who had organized us into an "inclusion" workshop and thus relegated us to last place on the conference's printed program and at the same time a member of the group, a comrade, one of the included others. An African American woman volunteered to chair the meeting. Much of the final language of the plenary flyer is hers, and it was her body that rose at the end of the conference, her voice that gave eloquent force to the words.

I did not know then that our positioning in the caucus program had resulted from conflicts among the leadership. I do remember that we were struck by it, as if this were some warped version of the Sleeping Beauty story—that, like the excluded fairy godmother, we would end up causing the caucus more trouble than they had bargained for. We knew on some level that we were tokens, but we were nonetheless going to make the most of the opportunity—to make it difficult for the leadership to simply use us for political window dressing. Collective anonymity was the position we had been assigned, but it was also importantly the position that we reclaimed by asserting that—in the language of item 2 on the flyer—"Women will no longer accept anyone else's definition of thier [*sic*] self value and the value of their work." It was not for others to name us. We were the nameless rank and file in defiant contrast to the headliners. With historical hindsight, I can see that we represented one of the fault lines along which women in the movement divided, but at the time it seemed patently obvious that any movement of women had to include all women.

The National Women's Political Caucus (NWPC) was formed in 1971 by a coalition of some 200 women including Bella Abzug, Shirley Chisholm, Betty Friedan, Patsy Minsk, and Gloria Steinem (Hole and Levine 426–27). They sought to increase the numbers of women and sympathetic men participating in the electoral process at all levels. The earliest meetings, held at various sites around the country, attracted a wide range of groups from religious organizations, the League of Women Voters, and various business and professional organizations for women, as well as trade unions, Welfare Rights groups, and a range of feminist organizations (Carden 139). But from the earliest discussions, a split opened up between those who wanted to focus exclusively on women's issues defined so narrowly as to exclude questions about welfare, abortion, sexual orientation, or racism (most prominently this was Friedan's position) and those—particularly Abzug, Chisholm, and Steinem—who urged a broader understanding of feminism and warned that the caucus could easily become simply a haven for the white middle class (Heilbrun 214; see also DuPlessis and Snitow 16). In part because of this split, radical women's liberation groups distanced themselves from the NWPC, and what little radical feminist press coverage there was tended to be negative.[4]

The 1972 meeting of the New York State Women's Political Caucus attempted to address the ideological split by including—ironically and tellingly—as its thirteenth of thirteen concurrent workshops a session titled the "Politics of Inclusion." According to the printed program, the workshop was supposed to consider how the caucus could "reach the unaffiliated, the poor, the aged, the young, the minority women." A representative from the NAACP, a National Welfare Rights organizer, and the chairwoman of the National Caucus of Spanish-Speaking Women served as the conveners and resource people for this session. Of the almost 150 conveners listed for the caucus, including nationally known figures such as Shirley Chisholm (who had just declared her candidacy for president of the United States, the first African American woman to do so), most but certainly not all represented relatively mainstream political, religious, and educational organizations (see the appendix). However wise any of these women were as individuals, in the context of the caucus they made too evident the organization's sense of priorities in relegating primarily poor and minority women to the last workshop, as if it had been an afterthought. Even though the sessions ran concurrently, and thus no session was temporally last, the women who participated in this so-called inclusion workshop understood that they were last and least.

But that is not the whole of the story. As Kathleen Weiler has argued, "people will use the means at hand, the power that they can employ to meet their needs and assert their humanity" (51). To look below or behind the caucus's apparent sidelining of difference requires that we consider how the workshop participants—knowing full well their positioning in this rhetorical context—nonetheless made use of rhetorical resources at hand. In discussing what she calls "fractured identities," Donna Haraway notes that among those who have asserted their historical identity as women of color in the American context, "this identity marks out a self-consciously constructed space that cannot affirm a capacity to act on the basis of natural identification, but only on the basis of conscious coalition, of affinity, of political kinship" (198). The flyer's we-saying suggests not a claim to unity that erases difference but something like the coalition-building that Haraway describes, one based not on "natural identification" but on claims to political kinship. Gay women, the aged, women in prison, single parents, ethnic groups, the young, and the working poor are all named as such in the flyer and in that sense given symbolic space in the workings of the caucus. We workshop participants were thus standing in the stead of such women even when we were not literally so representative. In standing for such a coalition, the workshop members were also pointing out the literal absence of this coalitional array within the caucus at large.

We were, in other words, making the absence visibly present. The coalition across difference, however, did not yet exist except on the page as the assertion of the collective authors' coalitional vision. The positionality of the individual authors is not stated explicitly, nor is the literal collective membership of the workshop; rather, the flyer projects a possibility for the assembled body of women. I want to call this an ethical and political projection. By not explicitly identifying the writers, the flyer attempts to create the occasion for the building of a coalitional "we." The we-saying is thus doubly valenced, offering ideal and critique at once. If the leadership wanted to include more women in the political process—to use for political purposes the women of workshop 13 and those they stood in for—they were going to have to consider the "mechanics—the system and tactics that keep women divided and that encourage oppressed people to fight each other," as the flyer urges. In a sense, the flyer's ethical appeal rests on the need for mainstream members of the caucus to join in coalition with an imagined and projected "we" (rather than the "we" they assumed as the default white, middle-class "we"), to locate themselves as part of a coalitional "we" in order to realize it, to make it real—not to speak for others, not to do all the talking, but to listen, to learn, and to educate themselves to a sense of political kinship across difference. As Adrienne Rich puts it, they had to imagine: "We who are not the same. We who are many and do not want to be the same" ("Notes" 225). To do this the authors of the flyer consciously chose not to identify themselves as separate individuals but to use the power and authority of a textual, choral anonymity. In this context, the workshop participants' rhetorical choice strikes me as the exercise of politically responsible authority. This ethos is projected as a possibility, as a challenge to the taken for granted.

In returning to this particular moment, I am naming the methodological challenge of this book and in a sense the beginning of the end for the historical period that I mark as subject of my inquiry. This book rereads a brief period of remarkable social volatility not as memoir but as what Houston Baker Jr. calls an act of "critical memory." To recover some fuller understanding of the literacy practices and pedagogies of the women's movement requires reading such fragments of movement activism in relation to a complex sociopolitical milieu. I am thus interested in returning to the early years of feminism's midcentury resurgence in order to understand how "women maneuver[ed] and to make their strategies visible and available to us now not as simple models but as a way to reflect critically on our work as teachers and scholars" (Friedman 32).

* * *

In 1970 I was part of a lucky group who enrolled in Alison Jaggar's course on the philosophy of women's rights, probably the first of its kind in the country. I had no plans then to teach in a university and could not have foreseen that I would return to the materials from that course to help me think through my place in the academy. But in fact those impressive materials served as a starting place for this project, and I thank Professor Jaggar for permission to use them. Many friends and colleagues have given me invaluable support along the way, asking me good questions, pointing me to resources, and joining in the kind of conversation that makes such work a great pleasure. Early on in the project, Allison Berg, Katy Borland, Caroline LeGuin, and Lori Robison raised for me anew the question of the relationship between teaching and feminism. More recently Rona Kaufman and Jennifer Sinor, two elegant writers, gave me ways of looking again with fresh eyes at the feminist conjoining of the personal with the political as a radical act of literacy. The poets Sarah Rothenberg, Lynn Wagner, and Stacey Waite enriched my understanding of the continuities between feminist underground poetry and contemporary poetic practice. Susan Andrade, Paul Bové, Brenda Glascott, Nancy Glazener, Jonathan Arac, Jaime Harker, Paul Kameen, Maggie Rehm, and Robyn Wiegman have each extended my thinking in invaluable ways. Dave Bartholomae, Jim Seitz, and Mariolina Salvatori have helped ensure an intellectually vital place in which to work. Sandra Kriz helped with research early on in the project. Special Collections librarian Mark Chaffee of the University of Michigan was a generous guide as I spent a year immersed in the Labadie Collection, a year that would not have been possible if it had not been for Anne Gere's fortuitous invitation to teach at Ann Arbor for a semester. Most generously, Marianne Novy loaned me her wonderful cache of periodicals and pamphlets from the early seventies, and she read and commented on an early draft of the manuscript. With Laurie Matheson of the University of Illinois Press, the manuscript has been in very good hands, and I am most fortunate in having had the careful advice of Jacqueline Royster and

Patrice McDermott, who served as readers for the manuscript. Not last, but first, this project would never have happened without Jim Flannery, whose patience, sanity, and deep sense of justice are at the heart of it all.

* * *

The author gratefully acknowledges permission to use the following material in this book:

"Cranky on Wheels" and "Africa in Chains." Reprinted by permission of Henry Lesnick.

Cover design by Joanna Vogelsang for *off our backs* 2, no. 2 (Oct. 1971). Reprinted by permission of *off our backs* and the University of Michigan Special Collections.

An earlier version of the preface appeared in *Professing Rhetoric: Selected Papers from the 2000 Rhetoric Society of America Conference,* edited by Frederick J. Antczak et al. An earlier version of chapter 2 appeared in *Rhetoric Review* 20 (Spring 2001). Both reprinted by permission of Lawrence Erlbaum Associates, Inc.

Every effort has been made to locate artists whose work is reproduced here. The author will appreciate any information that will help locate artists who are credited here.

Feminist Literacies, 1968–75

Introduction:
"Millions of Pockets of Insurrection"

> The fundamental object of history that aims at recognizing the way social actors make sense of their practices and their discourse seems to me to reside in the tension between the inventive capacities of individuals or communities and the constraints, norms, and conventions that limit... what it is possible for them to think, say, and do.
>
> —Roger Chartier, *On the Edge of the Cliff*

SUSAN STANFORD FRIEDMAN SUGGESTS, perhaps a bit wryly, that "Eve's desire for knowledge prefigures the drive for literacy, for access to books and education, that runs as a powerful current through the long history of intellectual women, as well as of women who struggle for the basics of literacy" (31–32). In contemporary and retrospective accounts of the women's movement of the late sixties and early seventies, however, relatively little has been said about literacy practices. Rather, the emphasis has more commonly been placed on women's interactions with one another, especially on the phenomenon Alice Echols terms "an ecstasy of discussion" ("Nothing Distant" 151). Certainly women were learning together face to face, drawing on their collective experiences to educate themselves. A fundamental tenet of women's liberation was that women had to learn to rely on one another because, it was argued, much that had been written was written by men for men, even when it was written ostensibly about or for women. Most visual images from the period reinforce the sense of women interacting face to face: women clustered together indoors, in intense conversation; women on outdoor platforms leaning forward to speak into microphones; women marching, arms raised, carrying banners. Like the images of suffragists before them, these are powerful pictures not of passive female bodies but of women full-voiced and mobilized.

Few of these images, however, portray women engaged in writing, reading, creating artwork or illustrating copy, running printing presses, or distributing print materials. Nevertheless, the material traces of such literate production—the very texts that surround the drawings and photographs of active women in movement periodicals and the often anonymous ephemera of movement organizing, such as free-university materials, theater scripts, leaflets, and reprints—make clear that women were indeed engaged in literate production on a remarkable scale. How then to account for the forgetting that leaves such production out of the narratives that chronicle the movement? Friedman argues that "subaltern people often produce histories that are ephemeral—in oral form, undocumented, unpreserved, difficult to locate, or hard for an 'outsider' to interpret" (19). The irony here seems to be that women, subaltern or otherwise, were writing themselves into the public sphere but forgetting their own acts of literacy along the way. This is in rather striking contrast to narratives of other liberation movements in which literacy has figured centrally. One might think, for example, of Frederick Douglass's account of learning first the ABCs and then words of three or four letters. When the slave master finds out that his wife has been instructing the slave, he forbids further instruction, warning that reading will surely spoil the slave, making him "forever unfit" (57). These words, Douglass recalls, "sank deep into my heart" and "stirred up sentiments within that lay slumbering" (57). He could now see that the white man's power to enslave the black man hinged on withholding literacy. "From that moment," Douglass declares, "I understood the pathway from slavery to freedom." Finding himself without a teacher, he thus committed himself to learning how to read. As David Blight has observed, the rhetoric of Douglass's narrative draws powerfully on Enlightenment notions of reason and a concomitant belief that literacy is the sign and substance of reason: "To be judged truly human and a citizen with social and political recognition, . . . a person had to achieve literacy" (4). "For better or worse," Blight adds, "civilization itself was equated with cultures that could *write* their history" (4). In these terms, literacy as the sign of reason and therefore of humanity is a refusal of slavery's cruel rationalization, for how can it be morally justifiable to enslave a fellow literate, and therefore rational, human being?

Unlike such narratives, which acknowledge the power of literacy as central to liberatory or revolutionary effort, retrospective accounts of midcentury feminism tend to discount literacy's role in the movement. Could women in an age of near-universal literacy still claim it to be a pathway to freedom, and if so, what sort of freedom? Some movement participants expressed considerable ambivalence about the role of literacy in women's lives because they recognized that it comprises not simply a benign set of skills but also culturally loaded practices that had operated historically as class marker, sign of patriarchal power, or a means to exercise hierarchical authority. At the same time, feminists were engaged in activities to increase women's access to the means of literate production and in the process reconceptualizing what literacy could be or do in feminist terms. But the recognition that literacy was somehow tainted often led to a refusal to notice how implicated movement women—and not just the media stars or headliners—were in practices they saw as inevitably compromised. The uneasiness created by the recognition of a tainted literacy was reinforced by a culturally widespread romanticism that placed greatest value on the spontaneous, the present, the immediate. The spoken word was perceived by some to be more present than the written word and thus more authentic and real.[1] At the center of consciousness raising—the educative process that helped to swell the ranks of the women's movement—is the immediacy of women speaking to women.[2] "Recalling and sharing our bitter experiences," as Kathie Sarachild put it, women learned to speak out loud and ideally to listen to other women speaking ("A Program" 79). Although consciousness raising was conceptualized to involve more than speaking, as I will discuss more fully in chapter 5, and many women in the movement expressed frustration when the process went no further than talk, women's sharing experiences orally and in person nonetheless has come to stand—sometimes as caricature, sometimes reverentially—as the prototypical process of the women's liberation movement as a whole. Left unexamined, this uneasy combination of a romantic embrace of the oral and a historically grounded distrust of literacy serves as a limiting origin for feminist praxis. Many feminists continue to identify consciousness raising as the core of feminist teaching, but assuming personal, face-to-face conversation among women as the originary pedagogical practice has tended to short-circuit a fuller discussion of what pedagogies have been engaged in by feminists and what pedagogies might be more fully consistent with feminism (see Kenway and Modra 150–56). As powerful as consciousness raising was for many women, it should be read as one practice among many—in particular, as an orality not disconnected from literacy but deriving part of its force from its relation to dominant and alternative literacy practices. But literacy, too, should be read in fuller terms, as a complex of social practices not delimited by formal schooling.

Commenting on "contemporary feminist movement,"[3] bell hooks observes that because many feminists are college-educated, we may take for granted our educational status and privilege and presume that such status and privilege are common to women more generally. She suggests that such an assumption may account for the movement's historical failure "to make education, especially basic literacy, a feminist agenda" ("Educating Women" 107). Despite efforts to end sexism in education, hooks contends that feminists "have not explored deeply the connection between sexist exploitation of women in this society and the degree of women's education" (ibid.). In "Black Women: Shaping Feminist Theory" and "Educating Women: A Feminist Agenda," hooks traces a path from the resurgence of feminism in the late sixties and early seventies to the present to suggest the complexity of this apparent neglect. There was a moment, hooks recalls, early in the movement when women tried to fight the isolation that separated them along class and color lines.[4] She cites several anthologies from the early seventies—*Liberation Now, Women's Liberation: Blueprint for the Future, Class and Feminism, Radical Feminism,* and *Sisterhood is Powerful*—all of which include articles "that attempted to address a wide audience of women, an audience that was not exclusively white, middle class, college-educated, and adult" ("Black Women" 6). As hooks reads these early years of the movement, the desire to create through print spaces for contact among a broad range of movement women eroded as "more and more women acquired prestige, fame, or money from feminist writings or from gains from feminist movement for equality in the workforce" (ibid. 7).[5]

Importantly, however, the problem has not been with print or literacy per se. Rather, as hooks sees it, feminists have failed to stress programs that would enable "all women to learn reading and writing," not simply as mechanical skills, but so that they would be able to critically engage with the ideas increasingly available only in print ("Educating Women" 108). Charlotte Bunch had earlier observed that "people who do not see reading and writing as basic are usually those who can take them for granted," and she too urges education in critical literacy ("Feminism and Education" 15–16, 18n5). Both hooks and Bunch contend that taking literacy for granted and failing to develop critical pedagogy have isolated feminist theorists from a larger public. Citing Paolo Freire's concept of a politically conscious literacy education, each defines an education in "basic literacy" as necessarily an education in critical consciousness.[6]

Although both hooks and Bunch criticize the class blindness of many highly literate women in the movement, neither argues that feminists should abandon print and rely exclusively on face-to-face contact. Indeed, both worry that the other side of a class blindness that takes literacy for granted is an anti-intellectualism that sees literacy as inevitably tainted and resists anything that seems abstract or analytical. In what might be called a Gramscian turn, Bunch observes that "our society... trains only a few people to think [systematically], mostly those from the classes it expects to control the social order." Historically women have not been expected to take control and, "in consequence, are not encouraged to think analytically" ("Feminism and Education" 14; see also Gramsci). She finds that many women thus expect theory to be arcane, having little to do with daily life. While they "regard something as properly theoretical only if it is very abstract," at the same time, they want all theory to be made easy ("Feminism and Education" 14–15). Similarly, hooks contends that "as a group, women have been denied (via sex, race, and class exploitation and oppression) the right and privilege to develop intellectually." Having limited access to "modes of thought that promote the kind of critical and analytical understanding necessary for liberation struggle," women are understandably insecure in academic contexts where they have to handle "new ideas and information." It is not surprising that some women therefore would discount the importance to their lives of new, complex ideas, ideas that are referred to in a kind of reifying shorthand as Theory ("Feminist Theory" 113).

Both Bunch and hooks argue for the importance of a literacy education that would work against the elitism and the anti-intellectualism that they believe converged to weaken the movement. Such an education would require, as hooks sees it, breaking down the false divide between theory and practice ("Feminist Theory" 112). If feminism "is not an unengaged study of women" (Bunch, "Feminism and Education" 8) but has "from the onset... struggled to unite theory and practice, to create a liberatory feminist praxis" (hooks, "Feminist Theory" 112), it would be well for us to look for sites where such struggle has taken place. To do so, I have chosen to consider literacy practices outside the classroom, on the edge of the university, and on the verge between the academy and the larger community, taking my cue from Adrienne Rich's 1975 essay "Toward a Woman-Centered University." Rich recognized the exciting resurgence of intellectual work among ordinary women that she saw all around her as a feminist renaissance. In an effort to rewrite history, women were "questioning and reexploring the past" and in the process "demanding a humanization of intellectual interests and public measures in the present" (126). While one might expect that much of this intellectual work was taking place within universities, Rich asserts that far more was taking place outside the academy in "unofficial, self-created groups" (126). She names this phenomenon the "women's university-without-walls": "It could be said that a women's university-without-walls exists already in America, in the shape of women reading and writing with a new purposefulness, and [in] the growth of feminist bookstores, presses, bibliographic services, women's centers, medical clinics, libraries, art galleries, and workshops, all with a truly educational mission" (126).

Rich saw in this loosely connected network of pedagogical spaces the potential to put pressure on the traditional university. Although universities had "gradually and reluctantly" admitted women, the system of higher education was structured to simply absorb their presence by using "exceptional women" to justify the status quo and thus blunt the possibilities for change. "It would be naive," Rich contends, "to imagine that the university can of itself be a vanguard for change" ("Toward a Woman-Centered University" 127). Rather, it is "probable that the unrecognized, unofficial university-without-walls . . . will prove a far more important agent in reshaping the foundations on which human life is now organized" (127). Rich does not discount the value of the university altogether: it can be a place where "people find each other and begin to hear each other," and it can be the source of "certain kinds of power" (127). But for it to be more than that, Rich urged that women in universities had to work to shift the "center of gravity," to make universities places where women could re-create themselves after "centuries of intellectual and spiritual blockading" (128). To do so, they would have to learn from the women working outside or on the edge of the university.

It is perhaps difficult now to imagine a time when so many women would see the need to undertake the difficult task of creating alternative structures and organizations. Despite what appears in hindsight as a period of unprecedented progress in civil rights for minorities and women, many feminists (like other political and countercultural groups of the sixties) found it necessary to develop separate organizations to better meet their needs and to provide space for creating and sharing ideas (Peck xiv; Kessler 74). Although the 1964 Civil Rights Act was not initially intended to address gender inequity—Congress had "held no hearings and . . . issued no reports on gender discrimination"—"sex" had nonetheless been added as a House amendment at the last minute, perhaps as a way to derail the whole bill (Farber, *Age* 246, 96–97). With the addition treated as a joke by some legislators, still others feared that including sex as one of the protected categories would dilute efforts on behalf of minorities. Just as the 1964 Civil Rights Act did not end racial discrimination, however, neither did it end gender discrimination. It would require the efforts of women (and sympathetic men) across the country, working in loose coalition on multiple fronts, to radically alter not only their status but their material lives. Women worked to gain greater access to education, job training, adequate health care, and reliable child care. They sought to secure their reproductive rights, as well as protection against domestic violence and harassment, as a matter not only of law but of societal expectation. They sought to change how—and by whom—women were portrayed in the media, in advertisements, in the arts, and in medicine. They challenged traditional understandings of female sexuality and dominant heterosexism. They began the process of rediscovering a forgotten history. Although the women's movement did not constitute a unified ideology and women did not agree about how best to go about effecting change, they did agree, in remarkable numbers, that change was needed.

When the first identifiably separate feminist newspapers appeared in 1968, the United States was in the midst of relative economic prosperity fueled in part by the Vietnam War. Like environmentalism and gay liberation, the women's movement gained momentum in the next decade, surviving the economic downturn of the early seventies (Anderson, *Sixties* 208). The nation had seen its Gross National Product increase by 93 percent in the course of the sixties. Unemployment had steadily decreased from a high of 6.7 percent in 1961 to a low of 3.5 percent in 1969. The minimum hourly wage had risen in constant (1996) dollars from $5.30 at the beginning of the decade to $7.21 in 1968 (Farber and Bailey 359). Such relative plenty encouraged a sense that the United States had the means to ensure equal opportunity for all and that only misplaced priorities, a lack of political will, a failure of social conscience, or even a conspiracy among those in power could explain why we had not followed through on the great promise. The 1964 Civil Rights Act had made it a federal crime to use race, color, creed, national origin, or sex as a basis for discriminating against anyone on the job or in places of public accommodation. Nevertheless, it became increasingly clear to a growing number of women and men that changing the law would not be enough to change the "system," namely, the conglomeration of corporate, military, religious, governmental, and educational interests that had a vested interest in maintaining the status quo.

Throughout the first half of the twentieth century, women had been entering the workforce in increasing numbers. David Farber has calculated that "between 1940 and 1960 the proportion of married women who had jobs [outside the home] doubled, from 15 percent to 30 percent," and that by "1960 about 38 percent of women were wage earners" (*Age* 243–44). The growing female labor force included mothers with small children, suburban housewives, working-class women, urban working poor, and the largely invisible rural poor, as well as a still small number of professional women. In 1960, however, a woman—whatever her line of work—could expect to earn only about 60 percent of what a man was likely to earn performing the same tasks (ibid., 244; the figure reflects median earnings). Although the 1963 Equal Pay Act made it generally illegal to pay women less than men for the same job, as David Farber argues, the bill had relatively little effect because employers commonly gave different titles to male workers and female workers performing the same tasks: "Segregation by sex, not unequal wages for identical jobs, was at the root of women's pay problems" (ibid., 245). Throughout the sixties and seventies women continued to earn sixty cents or less for every dollar that men earned, and the situation did not improve until 1982. In fact, women have not yet achieved wage parity: in 2001 women earned only 76.3 percent of what men earned (in terms of median earnings of full-time adult workers)—and that percentage holds whatever a woman's educational attainment (U.S. Census, table P-24). As I will discuss in chapter 2, the disparities were far greater for African American women, who experienced at least double discrimination.

The numbers of all citizens attending institutions of higher learning had tripled between 1930 and 1960 and then doubled between 1960 and 1970 (Farber and Bailey 344, 346). These numbers, however, hide significant disparities along racial and gender lines. More minorities and women were completing high school than ever before, and more were continuing on for postsecondary education, but a gap remained between the educational attainments of whites and blacks and between those of men and women. In 1960 the median for years of schooling completed for all people twenty-five years or older was 10.6. By 1970 it had risen to 12.2. As Sarah Schramm reported, however, whereas women accounted for about 51 percent of the population in 1970, they received only one of every three bachelor's and master's degrees and one in ten doctorates: "In 1968, 18% of the men entering public 4-year colleges had a high school grade point average of B+ or better; 41% of the freshman women had achieved such grades. In 1970, over 40% of the males aged 18–21, and over 20% of the males aged 23–4, were enrolled in college; comparable figures for females were 29% and 9% respectively. About 50% of the women high school graduates go to college, as compared to nearly 70% of the men. Between 75 and 90% of the well-qualified students who do not go on to higher education are women" (3). Those institutions of higher learning that admitted women—some of the nation's most prestigious schools did not—regularly set quotas to limit such admissions. Separate entrance requirements were common. Thus, for example, as late as 1967 Miami of

Ohio, a state university, admitted men from the top 25% of their high school graduating class but only the top 10% of women. Most medical schools and law schools limited the number of women admitted to fifteen or fewer (Women's Education Equity 1).

It was not until 1972, with the passage of Title IX of the Education Amendments Act, that sex discrimination was generally prohibited in public institutions of higher education and private ones that receive federal funding (U.S. Dept. of Education, "Title IX and Sex Discrimination"). Although its provisions exempt many institutions—for example, same-sex institutions, military academies, and social fraternity and sororities—Title IX is credited with contributing to a process that has led more recently to gender parity in higher education admissions (U.S. Dept. of Education, "Title IX"). Shortly after the passage of Title IX, however, as a record number of baby boomers were graduating from college and looking for jobs, the country was experiencing its worst economic downturn since the Great Depression (Anderson, *Sixties* 208). One could trace the beginnings of a more visible and vocal cultural backlash against civil rights initiatives to this moment, with the growing sense in the general population that there really was not enough prosperity to go around.

Changes in employment and educational opportunities were only a part of the picture, of course. Oral contraceptives were first approved by the Food and Drug Administration in 1960 and first marketed in 1963; by 1965, according to one manufacturer, "the Pill" had become the "leading form of reversible contraception" (Ortho-McNeil Pharmaceutical). Some states nonetheless still banned contraception based on nineteenth-century obscenity laws, deeming it obscene even to explain how to use birth control devices. Thus, finding reliable information about birth control, much less safe and effective contraception, was difficult if not impossible for many women. In *Griswold v. Connecticut* (1966) the Supreme Court determined that there is a right to marital privacy that allows a woman to use and a physician to prescribe contraceptives. But birth control information and contraceptive devices could still be withheld from unmarried men and women. Even though nearly half the students enrolled in universities in 1970 were women, over half of campus health services provided no gynecological services at the time, and "72% prescribed no birth control for women" (Yates 220). It was not until *Eisenstadt v. Baird* (1972) came before the Supreme Court that the right to privacy as applied to birth control was extended to single people (Kaplan 34). (It should be noted, however, that no right to privacy was extended to same-sex relationships, allowing the persistence of the so-called sodomy laws in various states and locales, as confirmed in *Bowers v. Hardwick* in 1986, and only recently successfully challenged in *Lawrence v. Texas.*) In 1972 a public-opinion poll commissioned by the U.S. Commission on Population Growth and the American Future found that "87% of American adults [thought] that the government should make birth control information universally available." Six out of ten adults polled favored birth control education at the high-school level. A higher percentage of adults—eighty percent—supported legislation allowing voluntary sterilization. Sixty percent favored abortion "for reasons other than saving a mother's life," fifty percent "would support lifting all legal restrictions on abortions" (Yates 220). In 1973 the Supreme Court, no doubt reflecting this level of public support, legalized abortion in *Roe v. Wade.*

The majority of laws affecting married men and women had been based on the common-law notion of coverture, wherein the man is assumed to head the family and the wife is legally "covered" by—protected by, incorporated into, subsumed under—her husband. The force of coverture eroded significantly through the nineteenth century as laws were passed to protect a woman's property rights, so that a woman could sign contracts, bring lawsuits, and have charge of her real property. Nevertheless, the general culture and the legal system continued to expect married women to give up a significant degree of independence. It was assumed legally and through custom that the woman would take her husband's name upon marriage, that children should have their father's name, and that women should be the primary child-care givers. Some women worried that to change marriage laws might jeopardize protective legislation, some of which had arisen as part of the efforts of an earlier "first-wave" feminism at the turn of the twentieth century. Others, however, saw in such legislation not protection for women but protection for male privilege. Proponents of the failed Equal Rights Amendment argued that "ownership and control of earnings and property should be held jointly by both spouses regardless of whether one or both work" outside the home." Further, "alimony, child support and child custody should not be based automatically" on the gender of the spouse; rather, it should be based "on the individual circumstances and need of the respective partners" (Hole and Levine 67). Similarly, the National Conference of Commissioners on Uniform State Laws drafted the uniform Marriage and Divorce Act urging that marriage be treated as a "partnership of equals" (ibid. 420). In 1970 California passed the first "no fault" divorce law, and other states followed. Changes in divorce laws, together with changes in cultural acceptability, made divorce increasingly more likely. Divorce rates had dropped significantly in the fifties after spiking in 1946 at 4.3 per 1,000 people. Divorces began to rise again in the late sixties, climbing from 2.6 in 1967 to 5.3 in 1979 (the divorce rate in 1997 was 4.5 per 1,000, meaning approximately 1,163,000 marriages ended in divorce that year) (Gender Issues Research Center 4).

Changes in marriage occurred in relation to the larger ongoing sexual revolution defined not only by conflicting notions of sexuality within the terms of heterosexism but, increasingly, through challenges to the dominance of heterosexism. As Beth Bailey astutely argues (249), efforts to blur gender boundaries were in tension with efforts to accentuate sexual difference. Men and women could be seen as the same in terms of sexual desire, a view flying in the face of marriage manuals and cultural commonplaces that presumed sex to be a man's right and a woman's duty. But men and women also could be seen as different—not necessarily because women do not feel desire (or at least not as powerfully and constantly as men do) but because the nature of their desire is unlike that of a man's. Bailey identifies three strands that constituted the "tangled roots" of the sexual revolution: a growing sexualization of culture, with sexual images an increasingly visible part of daily life; increasing numbers of young people living together outside marriage not only for sex but also to realize notions of "honesty" or "commitment" and a revised sense of "family"; and finally, the use of sex as a "new form of cultural politics," an "incendiary tool" (238). But none of these threads necessarily served women well. Women were more likely than men to be used as sexualized objects to sell America's goods and services. Living together could function remarkably like the old-style marriage sanctioned by law. And sex as an incendiary tool could mean that women still got burned. Some women and men sought to redefine heterosexuality by resisting sexualized images of women, organizing against pornography, arguing for more equitable distribution of domestic responsibilities within relationships (sanctioned by law or not), improving day care, and the like. Still others attempted to remove themselves from the heterosexist economy to explore same-sex relationships. As Bailey suggests, "in many ways the most important decade of the [sexual revolution] was the 1970s, when the 'strands' of the 1960s joined with gay liberation, the women's movement, and powerful assertions of cultural difference in America" (239).

Much had changed in the course of a decade and a half, but the changes in employment, education, marriage, and notions of sexuality made all the more visible the deeply embedded resistance to change within societal institutions and fueled a desire for more systemic and radical change. Because of a perceived societal intransigence, a growing number of women found it necessary to create alternative places to accomplish what neither law, the "system," nor the "establishment" seemed able or willing to do.

But who were these women? I have come to realize that I cannot easily or tidily identify women in terms of familiar ideological categories. In some cases their identities are simply not available. Some of the work I analyze is identified by pseudonym, or collectively authored, or accompanied by a name I cannot easily trace to a biographical or biological person. Many writers, however, did locate themselves variously in terms of age, class, race, sexual orientation, educational, or work experience. Additionally, photographs and artwork in movement publications represent women across a range of ages, sizes, and races, depicting women with children, with men, with other women, women engaged in various kinds of work. It would be a falsification to order this multiplicity into a unity. As DuPlessis and Snitow rightly observe, the "feminist movement was polyphonic," with "no central group, no central leader, no single political analysis, and no single moment of access" (11). The print traces of the women's movement thus suggest neither a single, unified movement nor neatly aligned cohorts of women but rather multiply affiliated women who entered into movement activities in various ways for various purposes.

While many of the participants in the university-without-walls would have self-identified as "radicals," what "radical" meant for the participants or to what extent "radical" signified a particular racial, class, or sexual identity was hardly a settled matter. Radical feminism embraced a range of activism that hinged on critique of the fundamental workings of society and sought revolutionary change. This broad definition allows for a more complex way of addressing questions about who constituted the movement. It has become commonplace in contemporary academic feminism to assume that second-wave feminism mistook a white, middle-class face for the face of all women (see Probyn 177; Bordo 141–42). While there is enough evidence in the writings of midcentury feminism of such politically loaded narcissism to fuel the critique, the other side of this critical coin is that it can effect a kind of double erasure. If it simply condemns midcentury feminism as racist and classist without looking further, contemporary criticism risks ignoring the range of women who were actually participating. In part because criticism of women's liberation's failure to live up to its utopian aims arose simultaneously with the movement itself, in looking back on that moment in time, we may find it difficult to notice the multiplicity of women who were actively contributing to the movement. Early criticisms of the movement came as much from inside as from outside the movement. From the outset women of color, working-class and poor women, lesbians, Chicanas, and women young and old challenged what they perceived to be oversimplifications and biases within the movement, but their presence as part of the movement has been largely ignored until fairly recently. Beverly Guy-Sheftall has voiced her frustration with the "erasure of Black women in popular and scholarly histories, television documentaries, and magazine articles about the 'second-wave' women's movement," noting how she has become "tired of seeing mainly white faces and hearing white women's voices in retrospectives about the women's liberation movement of the sixties and seventies" ("Sisters" 485–86).[7] A similar concern could be raised by lesbians and working-class women, whose presence in the movement is fully evident in feminist publications but who have not been adequately recognized in accounts that begin with the familiar originary story of young, college-educated women breaking from other movements for social change or that depend primarily on the default face that the mainstream media projected for women's liberation.

I cannot, of course, argue that women's liberation was representative of all womankind, recognizing that middle-class white women constituted the majority. But middle-class white women were not the whole of the movement. They were not the only women to construct feminist counterinstitutions or articulate a radical critique of systems of gender oppression, nor were they the only ones to contribute to the enormous outpouring of print. The traces of a greater range of activism are there if one looks beyond the relatively few women who caught the national media's attention, to the network of loosely affiliated women's liberation groups across the country. One can find a diversity of women entering into print in various forms, and much of that writing explicitly sets out to explore the breadth and range of women's experience and to recognize the differing paths that women necessarily created toward feminism. This is not to say that the periodicals and other movement ephemera do not also reflect tensions in the movement, but those tensions themselves evidence not the absence but the presence of a range of women, interacting across difference, who had the courage to disagree.

In reconstructing how the women's university-without-walls operated as a network of alternative pedagogical spaces, I will consider the extent to which the network of counterinstitutions women were building served as a powerful engine for change. I have demarcated 1968–75 as the time frame for my study because I take seriously hooks's contention that it was in this brief moment that feminists attempted the potentially radical task of addressing a wide audience. I am interested not only in understanding how and to what extent women attempted to write across boundaries but also in what sense, as hooks contends, such an effort was not sustained. This study opens a window onto this brief moment of possibility—from the first flush of identifiably separate feminist periodicals in 1968 to what one might call the "mainstreaming" of feminism in the midseventies.[8]

Others have constructed histories of the women's movement from national, political, and personal perspectives;[9] others, too, have traced the history of women's studies.[10] These histories are certainly valuable and I draw from them, but by themselves they do not get at what might be called the literacy practices of a highly decentralized women's liberation movement. I am interested in the ways in which a broader range of women—largely unknown, unremarked women—understood their educative roles and how they attempted to develop pedagogies to address particular and local concerns. I thus return to that moment of volatility and hope, the late sixties and early seventies—the moment that represents for hooks the opening of spaces for contact—to reconstruct how women worked to educate themselves into feminism, how they took cultural materials and practices not necessarily intended for them and turned those materials to their own uses. In particular, I am interested in how women made use of the literate practices available to them and how pedagogies emerged out of or in relation to such use.

Jane Kenway and Helen Modra define pedagogy as "what is taught, how it is taught and how it is learned and, more broadly, . . . the nature of knowledge and learning." To understand knowledge and learning in these terms, one must understand knowledge as "produced, negotiated, transformed and realized in the *interaction* between the teacher, the learner and the knowledge itself" (140). While more typically pedagogy is thought of as the function of schools, as the responsibility of formal institutions of learning, Jennifer Gore and Carmen Luke have each urged that we consider pedagogy more broadly as "an activity integral to all learning, all knowledge production" (Gore, *Struggle* xii), and as "endemic to all social relations . . . , fundamental to all public/private life and all communicative exchanges, from the nursery to the playground, classroom to the courtroom" (Luke 11). Indeed, as Luke puts it, "social agency in the world is about learning from and reacting to multiple information sources, cues and symbol systems" (11). In these terms, "learning and teaching . . . are the intersubjective core relations of everyday life," and they are "always gendered" (7).[11]

This broad understanding of pedagogy provides a starting place for rethinking the ways in which women deployed literacies as part of the women's university-without-walls. One must ask not only what was taught and learned, in what ways, by whom, and under what circumstances, but also how knowledge was conceptualized (what was considered knowledge worth teaching/learning, to what ends it was conceptualized, and in what sense it is "always gendered"). Additionally, what were the material circumstances that enabled or constrained literacy practices and the emergence of pedagogies in relation to those practices? These are questions that both literacy studies and print culture studies pose. A basic assumption in both is that literacy is understandable only if considered as a cultural practice or set of practices located in, and changing over, time and space. What counts as literacy, what it is assumed to be good for, and whose interests it serves are all questions that require understanding print as something made and used. The printed page does not, in other words, speak its own meanings independent of the practices that produced it or that shape its use. The material page may give some clues as to how it was made and how it was used, but neither the print nor the materiality of the page tells all. Further, practices of production and use do not themselves hold steady the printed page to lock in meaning over time, but rather the printed page can be put to new uses, transformed for new contexts.

Shirley Brice Heath has offered the literacy event as a "conceptual tool useful in examining within particular communities ... the actual forms and functions of oral and literate traditions and co-existing relationships between spoken and written language" (350). Heath understands the literacy event as "any occasion in which a piece of writing is integral to the nature of participants' interactions and their interpretive processes." In this sense, we might consider how women used writing to make sense of their situation within the larger culture and, most strikingly, depended on print to hold a dispersed coalition of groups together as a national movement. To study a literacy event, one must describe not only print materials circulating in the environment but also "the individuals and activities which surround print, and the ways in which people include print in their ongoing activities." The literacy event, Heath suggests, "can then be viewed as any action sequence, involving one or more persons, in which the production and/or comprehension of print plays a role.... Speech events may describe, repeat, reinforce, expand, frame, or contradict written materials, and participants must learn whether the oral or written mode takes precedence in literacy events" (351). In terms similar to Heath's, Roger Chartier urges that we keep in mind the extent to which literate practices are always embodied in "acts, spaces and habits" (*Order of Books* 3). They do not occur in isolation from other aspects of the social world. To reconstruct how texts work in the world—to understand, that is, their "actualization"—is to understand not only how they are produced and under what circumstances but also "the forms through which they are received and appropriated by their readers (and hearers)" (3). As Chartier puts it, "readers and hearers ... are never confronted with abstract or ideal texts detached from all materiality; they manipulate or perceive objects and forms whose structures and modalities govern their reading (or their hearing)" (3). To reread the literacy practices of movement women thus requires that I consider not only the forms of material production but the places, practices, and human interactions that animated the material forms.[12]

Any history of feminism is necessarily partial and fragmentary, and it is always mediated, as Susan Stanford Friedman observes, through intervening "reconstructions of what 'really' happened," the happenstance of whatever texts survive, and the interpretive work of the historian (13). In the case of relatively recent history, one might think that the problem facing a historian would not be a scarcity of materials on which to draw but rather an overwhelming documentary archive. The explosion of books on, by, and about women that literally spill off the shelves of university libraries might suggest that every nook and cranny of mid-twentieth-century feminism has been investigated and every shred of paper having anything to do with women has been found, cataloged, and analyzed. Nevertheless, as with social histories that attempt to reconstruct the literacy practices of earlier popular movements (rather than the privileged behaviors of elites), an attempt to read the pedagogical practices of second-wave women requires making sense of precisely the kind of partial and fragmentary traces Friedman describes. Part of the challenge is that much of the academic work on sixties activism more generally has relied on the establishment press and rarely on the fliers, posters, or underground newspapers produced by the activists themselves (Anderson, "New American Revolution" 201).[13] Because mainstream press coverage of the women's movement was often inaccurate or "openly hostile" (Tobias 203), relying on such accounts is particularly problematic. Without reading a broader range of primary documents, we risk perpetuating reductive versions of midcentury feminism. But to read in such a way that is neither nostalgic nor defensive also requires rethinking the analytical terms traditionally used to understand textual performance.

Ironically, given the fact that historians, dependent on print records, have had to learn to resist the tendency to read the social world in literocentric ways (Chartier, *On the Edge* 19), in the present case I have found it necessary to read literacy practices back into the social world. The challenge then is to recognize that the social world is not necessarily governed by textual or discursive logic, at the same time recognizing that literate practices always operate in the social world. The peculiar uneasiness about literacy among movement women that I noted earlier—the taking-for-granted of educational status and privilege, as well as a reluctance to make much of movement women's literacy accomplishments for fear that such recognition would be organizationally divisive—went hand in hand with a rhetoric of spontaneous conversation and action and a suspicion of outsiders who wanted to write about movement activities.[14] This complex of attitudes, reinforced by the movement's diffuse and decentralized organizational antistructure, made it less likely that materials would be archived in any systematic way. Much of the ephemera of movement activism (flyers, newsletters, just-above-ground newspapers, and the like—not to mention whatever material traces of the literacy work that went into producing these print materials or that deployed these print materials in various ways) simply does not survive. The very material form (cheap paper, cheap printing, often with the appearance of coming hot off the mimeo machine) and the conditions of production (mobile, volunteer, learning as one goes) signaled that these were bits of text to be used "right now," to be used up so that women could move on. The remarkable proliferation of such materials, with a marked degree of redundancy in content, no doubt contributed to their utility but also to the likelihood that the object per se mattered little, certainly not enough to be consistently archived. What does remain comes from individuals and a few important archives from which I have drawn, including the University of Michigan's outstanding Labadie Collection of activist materials, the State Historical Society of Wisconsin Library's collection of countercultural materials, and the Redstockings Women's Liberation Archives for Action. Augmenting these collections of actual material objects are online and microfilm resources, especially the Chicago Women's Liberation Union Herstory site and the Herstory microfilm collection developed from the Women's History Research Center.[15]

In the first chapter I consider the epistemological and pedagogical work of radical feminist periodicals as a key part of the women's university-without-walls. Not only did the periodicals report on women's liberation efforts generally, but they were themselves "counterinstitutions" created by ordinary women across the country in an attempt to "prefigure," as Alice Echols puts it, "the utopian community of the future" ("Nothing Distant" 160). The periodicals were laboratories in which women worked to construct alternative, participatory approaches to educating themselves as feminists. As Francesca Polletta has suggested, more than any other movement of the time, feminism made the "internal life of the movement the stuff of political experimentation and innovation" (149). It was thus not talk per se but process that was at the heart of feminist method. In this sense, we might consider Sara Evans's suggestion that we look at how women have rethought the schooling of citizens, "if citizenship is understood as something that must be learned and practiced," and the relationship of that schooling to "the linkage of public and private" ("Women's History" 126–27). Not only political analysis but also exploration of all aspects of women's experiences through a variety of modes was considered a necessary part of an education in radical citizenship. The periodicals evidence in their material forms as well as in the content of their pages a complex understanding of their educational mission in their self-conscious struggles to decide what would count as legitimate knowledge, what forms that knowledge should take to be most useful to women, and how best to engage women in the construction of new knowledge. The periodicals say a great deal about how they came into being, how they evolved over time (including, importantly, how many of them unraveled), and how they were used. They also make clear the extent to which they served to break down what were perceived to be the traditional boundaries between writer and reader, expert and novice, teacher and learner, not simply by delivering the news but by teaching women how to write for and participate in radicalized public spaces. In this chapter I consider the history and organization of the periodicals and then focus on the prominent knowledge domain of self-health, which was regularly covered in most periodicals, to look more specifically at the complex processes involved in knowledge production and circulation.

In chapter 2 I consider what might be called the rhetoric of knowledge production by focusing on feminist polemic. Many of what are now understood to be the inaugural documents of the women's liberation movement began as in-house papers circulated among women involved in other radical movements. These documents were often, in Patrice McDermott's terms, "concise expressions of rage and politics" intended to rouse other activist women to recognize their common cause and to fight on behalf of their gendered interests (32). Quickly printed in pamphlet form, in-house papers circulated widely. As Barbara Epstein recalls, "ideas traveled fast, partly because in the women's movement, as in the antiwar movement, people traveled a lot, and national networks were often as strong as local ones" (125). A paper delivered to a gathering in New York or Ann Arbor would be carried by hand, finding its way to Iowa City or Tallahassee or Seattle. Pamphlets were distributed through the growing number of women's centers, clinics, conferences, and concerts. Periodicals reproduced portions of pamphlets, and editorial groups asked delegates from local women's groups to report back from their travels about what they had heard at regional gatherings. While a much broader range of rhetorical practice is evident in the writings emerging from the women's movement, these inaugural papers were nonetheless a familiar and important form. Because many in the movement understood traditional forms of argumentation to silence women, they saw themselves as attempting to forge alternative discourses that would engage women more effectively in disputation. Little within late twentieth-century and early twenty-first-century feminist rhetoric, however, provides the analytical terms to enable a productive (rather than dismissive) reading of this material—that is, to read it as other than strident rant. To make better sense of the pamphlet literature, I have found it necessary to reclaim "polemic" for analytical use, as a term that operates in some sense outside traditional rhetoric, aligned as it was in movement publications more closely with dialectic.

If polemic was the founding genre, poetry was the form that invited the greater quantity and range of participation. Feminism was, as one participant put it, "this train full of poetry" (Belgrade 4). In chapter 3 I explore the political, aesthetic, and affective work women expected poetry to do by analyzing specific poems as material texts. Granting that the poems were on some level preread ideologically because of their location in feminist periodicals and pamphlets, I am struck nonetheless by how little of the poetry is reducible to simple political message. Indeed, it may be that the genre invited a greater range of participation in part because women perceived poetry as affording ideological and formal room to maneuver. Poetry was understood by some to be superior to dialectic or as an antidote to propaganda, offering a freer space to express the complexity of women's lives. As the poet Jan Clausen asserts, poetry fed women's "enormous appetite for *the evidence*" (11). Some of the poems indeed operated forensically, as linguistic artifacts evidently crafted less to be aesthetically pleasing objects than to operate as assertions of a raw kind of truth about a gendered world. But far more of the poems, even as they are on some level "personal" engagements with that gendered world, nonetheless are also simultaneously negotiations with cultural notions of Poetry and as such can be seen as attempts to stretch the formal bounds of the genre. It is not news to say that in poetry form and content interanimate. What is striking in much of the poetry appearing in feminist periodicals and pamphlets is the extent to which radical women understood this interanimation to be a vital, even necessary, way to intervene in the historical moment. The poems are thus sources of knowledge in a double sense—not only in terms of what they have to say "about" women's experience broadly conceived but also, as importantly, in terms of how they attempt to manipulate and extend the available forms of language.[16] In feminist periodicals poems were treated as part of the informational mix. One can find poems on virtually any topic, and significantly, the very presence of poems in such numbers served as incentive for ordinary women to compose poems and to contribute their work to feminist publications—to engage, that is, in literate acts.

In considering feminist performance work, chapter 4 may seem to move away from what are obviously literate practices. But, for all the ways in which participants in feminist performance work concentrated on the material body in motion, feminist performance events were also, in remarkable ways, literacy events. Literacy was part of the performance process not in the way that some traditional theater history would lead one to expect—not, that is, in the sense of the overriding importance of printed play or script—but as part of a temporally and spatially dynamic process. Organized feminist theater groups can be seen as among the counterinstitutions constituting the women's university-without-walls, but performance practices were also adopted by many women in the movement for the purposes of street actions and public demonstrations, consciousness raising within local women's liberation groups, and cross-generational educational efforts. In this chapter I consider how feminists crafted performance events in part by drawing on a range of literate practices. Feminist performance was conceptualized as something other than delivering a message to a passive audience, something other than propaganda. Rather, groups worked to develop performances that were radically pedagogical, intended to transform audiences into actors and composers of text.

In the first four chapters I reconstruct pedagogical principles primarily from feminist literacy practices. In the concluding chapter I focus more specifically on explicit pedagogical theorizing that provided points of contact between the women's university-without-walls and the establishment university. In a 1975 "do-it-yourself" introduction to women's studies, Sarah Schramm looks outside the academy for pedagogical models, observing that women's studies created itself from materials developed for continuing education settings, community programs, and other forms of alternative education (1). Although, as I noted earlier, it has become commonplace to argue that consciousness raising was the primary pedagogical approach of the women's movement—indeed, consciousness raising has been seen as a model for collaborative approaches to learning more generally (see Bruffee)—this chapter suggests a more complicated, osmotic relationship between *inside* and *outside.* Some students and teachers within the academy appropriated feminist models for interpersonal interaction, but more importantly they renegotiated questions of value, legitimacy, and access to the means of literate production. As the earlier chapters make clear, the university-without-walls generated critical knowledge in and through print. At least some of that print production served directly as material for university teaching. What was probably the first feminist philosophy course taught in the United States serves as a particularly striking example: in 1970 the feminist philosopher Alison Jaggar designed a course that brought material generated through feminist work outside the academy together with work more traditionally recognizable as academic.[17] This groundbreaking course confronted head on questions of legitimacy in its selection of reading materials, but it was also significant in that it required students to take greater responsibility for weighing the relative values of different sources and kinds of knowledge, to defamiliarize, in fact, the very notion of value. Value in terms of what? Value determined in relation to what systems of judgment and assessment? In this chapter I situate Jaggar's course in relation to other pedagogical materials from the time to suggest not an easy or superficial transfer of practices from one location to another but the potential of the women's university-without-walls to serve as radical critique of the academy.

In the course of the book, I suggest how a rereading of feminists' literacy practices can put pressure on commonplace assumptions about midcentury feminism that circulate in the academy today. In particular, the material traces suggest that the women's university-without-walls was not a phenomenon exclusive to or created solely by white, middle-class, straight women, nor did it unproblematically conjoin all women into "Woman." Indeed, this study makes clear that the decentralizing nature of the women's liberation movement—from the outset—worked with centrifugal force against an unproblematicized or politically naive rhetoric of unity and commonality. Packed into the very rhetoric of radical feminism was the double sense that every and any woman's experience could serve as the basis for the development of valuable knowledge at the same time that no one woman, nor any one group of women, could stand for the whole of womankind. One can read the ubiquitous first-person pronoun in movement literature as an attempt to register wariness of speaking for others, as a way to avoid universalizing and to acknowledge one's accountability for what was said. This is not to say, of course, that such rhetoric somehow was enough to inoculate the movement against deeply installed racial, class, or sexual blindness or bias or that it enabled the creation of a fully realized utopian space that made room for women to work together in coalitional celebration of both difference and commonality. Words by themselves were (and are) not enough. But it is to say that although the terms of current critique were present in the foundational discourses of the midcentury resurgence of feminism, they were so in part because a diversity of women, primarily below the radar of mainstream media, were contributing their intellectual and organizational energies to create counterinstitutions.

Reconstructing some of these counterinstitutions can contribute to the "archive of feminist intellectual activism" for which Linda Brodkey and Michelle Fine have called (128) by helping to counter the effects of the "recurring amnesia" that erases large parts of the history of women, especially radical women (Alexander 100). My purpose, however, is not to find in any simple way solutions for the present, as if what "worked" in the past could be transported like some pedagogical bag of tricks to another time and place, but rather to reconsider what circumstances, material conditions, and human actions made a set of practices work (or not work)—and what "working" meant—in a given time and place. Because such sites are never theoretically pure spaces, but always changing and messy, cluttered with competing ideas and interests, they suggest the very human, contradictory, and resourceful nature of activism. Such a volatile moment as the sixties and early seventies tends to get straightened in the telling, so that as it recedes from active memory, it becomes more and more difficult to see the initial generative tangle. Such straightened history makes it easier now to feel that we are somehow more theoretically or politically sophisticated, that we have righted the mistakes, or at least can see the naïveté and down-right silliness, of midcentury feminism. But to try to see the tangle, to resist the desire to straighten all the threads, can operate as humbling tonic to temper what might otherwise be historical arrogance.

1

Going Public with Pandora's Box: Feminist Periodicals

> My interest in print per se grows out of my sense that the basic tools of thinking, for being able to think imaginatively, for being able to think for yourself, grow out of people being able to read and write. I think it's not surprising that revolutionary movements have always seen literacy as one of the tools of revolution because the first process of literacy enables people, in this case women, to understand what our situation is; it also gives us words for our experience and helps us to figure out what we want to do and how things could be different.
>
> —Charlotte Bunch, "Charlotte Bunch on Women's Publishing"

> We want to put out a newspaper in our own way—a collective way. . . . We want to maintain no "professional" standards. "Professionalism" has been used as an excuse for the educated elite to corner the market on knowledge and communication. . . . We want new structures that do not allow people to fall into leader/follower, boss/worker, powerful/powerless roles.
>
> —*Ain't I a Woman* Editorial Collective

IN THE LATE SIXTIES and early seventies, as part of the women's movement, ordinary women engaged in literate production on a remarkable scale. In 1974 Ann Mather reported that more than 560 feminist periodicals had emerged between March 1968 and August 1973, including several hundred newsletters, some sixty newspapers, nine newspaper/magazines, and seventy-two magazines and journals ("History, Part I," 82). Much of this print production registers in its content, material form, and layout not only the excitement and volatility of newfound, newly rediscovered knowledge but also the sense that the knowledge was to be used, shared, and spread around to create new knowledge and to foster cultural and political change.

Figure 3. Joanna Vogelsong, untitled cover illustration, *off our backs* 2, no. 2 (Oct. 1971) (*source:* University of Michigan, Labadie Collection).

The physical object—newsletter, newspaper, or paperbound journal—was generally inexpensive, available as long as the mimeo machine or cheap deal on offset printing held out.[1] Produced largely through volunteer labor with scrounged materials, donated resources, and the very occasional foundation grant, feminist periodicals were distributed—often for free or at least "free to anyone who couldn't afford it"—through the informal network that constituted the women's university-without-walls (Mather, "History, Part II," 110; "History, Part III," 23).

The periodicals suggest a great deal about how they came into being, how they evolved over time, and how they were (and were intended to be) used. Feminist editorial groups were particularly self-conscious not only about the content and form of their publications but also about the processes by which the publications were produced and the mechanisms through which the readership was to play more than a passive or consumerist part. If pedagogy involves not only "what is taught, how it is taught and how it is learned" but also an understanding of "the nature of knowledge and learning" (Kenway and Modra 140), then one can read feminist periodicals as rich pedagogical sites. At first glance this print production might suggest a relatively familiar and transparent notion of knowledge transfer, but a closer look reveals something more: in explicitly reconceptualizing the relationship between text and reader by inviting active participation, and in struggling to negotiate the tension between authority and creativity, the editorial collectives sought to reshape what would constitute legitimate and politically effective knowledge. Teaching and learning, in this sense, operated less as stable oppositional functions and more as reciprocating activities: women who wrote for the periodicals had to teach themselves not only about feminism but also about writing, and as they taught themselves, they made their learning visible for readers, who could in turn teach themselves. Ideally the reader would become a writer and contribute work to the periodical by sending in a poem, an essay, a letter, a testimonial, a news item, or an announcement and thereby not only extend the domain of feminist knowledge but also increase women's access to the means of literate production.[2] The proliferation of print—and the editorial collectives' frequent expressions of surprise at the quantity of submissions—suggests something about the success of this mass process of lay pedagogy.

Reading through complete and partial runs of feminist periodicals from across the country, I have been struck by how anxious the editorial groups were to share with their readership not only aspirations and hopes but also struggles and failures. I am also struck by how difficult it is now in the early part of a new century to imagine a time when so many women believed it was possible to make a profound and material difference through their words. When a newspaper such as Denver's *Big Mama Rag* asserts that "knowledge is the first step toward gaining power to control [women's] lives," its editors are doing more than recirculating a cultural commonplace ("Women Must Control" 11). They are asserting a basic tenet of the women's movement, acting out of a belief that it is possible to effect real, deep change. Left-leaning academics of late have been inclined to emphasize the naïveté in such belief (while right-leaning cultural commentators within and without the academy have been inclined to attribute the fall of Western civilization to such belief). My interest here, however, is to reconstruct how the periodicals were produced and used by considering what ordinary women understood themselves to be doing and by respecting the complexity of their understandings. Because feminist periodicals sought to break down the traditional lines between writer and reader, expert and novice, and teacher and learner, they serve as particularly useful sites to consider how feminism negotiated difficult questions of value and legitimacy. I begin by considering how feminist periodicals emerged as entities identifiably separate from both mainstream publications and the male-dominated underground press, before moving to a consideration of their pedagogical workings.

The Emergence of a Separate Feminist Press

In their inaugural February 27, 1970, issue, the *off our backs* (*oob*) editorial collective, based in Washington, D.C., criticized both mainstream and alternative press. They asserted, "Existing institutions and channels of communication have ceased to meet the growing needs of the women's struggle" ("Dear Sisters" 2). In particular, the editorial asserts, women who had worked in the mainstream media were "well acquainted with the patterns of discrimination which define and confine their news within the 'Style' and 'Fashion' sections," and they could "expect to remain research assistants or be satisfied with the dullest and least important assignments." In a February 12, 1971, issue of *oob,* a member of the Newspaper Women's Caucus reported that, as of the previous winter, women at the *Washington Post* and *Evening Star* had begun to "challenge male dominance at the papers and the sexism on their pages" and, "more recently, . . . to challenge the male leadership of their union, The American Newspaper Guild." Nonetheless, even though the writer notes some changes in the treatment of women within news items, the number of women employed by the papers did not increase ("Newswomen at Work" 13). If women journalists expected the largely male-dominated underground press to offer an alternative, however, they were bound to be disappointed: as the *oob* editors put it, "so-called radical and movement periodicals usually retain token women on their staffs and print token articles while vital issues wind up on back pages or in wastebaskets." As other women who had worked on underground papers had discovered, women's stories helped to sell those underground papers, but the alternative press's "true consciousness and concern [were] revealed by their dependence on sex ads, nude photos, and 'hip' commercialism" ("Dear Sisters" 2). The failure of the radical underground press to take seriously women's issues was experienced as the betrayal of allies who should have known better. Not only did the acute sense of betrayal "from within" fuel the creation of a separate feminist press, but some of the most intense invective appearing in the early papers was aimed not at the mainstream press but at men in the movement.

Voice of the Women's Liberation Movement, Lilith, No More Fun and Games, NOW Acts, and *Notes from the First Year: Women's Liberation* all appeared for the first time in 1968, and they mark the beginning of an identifiably separate feminist press. Although such periodicals make clear that feminists objected to traditional, patriarchal forms of publishing, from content and format to organizational structure, they also make clear that women were appropriating readily available forms and structures to reimagine what writing for a public could mean when put to explicitly feminist purposes. Some women came to the process with no more experience in journalism than having read newspapers. Others had worked in mainstream publishing or the underground press. Many had developed skills in political organizing through New Left and civil rights activism. They pooled their varied and often vexed experiences to create feminist newspapers, newsletters, and journals.[3]

In a cogent account of the relationship between women in the movement and the male-dominated underground press, Patrice McDermott points out that by the late sixties, several underground papers had appeared to serve different politically and geographically defined audiences, peaking in 1969 with an "estimated five hundred papers with 4.6 million readers in the United States" (22).[4] The underground press had developed in reaction to a mass media perceived to be dominated by white, middle-class, mainstream editors and writers who seemed all too ready to support American foreign policy (Peck xiv). But, thanks in part to FBI infiltration, the underground press was unraveling (140–41, 161). Ostensibly to challenge censorship and sexual repression, but also as a way to sell their wares, such papers as the *Berkeley Barb,* the *Free Press,* and *Rat* sold space for sex ads and indulged in a practice McDermott refers to as "dildo journalism" (see also "Dear Sisters" 2). McDermott argues that the sex features compromised political coverage and motivated "a scathing feminist critique of the New Left's glorification of patriarchal politics" (23).

In 1969 women who took part in the Underground Press Syndicate Conference held in Ann Arbor urged the adoption of three resolutions:

> 1) that male supremacy and chauvinism be eliminated from the contents of the underground papers.... Papers should stop accepting commercial advertising that uses women's bodies to sell records and other products, and advertisements for sex, since the use of sex as a commodity especially oppresses women in this country. Also, women's bodies should not be exploited in the papers for the purpose of increasing circulation. 2) that papers make a particular effort to publish material on women's oppression and liberation within the entire contents of the paper. 3) that women have a full role in all the functions of the staffs of underground papers. (Mather, "History, Part II," 109)

As with attempts by other women's caucuses in male-dominated organizations (see chapter 2), this effort to change practices through an appeal to legislative process was not successful, and women turned to extralegislative means. The dissatisfaction with the underground press reached its symbolic height in 1970 when a women's liberation coalition took over the underground newspaper *Rat* to protest the newspaper's mixing of radical politics with what were deemed pornographic features and advertisements: "a particularly violent and pornography-filled issue of *Rat,* with articles trivializing women's liberation, so enraged the women on the magazine's staff that they joined with the Redstockings [a New York feminist group], Weatherwomen [a radical underground group], and members of the guerrilla-theater group WITCH [Women's International Terrorist Conspiracy from Hell] to seize the paper and produce a special issue by and about women" (McDermott 25). The coalition formed a feminist editorial collective that then took permanent control of the paper (ibid.).[5]

After the takeover, one member of the editorial coup, Robin Morgan—whose influential anthology *Sisterhood is Powerful* was published in the same year—offered a strong sense of the anger that precipitated the women's revolt. Her essay "Goodbye to All That" appeared in a February 1970 issue of the newly feminist *Rat:*

> It's the liberal co-optative masks on the face of sexist hate and fear, worn by real nice guys we all know and like, right? We have met the enemy and he's our friend. And dangerous. "What the hell, let the chicks do an issue; maybe it'll satisfy 'em for a while, it's a good controversy, and it'll maybe sell papers"—runs an unheard conversation that I'm sure took place at some point last week. And that's what I wanted to write about—the friends, brothers, lovers in the counterfeit male-dominated Left. The good guys who think they know what "Women's Lib," as they so chummily call it, is all about—and who then proceed to degrade and destroy women by almost everything they say and do:... The token "pussy power" or "clit militancy" articles. The snide descriptions of women staffers on the masthead. The little jokes, the personal ads, the smile, the snarl.... Goodbye, goodbye forever, counterfeit Left, counterleft, male-dominated cracked-glass-mirror reflection of the Amerikan Night-mare. (qtd. in Hole 273–74)

Editorial coups by women at other male-dominated papers followed, but still more women organized themselves to form their own network of periodicals. Importantly, while they worked to put into practice (at least) the three resolutions proposed at the Ann Arbor conference, they were at the same time "appropriating the conceptual frameworks of other movements" (Echols, "Nothing Distant" 158) and borrowing and reshaping the publishing forms and traditions that they had learned directly or indirectly from the underground press (McDermott 26).[6]

Women learned how to run a press with minimal resources, drawing on volunteers, sharing equipment and sources, often inviting others to make free use of materials, and borrowing from other textual sources with a relaxed or nonexistent sense of copyright.[7] They learned to use publishing as a form of political action, as a way to create a network of activist women, and most important for my purposes here, as a vehicle for education and the development of new ideas. "Limited in resources but significant in influence," McDermott asserts, "feminist publishing quickly grew into a large, varied internecine phenomenon that addressed increasingly complex questions and diverse constituencies... reflect[ing] the ideologies, issues, tensions, and challenges of its activist movement" (27). But, more than just "reflecting," the newsletters, newspapers and journals helped shape those ideologies and issues of the growing movement. With an often lacerating self-consciousness about process, the periodicals worked across a contested literacy terrain that celebrated the possibilities of print yet registered a wariness of the divisiveness that had historically gone hand in glove with emerging literate practices. They wrestled with how to enact their feminist principles not only in the content and form of their periodicals but also in their organizational structure and their relationships with their readers.

Pedagogical Aims: The Nature of Knowledge and Learning

> We are building a movement so that we may be freed from myth and prejudice. This movement seeks to understand itself and to build pride and courage by reaching back to claim as its own its long ignored and suppressed history. It actualizes itself in struggles against all forms of discrimination . . . to build new liberated forms.
>
> —"Dear Sisters," *off our backs*

> We did spend a lot of time debating what our mission was as the printed word. What were we conveying to people, to other women? Were we making women proud? We had a lot of really serious questions about what a newspaper would mean. We knew the power of the printed word and holding something in your hand and looking through it, and what were people getting from it? You know, I don't know.
>
> —Susan Edwards of *Lavender Woman*

Feminist periodicals register a remarkable faith in the power of the word and in the capacity of their readers to make intelligent use of information made available to them, even as they worried about how well they were succeeding and whether they were doing it right. The editorial collectives saw themselves as responsible for making the world a better place, and they understood that to be effective, readers had to join in the effort—at the level of self-understanding, sociopolitical critique, and collective action. It is useful, I think, to imagine readers encountering many similarly crafted editorial statements in the growing number of newsletters, newspapers, and journals, with the very repetition of hope engendering a sense of radical possibility. In the fall 1968 issue of the Seattle-based *Lilith*, Judy Bissell urges women to see themselves as "creative, able individuals, fully capable but denied any meaningful say in our society." She expresses the hope that "in working for this radical consciousness," the newspaper and its readership "will be able to work for radical social change" (1). The editorial collective of Detroit's *Womankind* sounds a similar note in linking causally the release of feminist creativity to the betterment of all society. They hoped to "share creative inspiration and information with other women," understanding their "major responsibility to . . . readers" to be an outgrowth of "the responsibility of all individuals to work for a better society." They wanted to bring readers "closer to a consciousness of [their collective] humanity and a greater development of [their] inner resources." Thus it was "the policy of this newspaper to expose the core of appearances. To expose the double standard of some businesses and institutions. To illuminate their true de-humanizing functions" ("Womankind" n.p.)

A celebration of women's power and creativity is often joined to such statements about women's responsibility not only to themselves as a collectivity but also to the whole of humanity. Although many of these statements refer in some way to a critique of patriarchy, they also make clear that women bear some responsibility for their own oppression. Addressing readers as "Dear Sisters," the *oob* editorial mission statement exhorts women to understand the part they play in their own oppression so that they can work not only for the liberation of women but also for "the liberation of all peoples": "*off our backs* is a paper for all women who are fighting for the liberation of their lives and we hope it will grow and expand to meet the needs of women from all backgrounds and classes.... Our position is not anti-men but pro-women. We seek, through the liberation of women, the liberation of all peoples" ("Dear Sisters" 2). Women will need to build "new liberated forms." In particular, the *oob* collective envisions not only an end result—"our own media"—but also the transformative potential in the creative process itself: "the very definitions of news will change as we gain the power to describe it as we see it and as we make it" (2).

Editorial collectives expected that the periodicals would be made by women and used by women generally, not just those who were members of an editorial collective, and that the periodicals would be instrumentalities that would further the work of radical social reform. The Chicago-based *Lavender Woman,* written by and for lesbians, was expected to be "a powerful weapon against the society that tries, in vain, to keep [lesbians] closeted and out of sight." In a November 1971 "Collective Statement," the editorial group adds: "More important, the paper will be a tool for growth. Through it, we can create a positive, viable Lesbian community; increase our political consciousness; communicate our feelings to one another; share with each other our knowledge and gifts and, above all, thank ourselves again and again for each other. We are not Lesbians in spite of ourselves, but because of ourselves. The paper will affirm that" (qtd. in Brody 12–13). But, for change to happen, words would not be enough. Women would have to act; they would have to work to effect change, as *Big Mama Rag* puts it in its opening dedication, October 1972:

> Our Hope is that this paper, with the help of all the women who read and contribute to it, will dedicate itself; that it will dedicate us to each other and

> to ourselves; that it will replace the often times empty rhetoric of "Sisterhood is powerful" with a viable and tangible reality. We believe that unity around problems common to all women will also give us the strength to destroy a system that exploits and manipulates not only women, but all people of all countries. And through this we will find that we have much more to share as sisters, as women, as friends, as human beings.... sharing and exchanging is the only solution to a problem that is not particular but personal to *all* women. ("Dedication" 1)

Throughout the pages editorial aspirations are reinforced through the very visible work of contributors: through their writing (primary material written for the periodicals, as well as reviews of, and bibliographies directing readers to, other work written by women); artwork (original work produced specifically for the periodicals, as well as photographs and reproductions of women's work); and photographic images, both contemporary and archival, that depict women, often in action. The editorial groups assert that women can do virtually anything, that they can (and must) take control of their lives. The material products—the papers, newsletters, and journals—themselves serve as proof of what women can do. Importantly, the pages make visible a racially, ethnically, and economically diverse female world by reporting what women have done in the past; by making space for what they were currently doing politically, artistically, spiritually; and by pointing the way to what they would still need to do.

While newsletters—sometimes simply stapled mimeographed sheets of typescript—often included few graphics, most newspapers and journals offered a visually striking mix of image and word. The winter 1971 issue of Baltimore's *Women: A Journal of Liberation,* devoted to the theme "how we live and with whom," can serve as a fairly typical example. On the green cover of this folio journal, below the logo with its women's liberation symbol (the female symbol containing within it a power fist), appears Su Negrin's black-and-white block print of four human figures in silhouette pushing out against the confining walls of a house suggested in outline. An editorial outlines the question posed by this special issue, addressing in particular the nuclear family, communal living, and sexuality. As part of this discussion, the editorial group is careful to qualify its position by describing its members: "Of the 16 members of the Journal staff, 1 of us lives in a women's collective, 1 in a female/male commune, 5 in extended families, 2 live alone, 2 live with husbands, and 5 live in nuclear families" (Editorial, *Women,* 1). They acknowledge that they are in the process of making "positive changes" in their family relationships and that such changes do not dictate any one kind of living arrangement. The editorial concludes, as do many of the editorials, by urging women to continue to explore options and to commit to print: "We need to put more of our thoughts down on paper to share with one another. Women today need to rediscover for themselves how and with whom they want to live. This can mean a room of one's own, a job for economic independence, a community day care center, or a women's commune. What alternatives we choose are only important insofar as they give us the power to share our lives as a part of the process of revolution" (ibid. 65).

As evidence of what such sharing might entail, the journal includes sixty pages devoted largely to its theme, including essays, personal narratives, a fictional narrative, an open letter, a diary, poems, news items, and political analyses. To the extent that the writers identify themselves (and many do in terms of race, class, sexual orientation, education and work), one can find a wide range of women contributing to the periodical. The photographs and visuals reinforce the sense of a richly various womankind. Sometimes to illustrate text, sometimes to extend or to qualify text, the journal intersperses black-and-white block prints, line drawings, and photographs. Archival photographs and reproductions of paintings, together with Greta Handschuh's pencil drawings, illustrate the fourth installment of a children's "book" about Elizabeth Blackwell, "the first woman in modern times" to receive a medical diploma (Heyn n.p.). Children's drawings appear as well: a crayon drawing of two women yoked by a plus sign (the work of "Ellen, Age 7, Baltimore") serves as a heading for a reflective essay titled "Thinking about Psychiatry" (58); Missy Ambrose of Manhattan, Kansas, contributed a two-frame, captioned cartoon with bubble dialogue showing two girls who give up dolls to play ball (58–59). Ruth Geller's thin-lined cartoon shows four female figures forming a circle of mutual creation: each female figure wields a pen, pencil, or (possibly) paintbrush to create the next figure (see figure 4). Photographs and graphic images present children and older adults, women embracing women, a multiracial child-care group, a woman playing the trombone, two little white girls with the women's liberation symbol on their tee shirts, women marching, farm scenes, women dancing, women in intense conversation with other women, women at play, and communal groups. Native Americans, African Americans, and white women all appear in this textual mix. That a spectrum of women writes for the periodicals and that a spectrum appears in the visual representations announces to readers that, unlike the mainstream media, the publications of the women's movement allow all women to participate in the women's movement through print, to find matter that speaks to their concerns and interests and ideally

Figure 4. Ruth Geller, untitled illustration, *Women: A Journal of Liberation* 2, no. 2 (Winter 1971): 19 (*source:* collection of Marianne Novy).

to contribute through print or graphics to the ongoing project of mutual education.

It is, of course, one thing to say what editorial collectives hoped to achieve and something else to say what real readers did with the periodicals they picked up at feminist bookstores, clinics, and demonstrations or passed along from hand to hand. Through interviews with women in the movement in 1969 and 1970, the sociologist Maren Carden found what she calls a "two-step model for the movement communication system, in which a relatively few members read and digest the literature, and then pass the ideas on in private conversations and group meetings," a process most evident in the movement's early years (69). This process of a few people reading and then spreading the word orally recalls what Harvey Graff has argued to have been the case in the nineteenth century—with an important difference. Following E. P. Thompson's assertion that "illiteracy by no means excluded men from political discourse," Graff notes that those who could not read could nonetheless "listen and participate in discussion—at work, in reading circles, in pubs, or at ports of call" (246). In the case of the women's groups, however, it was less a matter of the literate reading for the illiterate than of some literate women reading and making their reading available orally to other literate women. In this sense, literacy should be understood as involving not only those who wrote for and read the papers but also those who participated in the exchange of literate knowledge by listening to and talking with others who had read the papers. The literacy event, in other words, involved not only print but also talk.

Carden argues, however, that as the movement expanded and national mainstream coverage of the women's movement increased, fewer women learned about the movement first or primarily through interpersonal exchange, and more women learned about women's liberation through a variety of print media (32). With the increasing availability of key founding texts—available through periodicals and reprint services—more women came to an understanding of feminism via reading. While Carden tends to underestimate the importance of feminist periodicals for understanding the movement because she believes that the editorial groups were not representative of the movement as a whole—they were too radical, she contends, compared to what she understood to be the mainstream movement—she nonetheless offers a sense of their distribution as a way to gauge the movement's national scope:[8] "Toward the end of 1971 Boston's biweekly *Female Liberation*... was being distributed to 900 people; Austin, Texas' monthly newsletter *The Second Coming* had 200 subscribers; and Philadelphia's bimonthly newspaper *Awake and Move* had 137 subscribers and additional street sales of 200 copies, while New Haven's newsletter *Sister*, published every two months, had 400 subscribers. The largest newsletter circulation is reported by the Los Angeles Women's Center, which sent out 2,700 copies of its January 1972 newsletter" (65). Carden asserts that the number of people reading a given periodical was "usually three or four times the number of women known to be participating in consciousness-raising groups in the city" of publication. For example, approximately one hundred women were reported to be participating in the network of small women's liberation groups in Cleveland, and the newsletter jointly published by these groups was sent out to some 350 people (65). Such figures, of course, are notoriously difficult to interpret.[9] The fact that a periodical is distributed does not mean that it is read, and if it is read, that does not mean that it is read by a single person. Nor do the circulation figures indicate how a periodical is read or what a reader does in consequence of having read it. Nonetheless, the sheer quantity of print production, with a remarkable (and inexpensive) reprint and recirculation capacity, suggests a significant level of activist literacy aimed at spreading the word and tying local groups together through a relatively unstructured system of national communication (69).

Although Carden's early study provides some evidence, it is to the periodicals themselves that one has to turn in order to understand more fully what was expected of readers and to find traces of the extent to which readers met those expectations. This remarkable outpouring of print clearly shows how the traditional separation of reader and writer broke down, as the reader was expected to actively engage in the production of new kinds of knowledge. In the 1970 *Notes from the Second Year* editorial, Shulamith Firestone and Anne Koedt reflect on the success of their effort to offer an annual compilation of "major writings" of radical feminism. *Notes from the First Year* came out in 1968. Firestone and Koedt's call it the "first feminist journal put out by the new Women's Liberation Movement" (*Notes from the Second Year* 2), and very quickly it became a valuable resource, providing a meaty selection of interviews, excerpts from pamphlets, chapters of books, works in progress, and reprints of manifestos, spiced with brief boxed quotations and photographs. Firestone and Koedt express their surprise and pleasure that the first compilation was so successful that "one dare not leave one's tattered copy unguarded even now." At the same time, they see a continuing need for a radical feminist periodical "in which to debate, a forum in which to present the proliferation of new ideas and to clarify the political issues that concerned us" (2). Firestone and Koedt see the need for a periodical that will expand as the movement expands and that will represent the movement accurately, free from distorting intermediaries. They note that they have been "cautioned that to present our ideas undiluted to the public might be a mistake, that some if not all the writing we have included might scare off women unfamiliar with the movement, in the long run doing a disservice" (2). But Firestone and Koedt "give women more credit than that": "this movement belongs to all and every woman and they don't need a sales pitch;... women are smart enough to recognize their own interests;... *we are tired of being talked down to*" (2).

At the heart of movement periodicals is precisely this double recognition that, on the one hand, consistently and historically women have been talked down to and that, on the other hand, women are smart enough to recognize their own interests. The periodicals enact in their content and format the conviction that women can make intelligent use of all kinds of information that has been withheld, buried, watered down, or distorted. Women are thus best served when they have available to them a broad "spectrum of current thinking," as Firestone and Koedt put it (*Notes from the Second Year* 2). Although periodicals varied in emphasis, most attempted to move across knowledge domains, including in their pages a kaleidoscope of ideas about history, health care and nutrition, the arts, sociopolitical analysis and critique, consumer information, education, and religion. Rather than explain away contradictions or regularize ideas according to some a priori notion of feminism, most editorial groups, especially in the early publications, celebrated "authenticity," by which they meant the "uncut and only minimally edited" as opposed to the tightly policed, assuming "that if [women] see [the women's movement] directly and honestly—firsthand—they can decide for themselves how they feel about it" (2).

Firestone and Koedt recognized that it could be overwhelming to try to make sense of "so young and vital a movement" and that some assistance was necessary not just for those new to the movement but even for those who had been active from the beginning (*Notes from the Second Year* 2). They thus offer some pedagogical framing in the form of table of contents entries as a set of "roadmaps" to the movement. These roadmaps consist of broad categories that are not intended to be mutually exclusive or exhaustive but are designed for flexible use. The overlap among categories and among articles is taken to be a sign of the movement's vitality. Whether the category is "women's experience," "theories of radical feminism," or "issues involved in founding a radical feminist movement," Firestone and Koedt chose recent articles that they thought were important or influential from the prior year (roughly 1969), in part to create a "historical record" but as importantly to generate further thinking: the articles are not expected to "cover comprehensively all aspects of the category in which they are found, but rather to open up that category for further debate" (2). Even though the pedagogical framing is offered to assist old hand and newcomer alike so they would not be overwhelmed, paradoxically the ultimate aim is for women to "throw away our safety nets" (2). The categories are intended as a relatively nondirective assist, just enough to get the reader started. Once involved, once participating in the debate, women could be trusted to discover "a new daring, a willingness—eagerness—to tear down old structures and assumptions and let real thought and feeling flow" (2). That is what the movement was expected to offer: "for many of us this has been the most liberating thing of all: the freedom to think, say, do, and be anything we decide. Including freedom to fail. To unsmile. *To dare to be bad*" (2).

It may be difficult now, in a media-saturated culture such as ours, to imagine how engaging in literate acts could be socially and politically daring. While women in the movement knew that reading and writing by themselves were not enough—indeed, reading and writing as marks of "education privilege" were understood to have been used against women—but the periodicals nonetheless offered ways for women to "dare to be bad" through their engagement with print (Peslikis 81). Redefining what would count as knowledge and who could produce and have access to it was the core pedagogical mission of feminist periodicals. Literate acts were radical indeed if ordinary women could presume to explore areas of knowledge or ways of knowing that had been cordoned off as inappropriate to them, as the province of experts or a cultural elite, and if women could presume to produce knowledge or reclaim disenfranchised or subjugated knowledges about themselves and the world.

A reader could find in a given periodical and across a range of periodicals news articles, feature essays, mininovels, plays, poetry, self-help articles (how to change a tire, how to bake a muffin), cartoons, line drawings, women's history features, photographs, book reviews, gynecological instructions and other health-related information, advertisements for women-friendly services of various kinds, and a fair dose of often wickedly satiric humor. Much that was published owed as much to the carnavalesque as to any sanitized, disembodied theoretical system. As one of its cofounders recalls, "*oob* was the quintessential child of the sixties—born of native enthusiasm, a pinch of planning, and a little bit of dope" (Webb 5). Although "daring to be bad" meant a serious commitment to sociopolitical critique and change, that serious commitment could at the same time mean "acting out," whether by simply purchasing a "scandalous" periodical or by learning from that periodical how to get involved in political activism of various kinds or how to contribute images or words that set out to challenge cultural constraint. For all the seriousness of much that was printed, there were at the same time elements that played at the margins of conventional decorum, sometimes in ways reminiscent of the underground press many women had criticized.

The inaugural act of naming a periodical could itself involve wry, sometimes acerbic, critique. Alongside such straightforwardly named periodicals as the *Dayton's Women's Liberation Newsletter* and Kansas City's *Women's Liberation,* or Albuquerque's *Sisters in Poverty Newsletter* and *The Welfare Fighter* from Washington, D.C., punning and assertive titles proliferated.

Such titles—*It Ain't Me Babe* (Albany, Calif.), *Hysteria* (Cambridge, Mass.), *Just Like a Woman* (Atlanta), *Mutha* (Sacramento), *Pissed Off Pink* (Lansing, Mich.), *New Broom* (Boston), *Off the Pedestal* (Palo Alto, Calif.), *The Hand that Rocks the Rock* (formerly *Lysistrata,* Slippery Rock, Penn.), *Skirting the Capital* (Sacramento), *Statutes of Liberty* (Rochester, N.Y.), *Turn of the Screwed* (Garland, Tex.), and *Velvet Glove Magazine* (Livermore, Calif.)—promised something other than staid reporting.

Satire defines the founding gestures of many of the papers. A Seattle organization identified as the Women's Majority Union or the Order of the Lead Balloon (a name, the editors say, that is itself subject to change) named its paper *Lilith* based on the "Hebraic document The Alphabet of Ben Sira": "When the Lord created the world and the first man, He saw that man was alone, and quickly created a woman for him, made like him from the earth, and her name was Lilith. Right away, they began to quarrel" (Bissel 1). "Surely," the inaugural editorial observes, "Adam and Lilith were as equal as two persons could be, literally created from the same earth." But equality alone is not the issue for this paper: "When Adam tried to assert his superiority, Lilith just wasn't cowed" (Bissel 1). Fear of the "lavender menace" among straight and especially more mainstream movement women, expressed most notably by Betty Friedan, gives edge to the Chicago lesbian paper *Lavender Woman* as well as Cambridge's *Lavender Vision.* The journal *off our backs* was named to "reflect on the dual nature of the women's movement." "Women need to be free of male domination," the editors assert, but "at the same time, women need to be aware that there would be no oppressor without the oppressed. We must strive to get off our backs" ("Dear Sisters" 2). The title *Big Mama Rag* is a takeoff on the Band's 1969 song "Rag Mama Rag." The newspaper title replaces the song's "mama" and her "skinny little body" who is invited into the male singer's sleeping bag for some "relaxing" with a big mama who has political, social, and creative heft (and presumably can tell a line when she hears one). And of course, the title gets some punning traction from that word *rag.*

Such titles set the stage for the periodicals' contents. To critique the dominant cultural logic, often with darkly comic intent, feminist papers sometimes embraced language and images that had been used to attack women in general or women's liberation in particular. Since the liberated woman was disparaged as a castrating bitch, *Lilith,* one of the earliest (and in some sense, angriest) periodicals, literalized the image in two issues, including a cartoon and a line drawing that depicted scenes of castration. In the line drawing, one woman hangs by her neck from an erect penis while another female figure attacks the offending member with a hacksaw (*Lilith* vol. 2, 16). In the cartoon, from *Lilith*'s last issue, "a sinister event is in progress": a male addresses a crowd to explain that it isn't that men discriminate against women; it is that "none are intelligent enough to meet our standards." As one man in the crowd says to another, "mine is bigger than yours," a woman proclaims the "end to tyranny" and appears to castrate one of the men. The last frame ends with the woman calling on the crowd to "behold your leader" (*Lilith* n.d., n.p.). Working at the level of ironically inflected cultural etymology (rather than the crude literalizing of the cartoon), Jo Freeman's "Bitch Manifesto" attempts to retrieve *bitch* for positive use to signify "an organization which does not yet exist" and as label for women to embrace: *"BITCH does not use this word in the negative sense. A woman should be proud to declare she is a Bitch, because Bitch is Beautiful"* (5–6).

Many images and texts worked with satiric edge to reverse the binaries that undergird sexual politics. As a postscript to a transcript of a consciousness-raising session produced for WBAI-FM Radio in New York and entitled "Men and Violence," *Notes from the Third Year* added a boxed quotation from then Israeli prime minister Golda Meir: "Once in cabinet we had to deal with the fact that there had been an outbreak of assaults on women at night. One minister . . . suggested a curfew; women should stay at home after dark. I said, 'But it's the men who are attacking the women. If there's to be a curfew let the men stay at home, not the women'" (Meir 43). The April 25, 1970, issue of *off our backs* included a centerfold pinup, "Mister April," with a perfectly ordinary man posing naked on a fuzzy rug in front of a fireplace. He is posed, modestly enough, to show a side view. Another *oob* centerfold shows two nude men, the photo altered decorously to veil, with hand-drawn daisies, male genitalia. The caption asks, "Why Are These Men Smiling?" and answers in ad-speak: "Butter Balls by House of Pénus, deodorant for genital odor." This particular centerfold so offended *oob*'s Maryland printer that the paper's staff had to drive to New York to find someone to print copies so they could get the paper out (Nov. 8, 1970).

Nevertheless, although some images of men (or male body parts) appear in the papers, and many articles critique male domination, far more images and text represent women young and old. Women are sometimes represented as oppressed, as reduced to sexual function, as malformed, or as chained. In the fall 1970 issue of *Women,* for example, the title "Women and Rock: Sexism Set to Music" (24) frames an image of a smiling woman whose body is composed of a multicubicled box, each cubicle occupied by a female form, some reclining and others crawling, but all posed as if for an artist's canvas. The image is captioned to play on the sexual reference, "She's Young but She Has the Makings of a Good Box." Even when women are so represented, however, the mix of images and text almost always counterbalances the representation of female victimage. The page design for Lynn Bronstein's article in the same issue of *Women* is fairly representative. "CIMEMASCULINITY," the block-lettered title of Bronstein's critique of the male-dominated film industry, arches like a marquee over Karen Danaher's photograph of a mannequinlike female head and torso. With staring, oddly focused eyes, wiglike hair, and stage makeup, the head seems to belong to a department store dummy, but the bare breasts appear voluptuously, photographically real. This negative image does not simply illustrate some statement in the article but amplifies its emotional weight. The text of the essay itself is interrupted by small graphics—first by a childlike accordion cutout of dollar signs against the backdrop of the U.S. flag, then by a sequence of female symbols, and finally by a series of question marks with the caption "The New New Wave" (27, 29, 30). The linked figures are not explicated within the essay itself, but the interconnection of American money interests, the exploitation of women, and the need for a new kind of cinema is an underlying theme. The essay begins by critiquing the movie industry and ends by imagining a future that "holds interesting possibilities." "If a third film form arrives, a New New Wave in which human relationships will be shown as they *could be*" Bronstein surmises, then "we may find women of a new breed in films" (30).

These periodicals sometimes overlapped in their coverage, with one periodical reprinting an article from another across the country, but they nonetheless defy any attempt to specify some centralized theory or practice that could stand for the whole of the women's movement.[10] Especially in the early periodicals, "daring to be bad" meant, for both the editorial groups and their readers, daring to explore relatively unfettered and resisting the desire to reign in and make uniform. The cacophony of ideas may at times seem self-canceling or contradictory, and some writers complained that especially the political theorizing was too muddled to be useful. A founding member of the *oob* editorial group, Marilyn Webb, recalls, "At the beginning... we didn't really have such things as correct ideological lines" (Untitled 8). Nevertheless, whether or not some editorial group members would have preferred more carefully and consistently articulated ideological positions, the material products perform a riot of variations rather than a consistency of positioning, and this mix of ideas and forms required that readers exercise their critical judgment to pick and choose from among the range of ideological perspectives and kinds of information made available. The development of such critical literacy would be necessary if women were to create their own revolution.

In subsequent chapters I will look more closely at polemic and poetry as two of the more prominent forms of radical expression, but I want to turn now to one knowledge category, health care, to consider in greater detail how editorial groups worked to reconceptualize what would count as knowledge and how they engaged their readership in rethinking what would constitute legitimate ways of knowing. Health care was a pressing concern for women not only in terms of birth control but also across the range of women's health-care needs. Reflecting on the impact of the women's movement some thirty years later, Susan Reverby refers to the effects of the women's self-health movement as one of the "shining moments" of feminism (qtd. in Mansnerus 1). Periodicals were not only reporting on an important set of topics that were largely ignored by mainstream media and inadequately addressed by the medical literature, but by contributing to the creation of a "self-health" network, they were also participating in one of the more influential and long-lasting counterinstitutional efforts that defined the women's liberation movement.

Self-Health: Diagnosing a Need

> When doctors claim to know what's best,
> Make demands—not requests!
> —"Witching the A.M.A"

In a small Feminist Press pamphlet that traces the history of women's health care, Barbara Ehrenreich and Deirdre English point out that the "medical system is strategic for women's liberation" because "when we demand control over our own bodies, we are making that demand above all to the medical system" (*Complaints* 5).[11] Some sense of this demand for knowledge is registered in a call for the creation of the local Women's Health Project that appeared in Detroit's *Moving Out.* Kay Otter expresses the frustration many women felt with the state of medical care:

> As women, we are forced to deal with a medical profession whose chief experts—doctors—are 91% male. . . . We have medical needs . . . [that are] emotionally loaded in terms of societal values. From the doctors we get the following: lack of understanding, moral lectures, prejudice—simple and complex—patronizing attitudes, lack of concern, cruelty, ignorance, physical roughness, sexual assault, over charging . . . , forced or coerced sterilization,

> insults, disregard of our questions, failure to tell us the basic information that leads to HIS decision about what is wrong, what to prescribe..., incompetence, attitudes that make us feel WE are neurotic. (28)

What is required, according to a *Big Mama Rag* editorial, is "continual self-criticism and education" so that women will be able to "revolutionize... health care and be ready with a better system if [the] government is ever replaced with a system in which better ideas can flourish." As in "other areas of the Women's Movement," the editorial asserts, "knowledge is the first step toward gaining power to control our lives" ("Women Must Control" 11).

The "self-help" movement emphasized self-examination and self-knowledge and involved seizing medical technology "without buying the ideology," as Ehrenreich and English put it: "Self help has no limits beyond those imposed by our imagination and our resources. It could expand far beyond self-examination to include lay (though not untrained) treatment for many common problems—lay prenatal and delivery assistance, lay abortions, and so on" (*Complaints* 84). Feminist periodicals understood themselves to play an important role in the self-health network by regularly publishing on health-care topics, from critiques of the medical establishment to art work and poetry in celebration of the female anatomy. They provided information not readily available so that women could teach themselves what had been withheld and begin to change how women's bodies would be understood. Such knowledge was necessary so that women could act more effectively on behalf of their own health within the medical system while at the same time organizing alternative health-care facilities. Virtually every feminist newspaper and many of the journals and newsletters included regular features on health care, sexuality, and nutrition.

In their treatment of health care, as with other knowledge domains, the periodicals set themselves the complex task of reclaiming a "long ignored and suppressed history" ("Dear Sisters" 2), critiquing current conditions, and making available current knowledge to seed the creation of new knowledge. In part editorial groups wanted to emphasize the extent to which the new women's liberation movement was a continuation of historical feminism.[12] In their organizing principles published in the *Notes from the Second Year*, for example, the New York Radical Feminists declare that they were "dedicated to a revival of knowledge about our forgotten feminist history, and to a furthering of the militant tradition of the old radical feminist movement" ("Organizing Principles" 119). As Susan Edwards recalls, for the *Lavender Woman* collective, "finding our history has been actually one of the greatest challenges facing us" (qtd. in Brody 167). But re-creating the history was not enough. In an *off our backs* piece entitled "History—Heaven or Hell?" Betsy Auleta and Bobbie Goldstone assert that it would also be necessary to gain the strength to face that history (4). Periodicals saw in history the possibility for better understanding the origins of women's oppression and thus a firmer footing from which to counter that oppression.

In the case of women's health care, the historical understanding was intended to make clear the extent to which the problems an individual might have with the medical establishment in the present were not simply "her problem" but often a problem with a deeply and historically entrenched system that medicalized normal female functions and often failed to take a woman's experience of her own body seriously. It might seem cold comfort to learn that such treatment had a long history. On the other hand, if women could understand the extent to which they shared in a common experience, they might be better able to confront a medical system that failed to serve their needs. History could also provide the stories not only of exceptional women, such as Elizabeth Blackwell, the first woman in modern times to get a medical diploma (Heyn 33), but also the ordinary women who had banded together in the past to improve medical care not only for women but also for children, the poor, and the immigrant. Several papers included images from and references to another of Ehrenreich and English's pamphlets, one that traces the history of the contemporary self-health movement to an earlier era of female activism. The "know-your-own-body" courses that proliferated as a part of second-wave feminism could be traced to nineteenth-century "ladies physiological societies." Ehrenreich and English point out that the earlier "Popular Health Movement coincided with the beginnings of an organized feminist movement, and the two were so closely linked that it's hard to tell where one began and the other left off" (*Witches* 24–26). Ehrenreich and English argue that for the contemporary self-health movement to make a significant difference in women's lives, it would have to reach beyond those women who have the "leisure for self-help enterprises" and address "not just the uncomplicated disorders of youth" (*Complaints* 84–85). Self-help did not take the place of confronting the medical system but was conceptualized as a way to attain the level of self-knowledge necessary for demanding changes in existing systems. Such changes, as Ehrenreich and English emphasize, would have to extend beyond the women of means and leisure and work to change the system for all women because a "movement that recognizes our biological similarities but denies the diversity of our priorities cannot be a women's health movement" (*Complaints* 86).

Such historical perspective fueled a critique of current conditions. Critiques of the "medical-industrial complex" abound, including reports on medical malfeasance and surgical mistreatment of women, scathing critiques of doctors' failures to adequately care for women during childbirth ("Letter to Dr. Phillip Goldstein" 11), exposés of family physicians pushing addictive drugs and of abortion profiteers ("How to Get Hooked"; Mazanka). From the earliest periodicals, the question of racial and class bias in medical care was raised. In its first issue *Lilith* ran "two remarkable papers" sent by "Patricia Robinson of New Rochelle, N.Y." concerning birth control and racial genocide, different versions of which appeared in 1970 in Toni Cade Bambara's anthology *The Black Woman* as well as Robin Morgan's *Sisterhood is Powerful.* According to the first of the two papers sent by Robinson, the Black Unity Party had called on black women to refuse to take birth-control pills because the pill was seen to be a means of racial genocide ("Dear Brothers" 7). Patricia Robinson and a group of seven other women responded with a letter that recognized that the pill could be a form of "Whitey's committing genocide on black people" but that it did not have to be. In fact, they argue, "birth control is the freedom to fight genocide of black women and children." They charge that the men of the Black Unity Party who wrote the initial statement could not understand the importance of birth control because, as male members of the middle-class, they could not appreciate the needs of poor black women. Like the Vietnamese, South American poor, and African poor, the group asserts, poor black women would fight back against genocide, but they would have to do so "out of [their] own experience of oppression" ("Dear Brothers" 8).

As with other articles on health care for particular groups, such as *Mother Lode*'s feature "High School Women and Health" or a piece on the preponderance of women doctors in California's Yurok community ("Yurok Doctors"), the periodicals offered in the informational mix not only the overarching critique of medical care as inadequate for all women but also analyses of and reactions to the racially and classed marked differences in the ways health care was allocated. Simply recognizing the diversity of women's needs, however, would not be sufficient. Although it would be necessary to demand that the medical system respond to the "broadest possible range of women's experience," the very notion of "need" had to be rethought: "how much of our 'need' is manufactured?" (Ehrenreich and English, *Complaints* 87). Ehrenreich and English contend:

> There is no "correct line" on our bodies. There is no way to determine our "real" needs, our "real" strengths and liabilities, in a sexist society—any more than there is a way to understand what "female nature" may really be.... Our

> *bodies* are not the issue. Biology is not the issue. The issue is power, in all the ways it affects us. This is not to say that we do not need more hard information about our biology and about our health needs. We do.... But in our concern to understand more about our own biology, for our own purposes, we must never lose sight of the fact that it is not our biology that oppresses us—it is a social system based on sex and class domination. (88)

They thus conclude that women need to ask for more than the familiar mantra "control over our own bodies" suggests. Women must "struggle for... control over the social options available to [them] and control over all the institutions of society that define those options" (88).

While much attention was given to inadequate care, still more was directed at change. A special 1972 issue of *Mother Lode* devoted to medical issues, while laying the blame on the medical establishment for withholding necessary knowledge, urges women to take responsibility: "We must demand complete information from [the doctor] about what he is doing and must actively participate in his decisions about our body rather than passively accepting them" (Editorial 1). "ENOUGH!" Kay Otter declares; "We must begin to rely on ourselves, to break down those taboos about talking about our bodies so that we can share our knowledge with each other, learn what we don't know and search out the better alternatives for health care that exists now, so that we can survive long enough with energy enough to make changes" (29).

To meet the demand for "real knowledge," periodicals regularly included illustrated articles on self-examination, drawing on such sources as the Berkeley Women's Heath Collective or the LA Self-Help Clinic and often reprinting illustrations from the Boston Women's Health Course Collective's guide *Our Bodies Our Selves* or archival images of medieval medical practices. Along with information on pregnancy, birthing alternatives, non-Western medicine, nutrition, hygiene, birth control, cancer, and sexually transmitted diseases, bibliographies of resources appeared regularly, identifying materials from such local and national groups as Detroit's Radical Education Project, Ithaca's Women's Health Project, New York's Women's Health and Abortion Project, the Asian Women's Health Team, and La Leche League, as well as the organic farming organization Rodale. To read the periodicals is to see that useful knowledge was presumed to come from a variety of sources—not only from the medical establishment but also from women themselves—and in a variety of forms, not simply expository prose but also artwork (see figure 5), manifestos, poems, and personal accounts of experiences with health-care providers or alternative approaches to medicine.[13]

As in other knowledge domains, from sexuality to the arts, periodicals did not offer a "correct line" to which women were expected to subscribe, but,

Figure 5. Lyndia B. Terr, *Child in Pelvic Cup, Moving Out* 2, no. 1 (1972): 33 (*source:* collection of Marianne Novy).

consistent with Firestone and Koedt's editorial principles discussed earlier, they tended to offer a range of possibilities. As a *Big Mama Rag* editorial describes the self-health movement, there were a number of groups working on a number of fronts: "groups of women putting together such fine materials as *Our Bodies, Our Selves;* groups lobbying for less restrictive legislation of nurses, midwives and other paramedics; groups like the La Leche League who daily combat questionable obstetric and pediatric practices—these are the primary forces pounding away at the narrowness of U.S. medicine today" ("Women Must Control" 7). *Big Mama Rag* urged women to work for these groups, to help research and develop "an even larger body of knowledge with which to change what is poor but keeping the best parts of medical knowledge." Indeed, the success of the self-health movement within women's liberation was attributable to women's willingness to build from the ground up.

In the movement at large, and in the periodicals more particularly, authoritativeness and legitimacy of information were established in large measure through the visibility of the process by which knowledge was generated. One reason that periodicals relied so heavily on *Our Bodies Our Selves* was that the Boston Women's Health Collective made their learning process very clear; they made visible their limitations, invited others to help improve the guide, and continued to revise as they learned with and from women locally and through the national network. The Boston collective was one of the earliest (and most influential) feminist groups to study women's health care. As members of the collective recall in the preface to the 1984 edition, little information on women's health care was readily available in 1969 (xi). Spurred on by a workshop about "women and their bodies," part of a women's conference held in Boston in the spring of 1969 ("one of the first gatherings of women meeting specifically to talk with other women"), a group of women active in women's liberation groups in the Boston area decided to find out what they already knew about women's health care, what they had to learn, and where they could find the information they needed (xvii).

One of their earliest discoveries was that they were "capable of collecting, understanding, and evaluating medical information" ([1973 ed.; repr. in 1984 ed.] xvii). Based on their research—reading books and journals, consulting with doctors and medical students, and critically evaluating how the research connected to their own experiences as women—they developed a free course, "Women and their Bodies," and decided to distribute copies of their findings. After a year of "hard individual and collective thinking and working," with demand for the research material increasing, they decided to publish their research papers, raising the necessary money for the New England Free Press to run a 138–page newsprint edition ([1984 ed.] xi; Rimer 27). The first printing of *Women and Their Bodies*—a run of 5,000 copies in December 1970—sold so fast that three more printings, totaling 60,000 copies, quickly followed over the next year under the title *Our Bodies Our Selves*.[14] Not only the rapid success of *Our Bodies Our Selves* but also the criticisms in the periodicals of the book's omissions and biases made clear that women were demanding to know more about themselves as bodies living in the world, to develop knowledge about themselves that spoke to their lived experiences.[15]

In publishing *Our Bodies Our Selves* the Boston collective was making available what they refer to as "real knowledge": "We discovered that people don't learn very much when they are just passive recipients of information . . . and that by sharing responses we could develop a base on which to be critical of what experts tell us" ([1973 ed.] xix). They found that this real knowledge not only was personally liberating in the sense of enabling them to take greater control of their lives but also prepared them "to evaluate the institutions that are supposed to meet our [their] health needs—the hospitals, clinics, doctors, medical schools, nursing schools, public health departments, Medicaid bureaucracies and so on" (ibid. xviii, xix). The collective thus saw itself as sharing with other women knowledge they could use to care for themselves and demand better care from health-care providers.[16] And importantly, they saw their materials as in progress: they expected to give the course to a group of women who would in turn give it to other women, and so on. As more women worked on the course, they would add to it, transforming the body of knowledge. The collective intended the course to "increase consciousness about . . . women, to build [a] movement, to begin to struggle collectively for adequate health care." Significantly, they saw the research reports they had assembled to be less important than the process of inquiry they were intended to generate: "[These reports] should be used as a tool which stimulates discussion and action, which allows for new ideas and change" ([1971 ed.] 1). Although the women felt it was exciting to learn new facts about their bodies, they report that it was "more exciting to talk about how we felt about our bodies, how we felt about ourselves, how we could become more autonomous human beings, how we could act together on our collective knowledge to change the health care system for women and all people" (ibid. 2). Norma Swenson, a member of the original collective, recalls that "what was ground-breaking [about *Our Bodies Our Selves*] was the candor and honesty of women speaking about their experiences" (qtd. in Rimer 27).

Feminist periodicals across the country included *Our Bodies Our Selves* in their lists of resources, they reproduced gynecological illustrations from the book, they reviewed and critiqued the limitations of the work, and they cited the Boston collective's success to urge the formation of local collectives and clinics. The Boston collective's course was, as the group emphasizes, "only one way of spreading the word" ([1971 ed.] 2). When the collective decided to work with a commercial publisher rather than the New England Free Press, some papers registered the fear that *Our Bodies Our Selves* would be compromised, that the collective was selling out to corporate interests historically unresponsive to women's concerns.

Because the medical establishment had failed to take seriously women's knowledge and experience of their own bodies, feminist periodicals understood that part of their role was radically compensatory. Such woman-made guides as *Our Bodies Our Selves* were a necessary antidote to the neglect of women's health by the health-care system. The spring 1972 issue of San Francisco's *Mother Lode,* devoted to women and medicine, makes this particularly clear.[17] The opening editorial observes, "Throughout the women's movement, more and more information is being passed from woman to woman, group to group, city to city, on how we can learn to examine ourselves, how we can form health collectives and women's clinics to deal with our needs" (1). The editorial collective explains that they wanted to gather as much of the new information as possible "for the use of all women": "We want to pass on information to you, and in the process we want to make clear how important it is for us to gain control of our bodies through proper knowledge of them" (1). Doctors have so much power, they contend, because women are "prevented from knowing about [their] own physical beings" (1). In devoting so much space to health care, the periodicals were contributing to one of the counterinstitutions of central importance to the women's movement. They legitimated women's collective knowledge production, made that production available, identified resources, encouraged women to take part in creating clinics and improving the store of knowledge available about women's health needs, and pointed out areas in need of further investigation or development. As in all knowledge domains, the newspapers assumed not only that women would be critical consumers of the information but that they would participate in the generation of new knowledge. Readers, in other words, were expected to become writers.

Readers Becoming Writers

As is especially evident in their work on behalf of self-health, feminist periodicals both celebrated and fueled the rapid growth of the women's movement by trusting to women's intelligence and trusting that women would know what to do with the proliferation of knowledge made available in print.

The periodicals invited readers to involve themselves actively, to join in the work, not simply as consumers of the word but as creators of the word. Such creativity was seen not simply as a means to prepare for activism or to report on activism but as itself radical activity. Literacy in this sense was already a radical activity: the very fact of ordinary women breaking into print is itself a sign of social change. Most of the periodicals invited readers to get actively involved by contributing their own work. Anne Mather estimated that feminist periodicals devoted seven times more space to "reader response" than did traditional women's magazines ("History Part III," 31). But "reader response" does not quite convey the range of work readers contributed if one thinks only of letters to the editor. In the inaugural editorial of Detroit's *Womankind*, the editorial collective encouraged readers to "participate with well-written reportage, essays, fictions, and poetry" and "to submit photography and graphics." A multiracial group of women writing for a culturally and diverse public, the *Womankind* editors welcomed in particular "cross-cultural points of view" ("Womankind" 1). The twice-yearly magazine *Moving Out* asked readers to send any comments they might have about the publication; "better yet," they added, "why don't you write something for us?" ("On-Going Events" 2). Iowa's City's *Ain't I a Woman* wanted to be a vehicle for creating a collectivity of "all sisters in the mid-west," and to that end its June 26, 1970, inaugural issue asked individuals to send in articles and other "WL groups in the mid-west to do their own page" (Editorial 2).

The periodicals supported women's efforts by providing a venue, models, and a fair dose of empathetic encouragement. Because of the human scale on which the editorial groups ran their publishing operations—these were local, often grass-roots operations depending on face-to-face contact—they afforded plenty of opportunity for volunteers to get hands-on experience in every aspect of running a publishing venture. It proved enormously energizing for many of the women to learn in the company of others. But even for women who could not volunteer time to help run them, the papers modeled possibilities for writing. However old-fashioned a pedagogy modeling may appear now, the periodicals made visible radical—and iterable—acts of writing. Recognizing the sheer difficulty of writing, the editorial groups also made room in their pages for the expression of writers' struggles. In the May 1974 issue of *Big Mama Rag,* Elissa Meyer reflects on the newspaper's first two years of publication, registering the editorial collective's sense of both frustration and success in having learned how to "start with nothing and replace the emptiness with a reality" (5). The first issue of *Ain't I a Woman* ran a gentle parody of the novice writer accompanied by a line drawing of a figure padlocked into a yoke. In this short piece, titled "hang up," the novice writer agonizes over her limited abilities: "I can't write. If I try to write something, no one will like it, but they'll be afraid to say so, so they'll print it anyway, and it will ruin the paper; they'll hate me and I'll feel awful. Maybe I should just volunteer to type and paste up—no, just type; I don't know how to paste up . . . When we finish laying out our first issue, I'll spill coffee on it" (2).

Susan Jill Kahn, who had worked on Chicago's *Lavender Woman,* recalls that she "went through incredible intimidation around writing." She avoided writing for the paper even though "supposedly it was a paper that anyone could write on," because she thought she did not write well enough: "I have a fear of my own word on paper, that I'll be held to it or that I'll say something wrong." But she overcame her fears, thanks to the opportunity the paper afforded, recalling "putting [her] name to something" as her biggest accomplishment: "I wrote a little poem and stuck it in there once. And I wrote the editorial statement one month and I had my name on a couple things and that makes me feel good. You know, that was an accomplishment. To be able to do paste-up. To be able to work collectively" (qtd. in Brody 61). Similarly, Bonnie Zimmerman recalls the excitement she felt in writing for *Lavender Woman:* "People who didn't write began to write. They would try out writing, and that was exciting" (qtd. in Brody 84). Writing for the paper was one of her proudest accomplishments: "L. W. was when I began to be a writer. And that's one of the parts of my identity that is strongest now. I am a writer. So, L. W. gave me the opportunity to develop those skills, to develop a voice" (qtd. in Brody 85).

The response to the periodicals' open invitations could be overwhelming, and the sheer quantity of submissions fueled anxieties about who got to control another's creative work, how such work was to be evaluated, by what standards. In the fall 1970 issue of the Baltimore-based *Women: A Journal of Liberation,* the editors apologize to their contributors:

> Publishing this issue . . . has resulted in several painful encounters with our contributors. We received many, many manuscripts to consider for use in "Women in the Arts." Although we are excited that so many women are creatively expressing their personal and political insights into Women's Liberation, we also feel that in our attempts to include as much of this excellent material as possible, we drastically edited several articles. In a few instances, this editing may have somewhat violated the author's style and total purpose in writing the article. What is most difficult for us to assess, however, is the way the editing may have hurt women who struggled to write their articles in a particular way. ("A Letter to Our Contributors")

Even as *Big Mama Rag*'s editors wanted to make their newspaper a forum "for any woman to speak," by the third issue they were trying to figure out how to "upgrade the quality of [the] writing in general," proposing to expand their "journalism group" by adding more experienced women writers who could contribute their expertise part time (Editorial 2).

Editorial commitment to an egalitarian understanding of creativity was manifested through a resistance to the "creation of media stars" together with a celebration of the common woman, as suggested by a statement *Ain't I a Woman* reprinted from *Rat.* "Contrary to the aims of the movement," selecting out a few stars "puts forth the individual personalities as the originators of ideas and the source of inspiration rather than each and all women in common" ("Comments on Elitism" 10). But many collectives experienced a growing tension between such egalitarianism or collectivism and the desire to increase the quality of writing. This tension played out at the intersection of competing concerns: professionalism versus antiprofessionalism, individual versus collective, and authority versus creativity. In the inaugural editorial of *Ain't I a Woman,* from June 26, 1970, the fourteen women who constituted the editorial group declare their intention to put out a newspaper in their "own way": "We want no hierarchy of editor, assistants, staff, etc. All the people working on the paper should be involved in all decisions and policy. We want to maintain no 'professional' standards. 'Professionalism' has been used as an excuse for the educated elite to corner the market on knowledge and communication.... We want new structures that do not allow people to fall into leader/follower, boss/worker, powerful/powerless roles" (Editorial 2). Similarly, Shulamith Firestone and Anne Koedt justify their decision to only minimally edit selections for *Notes from the Second Year* in terms of their "anti-professionalism," which they see as a political stance (2). Antiprofessionalism can be seen as part of the utopian desire to create a "space... for action and creativity" where women could meet as equals and exchange ideas (Kearon 109). Professionalism had come to be associated with restrictively "male" (that is, rule-bound and inauthentic) writing. In a 1970 article in *Notes from the Second Year,* Pamela Kearon explained that "politics, the intellectual world, the arts and sciences, all belong to men," and thus "they set the standards and the goals." Women either had to "appeal to male standards or pass into oblivion" (109). In Kearon's terms, feminism was a matter not of putting women in positions of power as traditionally defined by men—not simply flipping the traditional hierarchy, in other words—but of creating alternative spaces in which women would collectively define the Real, not as "a static conceptual understanding but an active interpretation, always including how things shall become and the means for effecting change" (109).

It would not be news to say that women had historically been excluded by norms and rules not of their own making from participating fully in the political world. But Kearon is saying more than this.[18] Citing Hannah Arendt's *Human Condition* as a source for her thinking on the relationship between space and power, Kearon understands Truth as depending "on nothing so much as the power mobilized behind it" (109). That power is, as she sees it, not the "quality of an individual" but is created through collectivity (108). Creativity in these terms is always an assertion of power not as the act of individual genius but as the work of groups. While one can find in the periodicals many celebrations of the freedom of the individual to create according to her own lights, the privileging of collective process percolates through any number of periodicals in the period. Indeed, collectivism is itself sometimes seen as a way to ensure that the individual can work without constraint. As an *Ain't I a Woman* writer asserts: "The individual is truly free only through the collective" ("'Freedom' to Oppress?" 5).

In the winter 1971 issue of *Women,* the editorial collective reflects on the relationship between collectivity and creativity:

> The collective endeavor that we all (you readers included) engage in, year round, to get four issues of this journal to press has started us thinking about collectivity and the possibilities it offers as an artistic instrument. We have already said we deny the old myth of the "genius" artist who, ahead of her/his time, foresees and then suggests to the rest of us the vision of a new world.... And just as we deny this view of the artist as prophet and replace it with the view of artist as a historically and culturally-grounded creature, so too we want to deny the view of art as *individual* expression, and replace it with the view which we consider truest: that art is *social* expression. (Editorial 1)

Similarly, in the second issue of *Ain't I a Woman,* "the fanaticism of individualism" is seen to have "really warped our minds in this society" because "somehow we believe that if we do something all by ourselves it is done better." But readers are reminded of their collective responsibility for all women: "We cannot rise alone" ("Rising Up Together" 2).

This principle of collective responsibility found material expression in the collectivist organizational structure typical of most feminist periodicals. Of the feminist periodicals surveyed by Anne Mather in the early seventies, only three reported having a hierarchical structure, whereas 65 percent of magazines and newspapers and almost half the newsletters reported that they were collectively run ("History Part III," 23).[19] As is evidenced by the amount of print space devoted to the challenges of organization and process in feminist periodicals, editorial groups worked hard to articulate an egalitarian structure to replace what appeared to be either the hierarchical organization of the mainstream press or the haphazard workings of the underground press.

In an editorial in *Notes from the Third Year,* Firestone and Koedt reflect on some of the challenges facing the movement as a whole—and the editorial collective as a microcosm of that whole:

> In moving from the small amorphous rap group toward a more outward-directed group, the problem of "structure" arises. The women's movement will need to work out for itself a satisfactory form which can avoid the typical pitfalls of authoritarian leadership or inflexible ideology which so many other movements have experienced. With so many women's present dislike for authoritarianism, perhaps one of the major achievements of feminism will be to work out new ways of organizing ourselves that will encourage responsibility in all members, but discourage elitism—a form which can encourage strength in all women rather than create followers. Our success in accomplishing this goal will in no small part depend upon our ability to be as actively supportive of each other's new strengths and achievements as before (especially during consciousness-raising) we have been supportive and compassionate of each other's failures. (2)

Although many periodicals began this way, they often found that attempting to involve all members equally in all decision making was unwieldy and exhausting. When interviewing former activists, Francesca Polletta found that they were puzzled when "worthy antiauthoritarianism" could come to mean a leveling of all talents and "admirable collectivism" could become a "censoriousness that discouraged" dissenting voices (150). Even though collective organization was presumed to enable the development of political skills, she observes, some groups "minimized processes of learning and teaching" (170). Nevertheless, many of the periodical collectives register their ongoing commitment to making the process work pedagogically, as an opportunity for women to learn together. Many groups gradually tried to modify their processes without compromising their antiauthoritarian ideals.

The women who produced *Big Mama Rag* over a four-year period offer some sense of what it could mean to try to create a "new way of organizing." In editorials and "Where We're At" columns over the several years of publication, the members make clear that they did not have all the time in the world to put out a paper. They were all working full or part-time outside the paper to support themselves. With limited time, they had to come up with processes that were both equitable and practical. They report that they were "determined to carry sisterhood into the interactions of the group work." Disgusted by the hierarchy they found in their jobs and in society as a whole, they tried to find ways of running the paper that would "bring out each woman's unique contribution." Because they believed that no "person's potential is highly utilized when orders are handed down from the top," they experimented with alternative arrangements. They split into "task groups," and at each meeting they chose "by lot" a woman to prepare an agenda and chair the next meeting. They also chose a "process observer" whose job it was "to facilitate our evaluation of our interaction" (Editorial, *Big Mama Rag* 2). By January 1974, however, *Big Mama Rag* had altered its structure so that the paper was then run by three co-editors who split one full-time salary, with the money coming from a small foundation grant. Although they report that the paper's reputation was growing nationally ("presently Big Mama Rag is ranked among the most successful women's papers in the country, along with Ain't I a Woman, Off Our Backs, Women's Press")—and indeed, the paper is mentioned favorably in a number of other periodicals—they acknowledge that it had been something of a struggle to get a paper out "pretty consistently" (Meyer 5).

In the June 1974 issue they report that they realized that they had become more hierarchical in order to accommodate a flood of volunteers. But, in an effort to deal with "charges of elitism, Lesbian-overkill, and editorial authoritarianism" (charges that would seem to require some sort of diagnostic critique but are merely reported), they decided to "hold informal 'educational consciousness-raising' sessions" that returned them to their earlier procedure of making editorial decisions by consensus, with everyone sharing in the footwork ("Where We're At" [June 1974] 9). In the September 1974 issue of *Big Mama Rag,* the editorial group registers in their "Where We're At" column not only their exhilaration that the paper was actually working but also their sense of fatigue (16). In the midst of their ongoing struggles with tight finances, they record their continued attempts to work toward ways to share leadership equitably ("Where We're At" [June 1975] 4), including an attempt at a two-tier structure. The staff would be composed of the *Big Mama Rag* collective (the core group) and "Pals and Chums" (the various people who contributed from time to time) ("Where We're At" [July 1975] 1). Like other collectives, they found that not everyone could or would do the necessary work, so they had to create a structure that would ensure that the paper would come out and at the same time retain the support and advice of a larger group of women. By October 1975, however, the editorial group recognized that their "energies [had been] bound up in process rather than going into the product" (4). For the remainder of volume 3 and through volume 4, *Big Mama Rag* wrestled with competing approaches to feminism and financial difficulties. By November 1976 the paper reported that it was in crisis; it folded at the end of the year, having produced four volumes, from eight to twelve issue per volume.

Eventually the intense collective process exhausted many groups, even those with adequate funding. In analyzing the publishing history of *Lavender Woman,* Michal Brody identifies a "universal process, shared by any co-identified group in motion": "The steps of the process are conjoining, inspiration, activity, conflict, exhaustion, and dispersion" (183). Bonnie Zimmerman, who had been a member of the *Lavender Woman* collective, recalls the enormous amount of time and endless meetings: "Hours and hours of meetings, and what I think happens in collectives is that the people with the loudest voices—the people who are the most articulate and the most educated and the most trained in the use of verbal stuff—which tends to mean that it's related to class—those people tend to be the ones that end up making the decisions, because the other people feel frustrated and, you know, get silent and pull back" (qtd. in Brody 79). Zimmerman recalls as well that "some people do the work and some people don't," and "the people who do the work...have the most day-to-day decision making power" (79). However fair that might seem to be on some level, she remembers that some members of the collective resented the differential distribution of power that gave greater say to those who actually did the work.

Egalitarian process was understood to depend not only on organizational structure to ensure that all participants had an equal say but also on representation—a "collectivity of sisters," as *Ain't I a Woman* put it. It was not good enough simply to report on the diversity of womankind; it was necessary to ensure that the editorial collectives were themselves composed of such a diversity. I found that few of the editorial groups identified themselves in terms of race, ethnicity, or class. Some editorials mention sexual orientation and marital status, or indicate whether or not individual members had children, or whether they held outside jobs; a few include photographs of the editorial groups. A group photograph in the third issue of *Womankind,* for example, indicates that, at least within its first year of operation, the staff included blacks and whites. *Lesbian Woman* included a "Black and Lavender" page so that black lesbian feminists in the editorial collective had dedicated space to work. *Ain't I a Woman* included a "gay page." But designating separate space in this way could feel like acts of tokenism or co-optation and fed criticisms that women's liberation's counterinstitutions were run by white women who were not willing to give up their white privileges in any substantial way. Occasionally some publications register the absence of women of color, as does Iowa's *Ain't I a Woman.* Its June 26, 1970, editorial attributes the problem to geography: "Unlike our sisters in Chicago and Detroit, who have large brown and black populations and proportionately large working class populations, most of us tend to work in groups [that are] middle-class, university privileged and bourgeois mentality" (Editorial 2).

Although it is not clear to what extent editorial groups were themselves representative of the range of women who comprised the larger population, as was the utopian hope, it does appear that within the articles, poems, and graphics, some fuller sense of difference is represented. As noted earlier, writers often did identify themselves in terms of race, class, age, work status, and sexual orientation (and, far less often, ethnicity). It is thus in the content of the periodicals, more than in the makeup of collectives, that a greater diversity of women is evident. But editorial groups and contributors to the periodicals quickly realized that demographic representation was not by itself sufficient if all women were expected to write in accordance with an unexamined notion of standards. As soon as editorial groups had to decide what to include in their publications or how to suggest to a writer that changes needed to be made, they found that they were already implicated in the "professionalism" they sought to avoid. They had to confront the fact that they might be taking for granted their own privileged status as educated women. A white member of the *Lavender Woman* collective recalls how she did not at first understand that wanting the newspaper "to read a certain way" was a reflection of "skin privilege" (Brody 52). In retrospect, a black member of the *Lavender Woman* collective recognizes now that she left the group in part because the question of standards was so destructive: "It's stuff about standards of English, and how something needs to sound in order to be read and understood, and it didn't take me long, as I grew in terms of knowing myself and my own self-hate, to understand that those standards were totally arbitrary, classist and racist. But when I was working on the newspaper I didn't have that consciousness" (qtd. Brody 128). Although the periodicals began by assuming that they needed to break from what were understood to be traditionally male forms of literate practice, they could not escape the inevitable tensions caused when their desire for utopian inclusiveness ran up against their desire to put out "quality" publications. A romantic iconoclasm they shared with other contemporaneous movements was not enough to sustain many of the publications. But the fact that the questions were raised, that they were addressed with such seriousness, is worthy of our attention now.

To read the periodicals as part of the historical record of midcentury feminism is to be struck by how generative they were, how various the writing was in both content and form, and how exuberantly cacophonous a political forum they provided. They attempted to hold women together coalitionally to effect revolutionary change when from the beginning this heterogeneous movement born of centrifugal force was spinning out in a myriad of directions. They did not resolve (nor do I think they could have in any simple sense) that most basic of pedagogical dilemmas: how to make room for all women to contribute their knowledge and creativity to the articulation in print of a radical feminism and at the same time create enough critical friction to make movement possible. Collaborative process by itself was not the answer, as will be discussed more fully in chapter 5.

2

Virtue Sallies Forth and Sees Her Adversary: Reclaiming Feminist Polemic

Conscientious avoiders of grand moral claims . . . can be accused of restricting conviction to what propriety will tolerate.

—Anne Drury Hall, *Ceremony and Civility*

We have not yet spoken of that indignation, that rage—perhaps the essence of militancy—which never finds its way into movement writing but which surely must be the impetus of our commitment. Tonight I am with the rage, an old friend now.

—Beverly Jones and Judith Brown, *Toward a Female Liberation Movement*

Lenin said, "Dialectics in the proper sense is the study of contradiction in the very essence of objects." This . . . defines what we will be doing.

—"A Method for the Movement"

BEVERLY JONES AND JUDITH BROWN had been active in the Congress of Racial Equality (CORE) and Students for a Democratic Society (SDS) in Florida when they composed *Toward a Female Liberation Movement.* Dissatisfied with the "Women's Manifesto," a statement on women's liberation issued by the female caucus of the national SDS convention in the summer of 1967, Jones and Brown analyzed the condition of activist women in particular, as well as women in the larger culture, and urged the creation of a separate movement on behalf of female liberation. The resulting position paper, often referred to as the "Florida Paper" and widely reprinted in pamphlet form (see figure 6), has been considered one of the founding documents of radical feminism. What strikes me now, reading this pamphlet

Figure 6. *Toward a Female Liberation Movement* (*source:* author's collection).

over thirty years later, is a passage about rage that appears as a coda on the final page of their thirty-two-page pamphlet. There is in this brief moment of reflection the hint of an apology—"as I sit here in poorly controlled rage, I realize that there is one thing we have omitted"—at the same time, there is also the recognition that rage is potentially constructive, the "maelstrom in which I come to recall again my own alienation," an alienation that, oxymoronically, connects the writer to others. It is this double sense of rage—as something that "ought" to be controlled but is also at the same time a vital matrix from which empathetic understanding and action come—that interests me as I reflect on the proliferation of writing produced by midcentury radical feminists. What sense can I make of that rage now? What good does it do us to recall it, to try to make sense of it?

In *Why Women's Liberation?* a pamphlet reprint of a December 1969 *Ramparts'* article, Marlene Dixon argues that rage was at the heart of the women's liberation movement. Women needed to "learn the meaning of rage, the violence that liberates the spirit" (63). The process begins with "women's knowledge...that they are not inferior." The recognition of the mismatch between what they know to be true and how they are nonetheless constructed in the larger culture lights the fuse, and the ensuing rage then "impels women into a total commitment to women's liberation" (63). Rage is evident in action, Dixon argues, but it is also evident in words: "The rhetoric of invective is an equally essential stage, for in discovering and venting their rage against the enemy—and the enemy in everyday life is men—women also experience the justice of their own violence. They learn the first lessons in their own latent strength. Women must learn to know themselves as revolutionaries. They must become hard and strong in their determination, while retaining their humanity and tenderness" (63). In her study of the development of feminist academic journals, Patrice McDermott has described the earliest publications of women's liberation as "written in the angry, confrontational style of earlier underground press newspapers," often taking the form of manifestos, "concise expressions of rage and politics" (32). But Dixon's qualification that the rhetoric of invective is an essential *stage* in the movement toward feminist self-determination is important to emphasize. Although it has become commonplace to assume that the rhetoric of sixties radicalism in general was more rant than reason, that invective was the primary currency, feminist writings suggest a greater discursive range. To understand that discursive range, however, requires us to reconsider how women drew from available rhetorical resources to work out of (rather than be swallowed by) the "maelstrom of rage."

The coda to Jones and Brown's pamphlet suggests that women themselves were not unaware of the relationship between rage and politics, but the ways in which this relationship was manifested in and mediated through writing has not been adequately addressed. Part of the problem is that a full range of women's print performance is not readily available. Influential anthologies from the period, such as Robin Morgan's *Sisterhood is Powerful,* Toni Cade Bambara's *Black Woman,* and Sookie Stambler's *Women's Liberation: Blueprint for the Future,* begin to give some sense of the kinds of writing women were producing, but as the editors acknowledge, however inclusive they may have tried to be, the anthologies could reproduce only a relatively small sample. Without reading the texts as they were made available to readers, in their multiple forms and material contexts, the work is either unreadable or appears flattened and sanitized. But recovering the material traces is not enough. To read in such a way that is neither nostalgic nor defensive also requires rethinking the analytical terms traditionally used to understand textual performance.

The late sixties and early seventies, which Sheila Tobias calls the "first five years of sustained and politically inspired new thinking about women" (205), witnessed an explosion of feminist publication. As early as 1970 Robin Morgan reflected on the challenge she faced in selecting from this outpouring of print representative materials for the anthology *Sisterhood is Powerful.* Thanks to the "quicksilver growth and change" of the movement, Morgan observes, some leaflets and manifestos already seemed to be "historical documents." From the "voluminous amounts of literature" produced, Morgan could not hope to offer a comprehensive overview of the movement (xvii). Rather, she offers what she takes to be a reflection of the movement's potential, noting with delight "a blessedly uneven quality... in the book": "There is a certain kind of linear, tight, dry, boring, male super-consistency that we are beginning to reject. That's why this collection combines all sorts of articles, poems, graphics, and sundry papers. There are the well-documented, statistically solid pieces and the intensely personal experiences" (xvii). Similarly, in her preface to *The Black Woman,* Toni Cade Bambara remarks that her list of materials "grew and grew" so that she decided that she could only offer a "beginning," with the expectation that other books and journals would further the work (11). In what Benita Roth aptly calls the "crowded, competitive social movement sector," activist women with various affiliations not only circulated their writings in-house, often as mimeographed papers distributed locally, but also published in periodicals or with publishers associated with the New Left, antiwar groups, and civil rights organizations (70). Jones and Brown's paper was fairly typical in that it was first published by the Southern Student Organizing Committee and then given a wider distribution by the New England Free Press, priced at twenty cents a copy. As an identifiably separate women's liberation movement emerged, newsprint resource guides such as *PM3: The Women's Movement, Where It's At!* (with an initial circulation of 50,000) compiled bibliographies of such reprints, and feminist periodicals across the country reproduced many of the statements in whole or in part and thus spread the word more widely.

Because many movement women saw themselves as deliberately refusing traditional forms of argumentation (even as they borrowed from them), to the extent that such forms were seen to silence women, it is necessary to find language that can better register their sense of rhetorical wariness and self-consciousness. While much useful work has been generated through recent interest in conceptualizing feminist rhetoric, and while that interest can be traceable to ideas generated out of second-wave feminism, I have not found the traditional terminology, even as it has been realigned to better suit feminist ideas, adequate to make sense of much of the writing radical women were producing. Kenneth Graham has suggested that academics currently participate in a revalorization of rhetoric in part because it is consonant with antiessentialism (223). We are in a sense, then, professionally suspicious of claims to certainty (no doubt for important and sound reasons). For academic feminists this has meant a renewed interest in "ethos" and the foregrounding of the positionality of the rhetor, in part as a way to interrogate what is read as the "assumptions of unanimity and solidarity out of which second-wave feminism was born" (Code 2).[1] I take seriously this critical project, and yet, as I work with the writings of radical women, I find that I have to shift gears if I am also to take seriously the passion of conviction registered in their writings. In other words, even as I understand the ways in which any writer is located in time, space, and culture, and thus the writer's statements are always already contingent, I also have to try to come to terms with beliefs that are not offered as contingent or equivocal. I have thus looked to a term on the fringe of rhetoric, to the concept of "polemic," in order to get at the "anti-rhetorical directness" (to borrow Kenneth Graham's useful phrase) of much midcentury feminist writing.

Antirhetorical directness is not simply reducible to rant. While women used blunt language and in some cases deployed "impolite" terms in scathingly satirical ways (as in the *off our backs* parodic ad for "Butter Balls" or in such cultural analyses as the "Bitch Manifesto," both discussed in the previous chapter), the blunt language is rarely used simply to shock or arouse. Thus, when Alice Echols refers to the Jones and Brown pamphlet as polemical, she does so not as a dismissive gesture but to signal something of the political dynamics operating around and through the pamphlet (*Daring* 62). *Polemic* has been used as a term of opprobrium, signaling a reader's sense that the partisan or even propagandistic writer has exceeded the bounds of good sense and good taste, but it has also been used historically to signal a passionate commitment to a cause that generates assertions of truth. Polemic in this latter sense is antirhetorical in some of the same ways as dialectic; the polemicist writes out of a belief in a cause or a truth rather than in terms of the inevitable provisionality of a rhetorical gesture. Reading at least some of the enormous outpouring of print in terms of a reclaimed concept of polemic suggests a great deal about the complex and shifting political terrain women were attempting to negotiate, but it also has led me to think that we have been a bit too quick to assume that midcentury feminism was born out of unanimity and solidarity.

Rethinking Polemic

At first glance, *polemic* seems to be a near-synonym of *argument.* According to the *Oxford English Dictionary,* the word *polemic* derives from the Greek term for war and refers to "controversial argument, especially religious controversy." *The American Heritage Dictionary* defines *polemic* as "a controversy or argument, especially one that is a refutation of or an attack upon a specified opinion or doctrine." *Polemics*—with an *s*—is defined as the "art or practice of argumentation or controversy." Given this etymology, one might expect *polemic* to appear as a term of art within formal rhetoric, but I have found no reference to the term in English-language manuals, handbooks, or histories of rhetoric from the English Renaissance forward. For all the concern about *vituperare* in epideictic, for example, and the concern about the place of pathos more generally in argumentation from Aristotle, Cicero, and Quintilian on forward—both terms of art one might associate with polemic—polemic does not appear to be used as an analytical category within formal rhetoric. Rather, polemic operates in English outside the manuals, as it apparently operated in Greek—that is, adjectivally to name discursive processes or movements that threaten the regularizing bounds of rhetoric. Indeed, the most consistent element that marks polemic is that it puts into question the notion of boundaries or limits.

Benjamin Arditi and Jeremy Valentine argue that if one were to try to formalize certain styles or codes as polemical, "such styles would quickly lose their purpose and their place in proportion to the extent that they become familiar and ideal": "This was the fate of the classical manuals of rhetoric and argumentation that rapidly became merely procedures for performing allegiance to a doctrine or position rather than reflections on how it was possible for such positions to be open to dispute. In fact, they only ever really worked as displays or spectacles within quite specific institutional settings" (7–8).[2] In Arditi and Valentine's terms, rhetoric systematized the "topoi of engagement," whereas polemic emerges precisely through the failure of the traditional grounds of argumentation (8). Polemic depends on a recognition of traditional grounds of argumentation and at the same time comes into being to make evident the inadequacy of those grounds. This way of conceptualizing polemic strikes me as particularly useful for thinking about radical feminist print production. The very uneasiness that Jones and Brown register about "poorly controlled rage" suggests their understanding of how argument is supposed to work: as any number of rhetorics could teach us, it isn't that rhetoric makes no room for emotion, even the emotion of anger, but to be effective, the appeal to emotion is supposed to be deployed with care, harnessed if not fully subordinated to logos (see Blair 358–65). In rather polite terms, P. J. Corbett states the problem: "In some cases, there is something undignified about a rational creature being precipitated into action through the stimulus of aroused passions" (86).

Because women understand that they have traditionally been figured as inhabiting the domain of the irrational, the price of "poorly controlled rage" precipitating action could be especially high. And yet, to the extent that rage is recognized as generative (as Jones and Brown suggest), the price of observing the decorums may be higher still. Several articles in publications from the period critique psychotherapy for attempting to treat a woman's feelings as illness, as a condition to be medicalized or controlled. In an early statement on consciousness raising, for example, Kathie Sarachild observes, "We assume that our feelings are telling us something from which we can learn . . . , that our feelings mean something worth analyzing . . . , that our feelings are saying something political" ("A Program" 78). Although Sarachild argues that the larger culture assumes one must "master" one's feelings—"control, stifle, [or] stop" them—she asserts that feelings may *sometimes* direct us to "a new and better idea of where we want to go and then to action which might help us get there" (78). In reflecting on the ways in which the personal is the political, Carol Hanisch argues that "therapy assumes that someone is sick and that there is a cure, e.g., a personal solution," when in fact "women are messed over, not messed up" (76). Sarachild and Hanisch both argue that, rather than turn inward, the analysis of feelings must turn outward to consider what social forces are operating to "mess up" women and in what ways. Much of the enormous outpouring of radical feminist print production at midcentury focuses precisely on that political move outward: not resting on personal testimonial or assuming that the individual's story is sufficient, but tracing the patterns and variations of gender politics.

Such polemics as Sarachild's and Hanisch's can be said to emerge to make the traditional argumentative terrain of controlled emotion problematic. Polemic does not settle the problem or lead to the acceptance of rage for its own sake (as if emotion itself, or rage in particular, were the issue), but rather it begins to make visible the inadequacy of operant forms of argumentation and begins to consider when and how to deploy feeling, emotion, even rage, as sources of ideas that lead to knowledge and action. Indeed, in Arditi and Valentine's terms, such discourse *is* polemic as long as it *does not* settle the matter, as long as it remains volatile and disruptive. bell hooks has argued that as women "internalized the idea that describing their own woe was synonymous with developing a critical political consciousness"—that is, when women settled on the idea that describing their individual woes was enough—"the progress of feminist movement was stalled" (25). However, as long as women resisted the centripetal pull of introspection (Piercy, "Grand Coolie Damn" 422) and worked to "create a space for contact" that would allow them to break out of "the isolation from women of other class and race groups" (hooks, "Black Women" 6), the movement had a degree of productive volatility.

The prominence of polemical discourse evident in movement publications can be read as one gauge of how volatile were the attempts to create and maintain spaces of contact across difference. There can be no way independent of context to say what made or makes a text volatile and disruptive, and the context of a text's production is itself available to us always mediated, reconstructed from a patchwork of possibilities that inevitably say as much about our own investments as about the context of the text's production and immediate reception. In this sense, polemic names not form or structure that is simply available—visible on the page—to the reader, nor is it technē or compositional guidelines (in contrast to rhetoric); rather, it is a way of naming what is perceived as orientation, attitude, intention, or stance in relation to situation. Such perception of orientation, attitude, and so on signals much about the reader's relationship to the text, hinging on how one is positioned or perceives oneself to be positioned in relation to the text. Thus, one can understand why from the vantage of thirty years' remove, one might refer to the earliest publications of midcentury feminism as angry and confrontational in order to distance current practice from that point of "origin"—both to recognize (and derive political legitimacy from) that origin in the sociopolitical volatility of an earlier moment and at the same time to distance current feminist practice in the academy from the "excess" of such volatility in order to ground it in (and derive intellectual legitimacy from) more conventional forms of knowledge production. In short, the aim would be to ensure that women's academic work appear more rational. This is an understandable project in the midst of what has been characterized as a backlash against feminism and underscores the extent to which much of the material remains "polemical" in that it retains its potential to disrupt and unsettle.[3]

Polemic forces an awareness of one's relationship to a text, forces a recognition of how one is positioned by a text and thus is openly partisan, but partisan in particular ways. Evelyn Tribble suggests that polemical discourse emerges especially at those historical moments when differential power relations are especially evident, but I find that what might be called the polemical context is more particular than that. In reflecting on the sixties, Kenneth Cmiel observes that polemic seems to arise in the midst of a relatively unregulated civic forum (269). It appears that when the recognition of differential power relations combines with cracks in the well-regulated society (as when censorship or the means to enforce censorship weakens), polemic can be seen to sprout like weeds in the sidewalk and to open up the cracks further. One could trace a cycle from relatively regulated argumentative discourse abiding by the rules of manuals and socially regulated decorum to eruptions of polemic that may appear to those included in or invested in the well-ordered society as mere rant but are actually demands to reorder the civil (or not so civil) space. When approached thus, some notions of civic space can be seen as intended to quiet difference and dissent. Polemic can be used, in fact, as a kind of cultural barometer, as a way of registering—in terms of both what is produced and how it is read—how tolerant the civic space is perceived to be.

In early Christian religious dispute and again in the English Renaissance, I find that the polemical context has been understood to involve not only a recognition of differential power relations but something closer to internecine conflict.[4] Arditi and Valentine suggest that polemic "involves a tacit appeal to a space of commonality" (135), even though the fact of the exchange paradoxically suggests that the commonality does not exist. Put differently, in polemic "the mode of address... represent[s] that which is held in common to be both present as a stake in the dispute and absent as that which is to be settled" (Arditi and Valentine 1).

In the remainder of this chapter, I turn to specific instances of feminist leaflet prose, considering their modes of address to understand what is both held in common and in dispute. I start with Jones and Brown's pamphlet and then move first to prose works that contributed to the changing movement's evolving dialogue (specifically, two arguments for black women's liberation) and finally to a manifesto on behalf of a distinct women's culture.

Toward a Female Liberation Movement

In the case of Jones and Brown's pamphlet, Alice Echols has located the polemical context in terms of a disagreement among women within the movement, that loosely coordinated and loosely defined coalition of male and female activists associated with antiwar, civil rights, and student rights groups. As members of an SDS chapter, Jones and Brown were addressing other women in the national organization in some sense as fellow travelers. Jones and Brown appear to have followed a familiar path toward radical feminism, that of the many white women who became increasingly dissatisfied with their secondary status within the civil rights, antiwar, and students' rights movements, which they understood to reflect their collective position within the larger culture. They do not fit the familiar profile perfectly, however, in that at least Beverly Jones identifies herself not as young but as middle-aged. In a sense, these activist women were following the lead of both the Black Power movement and the antiwar movement. Black activists questioned the motives of white liberals in the civil rights movement and urged black people to "escape dependency" on whites through "group solidarity based on black consciousness" (Chalmers 31). At the same time, as escalation of the Vietnam War increased pressure on draft-age men, more male activists were drawn away from civil rights to antiwar activities. Similarly, increasing numbers of women stepped back from their involvement in what were perceived to be male-dominated political coalitions to attend to what were understood to be women's concerns conceptualized increasingly in separatist terms. As Adrienne Rich recalls, in declaring themselves part of "an independent revolutionary movement of women," an "autonomous women's movement . . . , women already active in movements for social justice were refusing to postpone issues of gender injustice, male chauvinism, and sexual politics till 'after the revolution'" (*Blood* viii).

Jones and Brown share in common with others in the larger movement a belief in radical democracy: "We turn [to] that central theme [in New Left philosophy] that human beings, by combining in organizations, by seeking to participate in decision-making which affects their lives, can achieve a democratic society, and hence a life-experience perhaps approximating their potentiality" (23). And yet the double absence of such democracy is registered first through what they call the "soft-minded logic" of the "Women's Manifesto" in having to ask for greater representation for women within SDS—and the perception on the part of Jones and Brown that the very mode of the request itself underscores the extent to which SDS is unable to actualize in its structures the radical democracy it proclaims (1). Jones and Brown note sarcastically that "lest the men get upset by all this wild talk [i.e., the "Women's Manifesto"] or even think of taking it seriously," the SDS women have added "a reassuring note" in the form of two oddly conjoined slogans: "Freedom now! We love you!" The implication here is that this juxtaposition of demand and appeasement is a too familiar accommodationist female gesture: women learn to smile to mute the threat, to suggest their willingness to forgive. They have not yet achieved the freedom to "unsmile," as Shulamith Firestone and Anne Koedt put it (*Notes from the Second Year* 2). In these terms, the accommodationist gesture cancels out the demand. Jones and Brown then ask, "What lessons are to be learned from this fantastic document, from the discrimination which preceded it, and the unchanging scene which followed?" (2). If the other women in the SDS really believed in radical democracy, the pamphlet suggests, they would quit pandering to the men in the organization and help form a separate organization.

Although there is a degree of recognition of commonality with the audience, Jones and Brown write in terms not of some communal "we" but of something more complicated than that. They occasionally use the first-person plural to designate themselves—as in "*We* have emphasized the plight of the married woman in her relationship with a power-oriented representative of the master caste" (19; emphasis added)—but they almost never use it to encompass either women in general or women in the movement. Their's is not groupspeak (or what Lorraine Code calls "we-saying"), but neither is it the personal testimonials of two disconnected individuals (a mode commonly associated with second-wave feminism). They write as a coalition of two, noting their historical connection to their audience at the same time that they distinguish themselves from their audience in terms of age and situation in life. The authors have belonged to an SDS chapter, but Jones at least is older than the majority of their audience, and they assume that most of the members of that audience are college students. Thus, part 1 begins with Jones locating herself briefly in relation to the audience as "a middle-aged female accustomed to looking to militant youth for radical leadership" who is then shocked by the manifesto that these supposed radicals have produced (1). Later, in part 2, Brown characterizes the relative privilege of white, female college students that tends to insulate them from what Jones and Brown assert to be the realities of a patriarchal society. The pamphlet is thus constructed as a dialogue in which differences matter not in idealized or essentialized terms but as manifested in real, material ways.

Early on in the pamphlet, Jones and Brown express empathy for women in the movement (in language tough enough to match the historical circumstances), even as they step back from their affiliation to make visible the grounds of their differences and their stake in the dispute: "No one can say that women in the movement lack courage. As a matter of fact they have been used, aside from their clerical role, primarily as bodies on the line. Many have been thrown out of school, disowned by their families, clubbed by the cops, raped by the nuts, and gone to jail with everyone else" (2). But "any honest appraisal of their condition," Jones and Brown assert, "would...lead people out of logic, impulse, and desire for self preservation, to shoot at the guys who are shooting at them. Namely, first of all, to fight their own battles" (2). The assumption that the writers share some values in common with their immediate audience and yet also disagree in fundamental ways underscores the internecine quality of the polemical context. What readers may notice as the relative emotional intensity of polemic—or what Debra Shuger calls "polemical immediacy" (3)—can be tied not simply to the degree of heat fueled by a commitment to a cause but also to the relative proximity of opposition. It is one thing to complain about some distant enemy and another when one shares much in common with the opponent, when the opponent perhaps has been (or may yet be) an ally. The heat seems to come, in other words, in part from the falling away of a friend—or the potential falling away of a friend—as much as the egregious behavior of an alien and unfamiliar Other. The heat of an internecine conflict may thus feel particularly acute.

But the polemical terrain is more complicated than a matter of infighting alone. The infighting plays out across a larger culturally contested terrain. In figuring the immediate, proximate opposition—in this case, the younger radical women—polemic also figures a more distant but very present opposition—patriarchy, or in the terms of the pamphlet, male chauvinism. In a sense, to the extent that the radical women ally themselves too closely with patriarchy, they make clear the extent of their political error. Consequently, although the pamphlet does not address men directly, as will be discussed more fully below, it must characterize patriarchy or male chauvinism to point out the limitations and dangers in the SDS manifesto's position. Jones and Brown offer a critique of patriarchy in drawing a portrait of SDS leadership when they assert that even if an "individual male leader may be able to rise above [the] personal threat" posed by allowing women to participate in the group on the basis of full equality, "he cannot deviate from the rules of the game without jeopardizing his own leadership and the group itself" (7). They then broaden their critique to suggest the taken-for-granted quality of physical and symbolic violence against women in the larger society (11–12, 16–17). The force of such criticism, however, has less to do with "taking on the men" and more to do with educating (warning) younger women about the "ways of the world," a role more experienced women have historically played in a variety of cultural contexts.

The proximate and the distant opposition are both constructed literally on the page. Polemic, in this sense, "peoples the page" (Tribble 109). While this means incorporating and redeploying the opposition's words, it is more than simply attributing a set of ideas to an author (as I've just done in citing Tribble), and something more than ad-hominem, personal attack or name-calling, to the extent that the opposition is figured as a collective. Thus, using a format remarkably like Renaissance religious controversialist writings, Jones and Brown quote from the very document they seek to discredit, and significantly, they "quote" with an important substitution of words. Jones and Brown see the "'radical women' demanding respect and leadership . . . and coming on with soft-minded NAACP logic and an Urban League list of grievances and demands." To emphasize what they take to be the "fruitless" rhetoric employed, Jones and Brown, substitute terms: *white* and *black* for *male* and *female*, respectively, while replacing references to SDS with "the city council" in order to show how the document is a "rather pathetic attempt on the part of the [women's] caucus to prove its credentials by mimicking the dominant group's rhetoric on power politics." Unlike other instances of women's liberation rhetoric in which women's oppression is compared with the oppression of blacks—a move excoriated by bell hooks for its erasure of black women and its refusal to recognize differences in kind and degree of discrimination[5]—in this instance Jones and Brown are attempting to expose the manifesto's rhetoric as "ludicrous" by reminding the audience of recent history: black groups had tried a similar approach with local white power groups to no avail. Women should learn from that history and recognize that those in power will not give it up. It is as if they were asking, "Why repeat a rhetoric that has already failed?" Their paraphrase thus functions as deeply skeptical parodic reminder:

> 1. Therefore we demand that our brothers on the city council recognize that they must deal with their own problems of white chauvinism in their personal, social, and political relationships.
>
> 2. It is obvious from this meeting of the city council that full advantage

> is not being taken of the abilities and potential contributions of blacks. We call upon the black people to demand full participation in all aspects of local government from licking stamps to assuming leadership positions.
>
> 3. People in leadership positions must be aware of the dynamics of creating leadership and are responsible for cultivating all the black resources available to the local government.... And so on. (1)

Only late in the pamphlet do Jones and Brown invoke the phrase "male chauvinism" (29–30), and as Echols reads it, they do so not as a direct address to a male audience but as a way of educating women by giving a name to the practices they have described through a series of scenes—workplace, marriage, and the "limbo" of college. They focus primarily on demonstrating to the immediate audience of younger, white women the need for a separate women's movement, a movement independent of such male-dominated organizations as the SDS: "If the females in SDS ever really join the battle they will quickly realize that no sweet-talking list of grievances and demands, no appeal to male conscience, no behind-the-scenes or in-the-home maneuvering is going to get power for women. If they want freedom, equality, and respect, they are going to have to organize and fight for them realistically and radically" (3). Drawing on their experience in CORE, Jones and Brown compare women's situation in the SDS with the situation of whites in the civil rights movement, a position that for all its good intentions could translate into a kind of noblesse oblige:

> What happened to [women] throughout the movement is very much what happened to all whites in the early civil rights days. Whites acted out of moral principles, many acted courageously, and they became liberalized but never radicalized. Which is to say, they never quite came to grips with the reality of anybody's situation. It is interesting to speculate on why this should be the case. At least one reason, it seems to me, is that people who set about to help other people generally manage to maintain important illusions about our society, how it operates, and what is required to change it. It isn't just that they somehow manage to maintain these illusions, they are compelled to maintain them by their refusal to recognize the full measure of their own individual oppression, the means by which it is brought about, and what it would take to alter their condition. (2)

Shifting the lines of comparison, Jones and Brown next compare radical women (and here they seem to mean, but do not say, white women rather than all women) to radical blacks who had left the "white controlled civil rights movement, [and] started fighting for [themselves] instead of the American Dream" (with the "American Dream" signaling a dangerous and misleading myth). The "best thing that may yet happen to potentially radical young women is that they [too] will be forced to stop fighting for the 'movement' and start fighting primarily for the liberation and independence of women" (3). Jones and Brown thus construct their proximate audience as too caught up in fighting other people's battles to "get radicalized." Perhaps more damning is their charge that the younger, almost exclusively white women in the SDS operate as the female equivalent of "Uncle Toms" to the extent that their manifesto is an attempt to ingratiate themselves with the "male power structure of the movement" (2–3).

It is important to reiterate Echols's reading of the pamphlet: that the white male power structure is not the immediate target in that what might be called the "polemic intention" can be seen as involving more than an expectation that the distant opposition will be won over: this distant opposition is perceived in fact to be so distant that it is not even within the reach of persuasion. One might think of English controversialist literature in which differing branches of Calvinism dispute against the relatively distant backdrop of presumably unpersuadable Roman Catholicism. In these terms, if the male members of the SDS had been understood to have been persuadable, Jones and Brown would not have needed to compose their own manifesto. They could have simply signed on to the "Women's Manifesto" already circulating and count on the reasonableness of the men to whom that manifesto was addressed. But they do not see the men as likely to be persuaded: "We cannot expect them to relinquish, by our gentle persuasion, the power their sex knows and takes for granted. They do not even know how" (19).

Reflecting on the First National Conference of Women's Liberation, held near Chicago in 1968, Marlene Dixon remarked that persuading the male left ought not to be the primary goal of women's liberation: "Women must face facts. Men will never, until forced by circumstances, place first, or even urgent, priority upon a struggle against the oppression of women. Witness the fact that there is not one male dominated organization, from the Left-liberal New University Conference to the radical Youth Movement, that has been willing to place top priority upon the women's struggle. Indeed the idea is so repugnant to many men that they cannot tolerate a woman who refuses male leadership in order to address her energies primarily to her sisters" (qtd. in Burris 103–4). Read in these terms, the men are not the primary concern of Jones and Brown, much less the primary audience, and in this sense the document cannot be called "male bashing" in a simple or direct sense, as was sometimes the charge leveled against feminist writing. Further, the document is not directed toward arousing male opposition and thus needs to be distinguished from eristic—that is, from fighting words or fighting as display of one's verbal dexterity. It is thus more than verbal pyrotechnics (see Vickers's reading of Plato's *Gorgias* [111]; Cmiel 263). Rather, by figuring within the text an immediate or proximate opposition of fellow radical women, Jones and Brown construct their pamphlet primarily as woman-to-woman discourse, and that gives them discursive license to speak frankly.

In describing "the Invisible Audience" of "'male heavies' who had ironically done so much to bring about the existence of a radical Women's Female Liberation Movement" through their refusal to take women's concerns seriously, Marlene Dixon contends that the women attending the first national conference on women's liberation were "decimated by the invisible male audience," and thus the "real split among the women hinged upon the significant audience that women addressed: other women, or Movement men" (qtd. in Burris 103). What is evident in the Jones and Brown pamphlet is that they directed their pamphlet to "other women," and they note that most women with whom they had shared their ideas accepted their "description of [women's] lot with little argument" (31). Not all women who contributed to the reemergence of feminism at midcentury would have seen themselves as hailed by this address, of course, nor do I want to say that the pamphlet was aimed at all women. Jones and Brown were addressing a specific group of women (and not men) who had been involved in the larger movement. In a sense the differential male/female power structure is treated as a given, and although clearly a source of "rage," it does not constitute the pamphlet's principal focus. Rather, Jones and Brown's purpose can be read as tactical, designed to redirect younger (primarily white) radical women's activism toward more effective strategies to combat gender inequity. Perhaps the effect of side-lining other potential members of the audience was all the more irritating to those excluded—and no doubt generated heat from another quarter—and in this sense, the move seems to be analogous to the contemporaneous black power movement's efforts to say "let's look to our own house and leave Whitey to his own problems." Indeed, in part 2 of the pamphlet, Jones and Brown suggest why "looking to one's own house" is a necessary move.

It should not surprise us that their account of the situation parallels the history of earlier suffragists, who were expected to defer their concerns first until abolition was achieved and then until peace was restored following World War I rather than recognize the common cause among and between these efforts (see Riley). Jones and Brown note that male leadership in the

SDS had attempted to keep militant women within the fold "for the good of the movement." More "sophisticated" male leaders might say to the militant women: "There is a war; radical men are being cut down on all sides; we know there must be merit in what you say, but for the good of the movement, we ask you to wait, to defer to the higher aim of draft resistance; besides, if you will fight along with us in our battles, you will receive equality when we return from the serious front" (21). Jones and Brown urge women to resist this "sophisticated" appeal by recognizing that there will always be another cause pushing women's liberation to the back of the line; if women want equality, if *they* want liberation, *they* will have to act to get it.

But what action is called for? Jones and Brown say that they are wary of utopian solutions, arguing instead for multiple short- and long-term tactics (including "emergency tactics for non-separatists," those women who maintained their ties to men) (26). Women must develop physical self-confidence by learning self-defense; they should force the media to portray women in "their total spectrum"; women must learn their own history, develop and use "scientific competency," demand equal pay for equal work (even if some radicals have as they say "pooh-poohed" such an effort), work against job discrimination, share what they know about themselves and about survival strategies with one another, develop strategies for overcoming "legal discrimination," and support newsletters and journals as writers and readers; and women have to claim the right to control their own bodies (16–18, 30). This is no doubt a familiar list.

Perhaps more striking from the perspective of historical distance is their approach to the question of homosexuality (the term that Jones and Brown use). As noted earlier, it is not uncommon now to assume that second-wave feminism in working for unity among women tended to negate difference, that it was a middle-class and white movement that tended to exclude working-class and poor women, women of color, and lesbians. But as part of the volatility that bell hooks has noted, feminist newspapers and pamphlets in fact devoted considerable space to the relationship between sexual orientation and feminism. If at the heart of women's liberation is "the primacy of women relating to women" as a polemic from the Radicalesbians puts it, then it would seem that "the issue of lesbianism" is not a side issue but central to an understanding of feminism (83–84). Others argued, however, that lesbianism would be radical feminism "only if it is then placed in the context of wanting to destroy the system as a whole, that is, destroying the sex role system as opposed to just rejecting men" (Koedt 87). Otherwise it is only a "personal" matter, not even necessarily a choice, and not yet a political solution (86–87). While radical feminists disagreed about the role of lesbianism within women's liberation, as Alice Echols notes, "many reformist feminists unalterably opposed any discussion" of the topic (*Daring* 212). Betty Friedan, who knew the consequences of red-baiting, is said to have warned against the "lavender menace," arguing that the issue would undermine the women's reform efforts. Susan Brownmiller recalls her own retort that there was no menace, at best only a "lavender herring"—that is, a smokescreen to deflect women from the work at hand (Brownmiller 71, 82). Indeed, it would be more accurate to say that lesbian participation was a driving force in the women's liberation movement and in the creation of counterinstitutions within the women's university-without-walls (see Taylor and Rupp). What is certain is that in the early years of the movement, the question of sexual orientation was a defining issue of the polemical terrain feminists would continue to try to negotiate.

It is thus useful to look at Jones and Brown's pamphlet, appearing as it did early in the movement, to see in nascent form some of the issues that would continue to charge the feminist debate. Jones and Brown observe that "underlying much of the evasiveness, the apparent lack of self-confidence, and even the downright silliness among women when confronted with the possibility of a female liberation movement, is the big male gun—the charge of homosexuality" (27):

> Indirect male sniping, insinuating homosexuality . . . has some interesting analogies in our movement experience. It's like the signals southern whites put out: "If you leave a white and a black alone for five minutes, there's no telling what might happen." And it's a lot like red-baiting. Our answers to red-baiting will serve us well here. The charge of homosexuality . . . stands for a fear of something greater, as did the charge of communism against southern blacks and whites getting together: that they might get together. An indigenous movement of any people determined to gain their liberation is a more serious threat than "communism" and "homosexuality," and the charge is merely a delaying tactic to obstruct organization. (28)

While one might want to complicate the assumptions about what is the "more serious threat," one can nonetheless see how Jones and Brown are attempting to work through a problem that they see as standing in the way of political action. Although they compare the charge of homosexuality to red-baiting, they do not suggest that the response to the charge ought to be either ignore the question or to keep lesbians closeted. Many of the "hassles" in the movement in fact are attributable, as they see it, to women's unwillingness to openly consider what it means for women to love women, and such love is not presented simply as an expression of political solidarity or as ever not political.

Jones and Brown reflect on the "curious paradoxes in the movement," in particular, how movement people maintain "some Puritan mores to excess." Even though activists may be willing to "combat the social order... [and] accept ostracism from [their] families..., [they] have learned a thousand tricks to forestall the ultimate bust—legal or psychological." Homosexuality seems to be "too much to add to an already strained relationship with the society in which we dwell" (27). And yet "fear of homosexuality may be the one last strand by which the male order can pull us back into tow. It has been our past error to repress the political attraction we have for our own kind. It would be equally wrong to turn female communes into anything less than a tentative experiment with a new domestic arrangement; political content will not suffice to fill the need every human has for that place where one 'slackens the pace at the crossroads, and takes a chance to rest'" (27–28). It is not entirely clear whether such a crossroads is a place to rest for the long term or only before returning to heterosexual relationships. The sentence, as I read it, is ambiguous and at least hints at the idea that homosexuality could be a "simple" matter of choosing a "lifestyle" one could simply abandon without experiencing any real repercussions, an idea that irritated many in the gay liberation movement. However they imagine the crossroads, Jones and Brown assert that it is through acts of "female rediscovery that we may learn to design new living arrangements which will make our coexistence with men [whether domestic coexistence, simple coexistence as humans on this planet, or both is not clear] in the future all the more equal and all the more humane." Indeed, they say with a hint of the utopian, "exploring the possibilities of non-elitist, non-colonial love may teach us forms of political strength far more valuable than guerrilla theater" (28).[6]

I read this sentence as putting the weight on exploration and the ways in which women's fear prevents them from exploring a fuller range of possibilities. If polemic is marked by a passionate conviction—in this case, the conviction that women have to create a separate movement for their own liberation—that conviction, as I read it, does not have to lead to a doctrinaire sense of method. Having established the need for a separate movement, Jones and Brown do not then determine a single path to follow toward radicalization. But neither do they minimize the risks involved. While, as Arditi and Valentine have argued, polemic hinges on identifying areas of contestation, in this case the polemic does not work to smooth over those contested areas or to make them go away (as polite discourse might aim to create a civil space of commonality) but rather seeks to resist closure in order to activate agency among the proximate audience. Indeed, the vehemence expressed in this pamphlet directed toward other women in the movement (more than to men, I would argue) suggests an understanding of how much strength or courage it would take to change a system of inequities deeply embedded in or definitive of the culture.

Although Jones and Brown's pamphlet has been considered an inaugural document of the women's liberation movement, I do not want to treat it as either marking an origin or standing for all midcentury feminist polemic. By definition, polemical ground is unstable: the participants do not remain static, the terms of dispute shift, and polemic invites polemic. Indeed, as feminist polemic makes clear, the very idea of *a* women's movement was itself a matter of contention. Radical feminism was, in that sense, polemical from the outset. I thus turn to two polemics that do not share Jones and Brown's vision of a separatist feminist movement. Mary Ann Weathers and Frances M. Beal can be read as navigating a somewhat more complex polemical terrain, and their work thus serves to complicate an understanding of feminist polemic.

Arguments for Black Women's Liberation

Mary Ann Weathers's "Argument for Black Women's Liberation as a Revolutionary Force" and Frances Beal's "Double Jeopardy: To Be Black and Female" each appeared in influential anthologies in 1970. Both Weathers and Beal were part of SNCC's Black Women's Liberation Committee, which was evolving into the Third World Women's Alliance around the time that their polemics were published (see Anderson-Bricker; Roth). With somewhat different emphases, both writers contend that for women's liberation to be revolutionary, women would have to recognize the interconnectedness among categories of oppression. A number of polemics circulated in feminist pamphlets and periodicals written by black women who argued that feminism and black consciousness ought not to be incompatible.[7] But this polemical terrain was fraught. If radical white women were taking heat from radical men—white and black—for embracing what was characterized as a frivolous cause and thus "neglecting" the far more serious issues of racism, militarism, and classism, the charge was magnified for black women. What, historically, would lead a black woman to see that her interests were well served by joining together with white women? And if she did see that a real coalition was possible (something more than a white, middle-class woman's movement legitimated through the presence of women of color or other than a matter of the poor sister requiring the white woman's leadership), must she conceptualize such a coalition in separatist terms? Must women's liberation mean disconnecting oneself from movements for racial justice? The polemics I consider here suggest that there was no single response to these questions and that addressing them required not only a complex approach to audience but also a fair degree of rhetorical dexterity to negotiate the polemical terrain.

These polemics were written following the murder of Martin Luther King Jr., which felt like a terrible defeat after years of civil rights struggle. Legislative progress, the momentum from the Civil Rights Act of 1964 and the Voting Rights Act of 1965, seemed stalled. A more conservative Congress finally passed the Housing Act of 1968 after King's death, but that was to be the last federal legislation addressing the civil rights of racial minorities—and that act was complicated by a rider that made it a crime to cross state lines to provoke a riot. Although this rider made it possible to prosecute civil rights murder as a federal crime, it was also used to prosecute the "Chicago Eight" for street demonstrations at the 1968 Democratic National Convention (Chalmers 44–45). In other words, the housing act became a vehicle allowing what many perceived to be an infringement of free speech and a curtailment of political protest. A pamphlet circulated by the Chicago Defense Fund claims that the Nixon administration, unable to "cope with the problems of [the] times," was forced to "jail the militant leadership of the anti-war, ghetto, and student movements" (*The 'Anti-Riot' Act* n.p.). If there was an "unraveling of faith in existing arrangements [among] a broader American public," the sense of unraveling was all the more acute among activists who felt that repressive forces were closing in (Sandel 296). Urban riots in the wake of King's assassination, an increasingly more conservative Congress, the Vietnam War's draining economic resources away from social programs, Robert Kennedy's assassination, the fear that the FBI was infiltrating radical groups, and the election of President Richard Nixon defined a climate in which radicals felt embattled and talk of revolution was not abstract.

Within this larger, highly charged context, black feminist polemic had to stake a claim. A polemical lightening rod was the widely circulated criticism that black families were matriarchal in structure and that such a structure emasculated black men. Several selections in Toni Cade Bambara's anthology *The Black Woman* address these conjoined ideas, "to set the record straight on the matriarch and the evil Black bitch" (11). In one essay reprinted from a 1969 issue of *Liberator* magazine, Jean Carey Bond and Patricia Peery reference "[Daniel Patrick] Moynihan's Black matriarchy proposition . . . based, incredibly, on the statistic that one-quarter—only one-quarter!—of all Black families are headed by women" (115). In "Black People and the Victorian Ethos," Gwen Patton asserts that "Daniel Moynihan . . . was partly responsible for dividing black men and women," who had been "a unifying force," marching "side by side [until] Moynihan stopped that force" (145). In the polemical literature reactions to Moynihan's thesis ranged from the dismissive (e.g., Mary Ann Weathers's reference to "this nonsense about the 'Matriarchy' of black women" [163]) to the more oblique (e.g., Frances Beal's assertion that it is "fallacious to think that in order for the black man to be strong, the black woman must be weak" [48]). Writers refuted the charge by drawing on history to celebrate the strength of black women in the face of great adversity, by reference to African culture to denaturalize claims to an origin for either matriarchal or patriarchal black culture (Weathers 162; P. Robinson and Group 201), or by contending that a black matriarchy could only be "illusory," because American society as a whole "is patriarchal" (Bond and Peery 117).

Black feminists hinged their critique of the problematic notion of a black matriarchy in part on how it was imposed on the black community by a white scholar, thus underscoring the painful irony that such a notion could be embraced by black radicals. On the one hand, Moynihan was a powerful enemy to indict; on the other hand, the more immediate and intimate affront came from the very black men with whom the women had worked. In 1965, while serving as assistant secretary of labor under Lyndon Johnson, Moynihan issued a report on black poverty, *The Negro Family: The Case for National Action,* that proved influential in shaping public policy. A Harvard professor of education and urban politics trained as a sociologist, Moynihan had served under John F. Kennedy and later became a domestic advisor to Richard Nixon. In his study he places the blame for poverty among blacks on family structure—in particular, on the percentage of children born to unwed mothers.[8] This was an argument similar to one made in 1939 by the African American scholar E. Franklin Frazier in *The Negro Family in the United States,* a project undertaken in response to a request from Mayor LaGuardia after the 1935 Harlem riots to study the "state of things in Harlem" (Sugrue 4; K. Clark 118). And the idea was not unlike that developed by Kenneth B. Clark in *Dark Ghetto,* published the same year as Moynihan's study (70–74). Whatever the similarities among these studies, however, it was Moynihan's that drew the most fire because his political power stood behind the moral judgment of family structure and sexual behavior. In appearing to condemn black women, he appeared to be conflating women's strength with destructiveness. Moynihan was thus the "oppressor" who created "havoc and discord among the colonized, particularly in internal and family relationships" (Patton 145).

But polemical immediacy in this case was defined less by Moynihan than by black nationalists who, as David Chalmers points out, had also criticized a "black matriarchy." Kristin Anderson-Bricker makes clear the complex relationship between black nationalism and the formation of the Black Women's Liberation Committee (BWLC). She argues that "understanding Black nationalism in its international context and rooting Black inequality in racism, capitalism and imperialism provided the intellectual environment necessary for Black women in SNCC to identify themselves as Blacks and also as women and workers" (57–58). But Beal, Weathers, and the other BWLC women felt that black nationalist men had "accepted discriminatory notions such as the matriarchy myth" and were using the "Black liberation struggle to search for manhood and to assert their masculinity" (Anderson-Bricker 59). To the extent that the black nationalist movement became "a male consciousness movement," in David Chalmers's terms (162), it conceptualized strong black women as part of the problem in the sense that Beal criticizes; that is, to the extent that black women were strong, black men were presumably made proportionately weaker. That some black men would embrace an idea promulgated by a powerful white man, that they appeared to accept white bourgeois notions of gender roles, was thus especially painful.[9]

The polemical challenge then was for black feminists to address the zero-sum argument without "step[ping] back into a submissive role," because to do so would have been "counterrevolutionary" not simply for women but for all peoples (Beal 48). Weathers and Beal both construct their immediate audience as other black women who feel the pressure to accept the myth of the black matriarchy and who might have subordinated themselves in the name of supporting black manhood. They do so, however, not by distancing themselves from that audience but as black women who share in the same struggle. Unlike Jones and Brown, who figure the younger white women in the SDS as a proximate opposition, as themselves affiliated but not one with them, and who do not include white men as among a persuadable audience, Weathers and Beal attempt to maintain a space of commonality not only with black women but also with radical black men. To further compound the rhetorical challenge, these polemics also addressed white women and a women's liberation movement that, in some of its manifestations, seemed blind to women of color. Weathers and Beal thus attempted, in ways not evident in Jones and Brown's work, to address directly and explicitly a larger, more inclusive audience of radical women.

Benita Roth has argued that studies of second-wave feminism pay insufficient attention to the "simultaneity and *interrelatedness* of Black and white feminist emergence [and] the very mutual influence that some feminists had on one another across racial lines" (75). Weathers's and Beal's were clearly crossover texts, made available to a wider readership because they were reprinted in a variety of publications. But such publication was not without its risks. *How* the writings were made available made clear the difficulty of sustaining contact across difference. Both Weathers and Beal composed their papers for circulation among Black Women's Liberation Committee members, but very quickly they were reprinted in women's liberation newspapers and anthologies. Boston's *No More Fun and Games* published Weathers's short "Argument" in 1969. It was reprinted a year later in two anthologies, Leslie Tanner's *Voices from Women's Liberation* and Sookie Stambler's *Women's Liberation: Blueprint for the Future.* Beal's lengthier treatise was reprinted in Toni Cade Bambara's *Black Woman;* Robin Morgan's *Sisterhood is Powerful;* and *The New Women: A MOTIVE Anthology on Women's Liberation,* edited by Joanne Cooke, Robin Morgan, and Charlotte Bunch.[10] The rapidity with which these papers were reproduced is underscored by the fact that names were misspelled; biographical data, if supplied, were inconsistent from publication to publication; and organizational affiliations were left hazy.

The emphasis was on ensuring a range of voices with a minimal level of packaging. A back-cover blurb for Stambler's small paperback, for example, calls it "a comprehensive study of the theories, actions and goals in the fight for Women's Rights," but Stambler herself locates the collection more narrowly in relation to women's liberation—that is, as a radical movement rather than the reformist movement the label "women's rights" might suggest—and she acknowledges that "so diverse is the movement that one book cannot reflect all of its ideas" (12). Thus Weathers's "Argument" is offered among an eclectic sampling of possible positions *within* a capacious understanding of women's liberation rather than as either an offshoot or a separate phenomenon. Stambler places the piece under the subheading "Women on Liberation" (following "Women on Women," "Women on Men," and "Women on Law and Education") and in the company of writings by Susan Brownmiller, Kate Millett, Alix Schulman, and Rosalyn Baxandall, among others. The category is broad, encompassing personal testimony about consciousness raising, a theory of sexual politics, a call for cooperative nurseries, a critique of communal living, and a report that verges on parody about a feminist sit-in at an Irish pub in New York City ("Inebriates of action were we, debauchees of daiquiri" [Reisig 230]).

Like the periodicals from which it draws, the anthology juxtaposes differing orders of seriousness, leaving the reader to weigh the relative value of the various selections. Unlike the periodicals, however, the paperback tends to regularize and flatten through the uniformity of commercial printing. No graphics or typeface changes set Weathers's "Argument" apart, that is, from the inebriates and debauchees on one hand or theories of sexual politics on the other. Unlike other key anthologies published that year, no contributors page identifies "Maryanne Weathers" to frame the selection in terms of her political affiliations beyond the indication that the piece had first appeared in a feminist paper. The force of her polemic has to rest then largely with her words.

In contrast, *Sisterhood is Powerful* identifies "Frances M. Beal" in "Notes on Sister Contributors" as having attended the University of Wisconsin, with a diploma in French history from the University of Paris, and as the New York coordinator for SNCC's Black Women's Liberation Committee (Morgan 594). Under the heading "Go Tell It in the Valley: Changing Consciousness," Morgan includes Beal's "Double Jeopardy," following sections entitled "After the Oppressed Majority: The Way It Is" and "The Invisible Woman: Psychological and Sexual Repression." Beal joins Eleanor Holmes Norton and the "Black Liberation Group, Mount Vernon, New York" (whose work other publications attribute to Patricia Robinson), as one of three views in the section "Women in the Black Liberation Movement." Together with "High School Women: Three Views," "Colonized Women: The Chicana," and "Experiment in Freedom: Women in China," this section marks off the other in contrast to the majority. Neither the credentialing nor the positioning as representative Other, however, quite contains Beal's polemic. Both Weathers's shorter piece and Beal's longer "Double Jeopardy" are multilayered polemics directed to a multiply situated audience.

Weathers opens her "Argument" with the premise that "nobody can fight your battles for you; you have to do it yourself." She acknowledges that this is not the most important argument to be made on behalf of black women's liberation, but it offers a place to begin. At first it is not clear to whom Weathers is addressing her case or how she is implicated in the argument. The first-person plural pronoun seems separate from the black women who are being described (rather than addressed): "Black women, at least the black women we have come in contact with in the movement have been expounding all their energies in 'liberating' black men" (161). But what seems at first to be a magisterial "we"—there is no indication that the piece was collectively authored or any indication of who else other than the writer the "we" might entail—begins to resolve itself within a few paragraphs into first a relational "we" identifying speaker with audience and joining them in common cause: "We have found that Women's Liberation is an extremely emotional issue, as well as an explosive one. Black men are still parroting The Man's prattle about male superiority. This now brings us to a very pertinent question: How can we seriously discuss reclaiming our African heritage—cultural living modes which clearly refute not only patriarchy and matriarchy, but our entire family structure as we know it" (162). Then the pronoun use shifts again, signaling that the proximate audience is not people of African descent in general but specifically other black women who are engaged in women's liberation. Weathers then addresses these specific women through a series of warnings and exhortations, putting the issue of a supposed black matriarchy at the emotional center of her exhortation: "Realizing fully what is being said, you should be warned that the opposition for liberation will come from everyplace, particularly from other women and from black men. Don't allow yourselves to be intimidated any longer with this nonsense about the 'Matriarchy' of black women.... The myth of the matriarchy must stop and we must not allow ourselves to be sledgehammered by it any longer—not if we are serious about change and ridding ourselves of the wickedness of this alien culture" (163). Like Jones and Brown, who offer advice to other women with whom they have been affiliated but with whom they disagree, Weathers councils other activist women who may be persuaded by the "myth" and need to be set right. But Weathers situates herself not as separate from those women but as someone who feels the same pressures. Other women beyond this group could certainly read the "Argument," just as women outside the immediate polemical context of disagreements over the SDS women's manifesto read Jones and Brown's pamphlet, applying it beyond its immediate context. Presumably the readership for both *No More Fun and Game* and Stambler's anthology extended beyond those most directly addressed. But while the proximate audience is clear and an extended readership can be presumed, the question of the textually constructed audience is yet more complicated.

Weathers knows that she is raising an emotionally charged issue. To the extent that she is criticizing black men, she leaves herself open to the serious charge that she is undermining the revolution at a moment when repressive forces are closing in. Cellestine Ware argues in *Woman Power* (1970) that the negative reaction of black men to black women who assumed positions of equality should be instructive for all women as a "forerunner of what all feminists will face as they grow in strength" (21).[11] But an acute awareness that black men and women were linked together as an oppressed group tended to bifurcate the proximate audience for black feminist polemics in ways less apparent in white feminist writing. One can see this bifurcation in Frances Beal's "Double Jeopardy," where she criticizes "certain black men [who] are maintaining that they have been castrated by society but that black women somehow escaped persecution and even contributed to this emasculation" (47–48). At the same time she offers reassurance: "Black women are not resentful of the rise to power of black men. We welcome it. We see in it the eventual liberation of all black people from this corrupt system of capitalism. However, it is fallacious to think that in order for the black man to be strong, the black woman must be weak" (48).

Beal thus imagines a larger black community that could serve as vanguard for revolutionary change, and while she addresses black women in particular, her utopian desires project a vision of a revolutionized future that encompasses all people. She reminds her readers, female and male, of the revolutionary aims they share (or ought to share) in common:

> A people's revolution that engages the participation of every member of the community, including man, woman, and child, brings about a certain transformation in the participants as a result of this participation. Once we have caught a glimpse of freedom or experienced a bit of self-determination, we can't go back to old routines that were established under a racist, capitalist regime. We must begin to understand that a revolution entails not only the willingness to lay our lives on the firing line and get killed. In some ways, this is an easy commitment to make . . . , [but] to live for the revolution means taking on the more difficult commitment of changing our day-to-day patterns. (56)

Such patterns include the ways men and women interact, how parents treat their children, and how workers treat one another. The new society will need to eliminate "the oppression of *all members,*" else "the revolution will have failed its avowed purpose" (56–57).

Weathers, too, figures the black male on the page when she makes sharp reference to how some "are still parroting The Man's prattle about male superiority" (162), and she also seeks to reassure male and (at least some) female readers that "black women's liberation is not anti-male" (163). There is in both Weathers and Beal the sense that black men cannot be, or at least ought not be, the distant opposition in the same way that white men are for white and black feminists but that they have to be positioned within black feminist polemic as not only needing to hear but capable of hearing, and their hearing is necessary for real change to take place. But still another layer comes into play. In a sense, black men oscillate with nonblack feminists for position within a middle space in this polemical terrain. While Beal addresses first and foremost other black women, she is also trying to educate (and reassure) black male radicals, even as she warns white feminists that unless they embrace an anti-imperialist and antiracist position, they will have "nothing in common with the black woman's struggle" (54). Black women are thus arrayed as the innermost circle in this polemical forum, with black male radicals circled in the next tier, white women further back, and white men at best outside the auditorium door.

This structuring of audience is tied to Beal's analytical priorities: for her, male chauvinism is not the primary cause of human oppression (nor is racism); global capitalism is. She addresses "bedroom politics"—in particular, programs of forced sterilization of nonwhite women—as an extension of economic oppression into the domestic sphere. To the extent that nonwhite males, white females, and nonwhite females are all systematically exploited by the economic system, they share a common enemy (50).[12] If white women's liberationists "do not realize that they are in fact fighting capitalism and racism," Beal warns, "we do not have common bonds." If they fail to recognize "that the reasons for their condition lie in the system and not simply that men get a vicarious pleasure out of 'consuming their bodies for exploitative reasons'..., then [black women] cannot unite with them around common grievances or even discuss these groups in a serious manner" (55). Beal thus challenges white women to understand the "fundamental cause of the condition of females" and invites them to join in common struggle to confront that "main enemy" (55).

Weathers, in contrast, begins with what she understands to be the common bonds all women share, and she thus puts greater emphasis on bringing nonblack feminists more closely into closer proximity. Much of her polemical effort, in fact, is aimed at identifying a broad and inclusive agenda for women's liberation, one that would encompass "all women [who] suffer oppression, even white women, particularly poor white women, and especially Indian, Mexican, Puerto Rican, Oriental and black American women whose oppression is trippled" (164). "Women's liberation," she urges, "should be considered a strategy for an eventual tie-up with the entire revolutionary movement consisting of women, men, and children" (162). While she recognizes differences in economic circumstance among women, she does not mount an economic argument per se but places human relations at the center of the movement. Thus, she urges women to rid themselves of their "hangups" before they "begin to talk about the rest of the world," adding that she means "the world and nothing short of that" (164).

For Weathers there is great, yet unrealized potential in the women's liberation movement, and she does not assume that it is a white women's movement. She recognizes that primarily younger black radical or militant women had been attracted to the movement at first, while "the very poor, the middle class, [and] older people . . . have not become aware or have not been able to translate their awareness into action" (163). But the women's movement has the potential to bring disparate women together so that they can learn from one another. Even though, she contends, middle-class black women have not suffered the same kinds of "brutal oppression as poor black people," they have nonetheless experienced male chauvinism and thus should be able to help the cause through teaching, "verbalizing the ills of women and this society," and organizing. All women, in fact, have knowledge to share: "older women have a wealth of information and experience to offer" because they have lived with oppression longer; "poor women have knowledge to teach us all" because they are likely to be more realistic about societal ills; "even white women" have something to say, because they too suffer oppression (163–64). As long as women fight against one another, she concludes, "this man playing the death game for money and power" wins (165).

The differences between Beal and Weathers are not merely differences in the relative proximity of addressees, of course. There are clear areas of overlap, but differences in how the proximate and nearly proximate audiences are constructed speak to somewhat different notions of how black women (and women in general) ought to invest their revolutionary energies. In some sense, they mark off differing affiliative priorities. For Beal, there is a larger revolutionary life-and-death struggle, of which women's liberationists can be a part if they understand the systemic causes of both racism and sexism. For Weathers, women's liberation is a movement in its own right, encompassing all women, serious in its opposition to the "death game for money and power," a movement that needs to create alternative social structures to combat racial, gender, and class oppression. As will become evident in the next section, the question of how and to what extent women's liberation should join with or be subsumed under other movements for social justice hinged in part on what was understood to be the underlying causes of oppression, and this complex issue continued to fuel feminist polemic.

"The Fourth World Manifesto"

In 1971 *Notes from the Third Year* reprinted an expanded version of "The Fourth World Manifesto," which had been composed originally as "a reply to the way in which a 'women's liberation' conference was planned" (Burris 102). Barbara Burris, "in agreement with Kathy Barry, Terry Moon, Joann DeLor, Joann Parent, [and] Cate Stadelman," a group of women from Detroit, composed the manifesto to protest what they saw to be the misleading arguments mounted by a group of "anti-imperialist women" who had planned the conference for the spring of 1971 to bring together Indo-Chinese women and women from North America (Echols, *Daring* 245). The conference was planned in the wake of the spring 1970 invasion of Cambodia. Nixon had been withdrawing troops from Vietnam and was publicly promoting the "Vietnamization" of the war, but the secret bombing and subsequent invasion of Cambodia seemed to signal that he was reneging on his promise and expanding the war in Indochina. Nationwide protests ensued. In May 1970 National Guardsmen opened fire on a crowd of students at Kent State University, killing four and paralyzing another. Ten days later state police in Jackson, Mississippi, fired at protesters on the Jackson State College campus, killing two students and wounding nine. Across the country students at four hundred colleges and universities went on strike in protest of the killings, marking the first general student strike in U.S. history (Zinn 481). By the spring of 1971 some 61 percent of the population—not simply college students, not simply civilians—opposed U.S. involvement in the war (Zinn 483). Of course, the conference participants could not have known that it would be more than two years before the United States agreed to withdraw its troops from Vietnam and another two years before the fall of Saigon.

Understanding this sense of urgent priorities helps to frame a reading of "The Fourth World Manifesto." Even in the midst of national crisis, the writers of the manifesto felt it necessary to resist what they saw to be an attempt to co-opt women's liberation for anti-imperialist ends. The writers distinguish between, on the one hand, opposition to the Vietnam War and all wars and, on the other hand, abandoning women's liberation to work for "male-dominated, very narrowly defined anti-war and anti-imperialist movements" (104). They charge that the conference planners ignored "the roots of domination, aggression, imperialism, and war in male-supremacist society" (103). If the conference planners had understood imperialism and war "in their deepest aspects" to be expressions of a male-supremacist society, the manifesto states, they would have understood that feminism would necessarily be deeply anti-imperialist by being anti-male-supremacist.

The manifesto sets out to refute the "emotional, psychological, and social assumptions underlying the attitude that women's liberation is less important than black liberation, anti-imperialism, anti-capitalism, etc." (103). In particular, they "criticize the male definition of oppression which does not recognize the unique position of females as a subjugated group" (103). Although the first version of the manifesto addressed directly the planners of the conference (and in that sense bears some similarity to Jones and Brown's polemical address), the expanded version broadens the audience and complicates the terms of critique. Unlike Jones and Brown, who were envisioning a separate women's movement that was not yet a force, Burris and her colleagues assume the existence of an independent women's movement and speak from within what they conceptualize as a separate space. They address other women whom they see as not yet free of the male-dominated left, women who need to understand that "the male Left has absolutely no interest in a female revolution" (105). The anti-imperialist women thus stand in for all those (female and male) who want to "get a finger in the women's movement pie" (103). And that list is long:

> Over the last year and half the SWP-YSA [Socialist Workers Party–Young Socialist Alliance] has made a nationally coordinated attempt to infiltrate and take over women's centers and organize women's liberation groups (which they hope to mold to their "single issue" approach and subordinate to their organizational aims).... What is said of the anti-imperialist women's manipulation of the women's movement applies equally well to every other Left group—the Communist Party, Socialist Workers Party, Young Socialist Alliance, International Socialists, Students for a Democratic Society, Progressive Labor, Youth Against War and Fascism, etc. (103)

With hindsight it might appear that Burris and her colleagues were worrying about an already disintegrating political fringe. Echols ventures to say that "the rise of women's liberation is related to the collapse of the left as a national movement" (*Shaky Ground* 65). But what Michael Harrington refers to as the "defeated remnant of an already defeated remnant" of the political left continued to exercise considerable force in activist politics, if for no other reason than that the left provided a developed set of analytical tools (*Long-Distance Runner* 14).[13] Even those feminists who wished to dissociate themselves from the male-dominated left nonetheless deployed at least a part of its political vocabulary. Burris and her colleagues thus take seriously the criticisms coming from the left in part because they share some of the same ideological ground. But they make somewhat different use of the analytical terminology in defending the independence of a women's movement against those who would dilute or subvert it. In defending, they are also defining what will count as legitimately part of the movement and who can legitimately claim to be a part of the movement. Rather than a heterogeneous coalition with multiple affiliative modes, of the sort imagined by Weathers, the movement is figured in the manifesto as defined by a centering ideology to which all who belong have to subscribe.

The manifesto briefly outlines organizational tactics used by the male-dominated left to impede or co-opt the energies of feminists before focusing on a key argument used to intimidate women "into not taking a strong and independent stand" (106). Like the "lavender menace" and the "myth of the black matriarchy," discussed earlier, "the myth of the white middle-class woman" was intended to undermine expressions of radical feminism. The manifesto sets out to refute the myth first by unpacking its terms. While Burris and her colleagues assert that "the Female Liberation Movement must cut across all (male-imposed) class, race, and national lines," they also acknowledge that "any false identification of women with privileges that are really male (such as whiteness or class, etc.) will be fatal to our movement" (107). Even so, the polemical "we" appears to embrace primarily white women (107). It is white women who are expected to feel guilty when they are told that the women's movement is "only a bunch of white, middle-class women," and so it is white women to whom the writers direct their critique of the charge (106). The manifesto does not address the charge directly, in the sense of demonstrating whether or to what extent the movement involved more than white, middle-class women, what might be called the "head count" defense.[14] Rather, Burris et al. argue that women's liberation as a cause encompasses all women to the extent that women constitute a sexual caste, a category of oppression that cuts across race, class and ethnic boundaries. As they see it, the sexual caste system is historically prior to racial discrimination (106). Whiteness is defined as a sign of male privilege, as is class. Because "a woman's class is almost always determined by the man she is living with," if a woman is on her own, she will almost certainly be "lower or working class"—no matter what her class position before (107). "Class," the manifesto contends, "is therefore basically a distinction among males, while the female is defined by her sexual caste status" (107).

The manifesto works to denaturalize whiteness by showing that not all white people enjoy the same privileges. Citing comparative wage data

("Doesn't everyone know the statistics by now?"), the authors point out that not only do men earn more than women, but the situation was worsening: "In 1955, the median wage of women working full time was 64 percent of that of men; in 1967, it was down to 60 percent" (106–7; see also note 12). Echoing Beal's double-jeopardy argument, they note that "the black female is doubly disadvantaged as a female and black, and has the lowest pay level of all." They grant that "many women do identify with white and class privilege," but because the writers presume women to be educable, they do not see this identification as anything more than temporary. Part of the task of women's liberation, as they define it, is to "patiently discuss and communicate with women, as sisters, what true caste position in society is" (107). Once women understand their true situation, they can begin then to "understand other groups' oppression—but not before" (107). Women's liberation is thus prior to other movements not only because sexual caste is prior to other forms of oppression but because educationally and psychologically, one has to understand one's own oppression before understanding the oppression of others. Self-understanding thus comes before empathy.[15] Recent history might have suggested otherwise to the extent that many women had become aware (or more acutely aware) of gender as a category of oppression through their experience working in civil rights and antiwar movements. The manifesto, however, carries forward the logic of Brown and Jones's polemic, which was in turn appropriating the logic of black nationalism, arguing that one must attend to one's own house first.

Having addressed the myth of the white, middle-class woman, Burris and her colleagues turn to the related rhetorical ploy used by the male left to "play one oppressed group off against another oppressed group" (107). If "who is most oppressed" is one side of this rhetorical coin, then "who is more guilty" is the other (107–8). But this hierarchizing of guilt and oppression, the writers contend, is a no-exit game: "If we can only identify with our oppression and not see how we also oppress others we are fooling ourselves"; at the same time, "if we feel only guilty about being oppressors we are also fooling ourselves" (108). How then to think past guilt toward change? The writers of the manifesto develop an answer by turning to the theories of their proximate audience, the anti-imperialist women. They "people the page," in fact, by giving over the bulk of their manifesto to a critical reading of anti-imperialist theory. They do not offer caricature but take seriously the analytical power of ideas that were developing especially out of the black liberation movement. They thus begin with an "extended . . . definition of imperialism or colonialism" before turning to a close and critical reading of Frantz Fanon's work (108). Although Fanon's work is ultimately rejected for its failure to take seriously the Algerian woman's plight in the sense that Fanon is understood by the writers to offer only a defense of Algerian male culture, it is his idea of "culture" that proves most useful to them as a way out of that no-exit game of guilt and oppression.

The concept of colonialism had been extended by black nationalists to refer to the process by which "a group is prevented from self-determination by another group—whether it has a national territory or not" (108). The writers of the manifesto emphasize that the harm that is done through colonialism—"the psychological and cultural mutilation"—is especially brutal when the opposing groups differ in "physical characteristics" (109). While the extended definition was used to describe the situation of blacks in America, the writers of the manifesto argue that the term applies as well to the subjection of women. Women are set apart by physical difference, and the territory that is colonized is their bodies. According to Fanon, however, it is not enough to control the colonized territory; the colonizer has to "destroy the culture and self-respect of the colonized" (109). Fanon argued that "colonialism . . . turns to the past of the oppressed people, and distorts, disfigures and destroys it" (qtd. in Burris 109). If—following Fanon's directive—blacks in America have to prove that a black culture exists, then so too do women, because the history of women has also been "distorted and almost completely censored" (109). It is thus the task of women's liberation to make that culture visible.

The writers emphasize their primary thesis by setting it in boldface: "A female culture exists. It is a culture that is subordinated and under male culture's colonial, imperialist rule all over the world. Underneath the surface of every national, ethnic, or racial culture is the split between the two primary cultures of the world—the female culture and the male culture" (112). Although they acknowledge that there are variations in degree from country to country, they nonetheless contend that women across the globe experience repression as a defining characteristic of female culture. Women may well identify with a national culture, but they need to recognize that national culture is always dominant male culture (112). Fanon's theories are thus useful only up to a point because, the manifesto's writers contend, Fanon fails to recognize that what he calls national culture is actually only male culture and that colonized women are in fact doubly imposed upon: first by the colonized male and next by the colonizing male. They cite Fanon's explanation that Algerian women have chosen to limit the scope of their existence—their's is not a "limitation imposed by the universe"—and in so embracing limitation, the Algerian woman most clearly declared her alliance to Algerian men who were fighting against the French colonizers (Fanon qtd. in Burris 113). The manifesto writers add as sarcastic gloss that "a united front means women must give up their 'silly, trivial' ideas of a female anti-colonial movement and fight in the male-dominated 'anti-' colonial revolution" (113).

To the extent that Fanon's theory can stand for the anti-imperialist position, by critiquing his ideas, the manifesto's writers expose the faulty reasoning of those closer to hand who have sought to turn women's liberation from its proper path.[16] Part of the polemical move is to give space to the opponents' words, to embrace a core principle—in this case, the free exercise of one's culture—and then to expose the failure on the part of the opponents to carry through the logic of the core principle they supposedly espouse. What is especially striking about the manifesto, however, is that the writers not only cite Fanon (who is used to stand for the anti-imperialist position)—giving over a fair amount of space to his words in fact—but also enlist the words of Algerian women to help them make their case. They cite, in particular, Fadela M'Rabet's *La Femme algerienne,* in which the position of women in Algeria is compared to that of blacks in South Africa. Algerian women who fought in the resistance were expected to return to their prerevolutionary state of subservience, whereby the man is "allowed to . . . completely dominate her" (M'Rabet qtd. in Burris 116). M'Rabet urges: "If we really want to end our underdeveloped status, then let's not wait. Let's ban apartheid. . . . Must we wait several generations under the pretext that our society is not 'ready'? We [Algeria] are the product of 130 years of colonialism. *But how many centuries of exploitation have women lived under: Their colonizers have been the men* (ibid.; emphasis added in "Manifesto"). The manifesto's writers conclude that no "anti-capitalist, working class, Third World, anti-imperialist etc. movement will ever free women" because "there is too much at stake for male colonialists to ever give up their privileges without a struggle" (117). The ruling culture will always betray the female culture, and so it is necessary for women to defend themselves. Thus, unlike Weathers and Beal, who figure the black male as within the range of hearing, as potentially persuadable, Burris and her compatriots make clear that no men are capable of giving up male privilege without concerted pressure from all women banded together.

Although Burris adds in a postscript that neither female culture nor male culture is "natural" but both are "social definitions only," and that "many people are not molded wholly into either category," the manifesto nonetheless concludes with a call for "women of all races, classes, and countries all over the world" to celebrate the "Fourth World," that "long suppressed and ridiculed female principle" that is necessary for a "truly human society to come about" (118–19). The manifesto does not find a way to reconcile the "Up with the Female Principle" conclusion with the postscript's notion that the "women's movement has to be free enough to explore and change the entire range of human relationships and it must be open enough to heal the split between the female and male and draw out the total human potential of every person" (119). Is it possible to have a separatist movement that can also heal the wounds of the whole of humankind? Does separatism come first, as the manifesto asserts earlier, before one can understand the oppression of others? Or is the fullest expression of the female principle to be a willingness "to end the split in the human personality that has cut men off from a part of themselves and which has caused untold suffering to women" (119)? These questions are left unresolved.

Like the other polemics I have discussed in this chapter, "The Fourth World Manifesto" presumes a space of commonality that could be shared with those to whom the polemic is addressed. The writers invoke a utopian future that could be realized if women would understand the ways in which they have been mislead—by myth and false notions—and if they could understand the root causes of human oppression. But it is precisely the hinge ideas about root causes of oppression that cannot be agreed upon, and it is the resulting disagreements that have defined much of feminist debate in the years since. However much the writers of these various polemics might agree that women have to learn to fight their own battles, they cannot agree on either the cause of the conflict, the most salient features of the battlefield, or the best means of ending the conflict. In each polemic the anger that could have been directed vituperatively against the distanced opponent—an anger more directly evident in satiric pieces in the periodicals, for example—is redirected instead toward a passionate embrace of an ideal future. Part of the power of this writing rests not in the realization of a unified women's liberation front but in the very proliferation of ways of addressing foundational questions. The seriousness with which women argued over foundational questions and imagined alternative ways to address the oppression of women was a large part of that centrifugal force that drove radical feminism.

Reading feminist prose this way, as polemic, challenges some of the preconceptions that shape our current understandings of second-wave feminism by showing how the movement from the beginning was defined by decentering. Polemic also has the potential to put pressure on a too-limited view of feminist rhetoric. In *Notes from the Second Year* Shulamith Firestone and Anne Koedt explain that they wanted to present "the spectrum of current thinking on radical feminism" not because they agree with all that is said in the various articles but because they think the very contradictions made evident through difference are themselves important: "One of the most exciting things to come out of the women's movement so far is a new daring, a willingness—eagerness—to tear down old structures and assumptions.... there is no right (stylish) opinion to have..., no longer a fear of being called 'unfeminine' or worse, no more 'style'—unless by that is meant courage to say what you mean however you choose as clearly as you can" (2). To read this "spectrum of radical feminism" now requires not only that we rethink the commonly accepted view that second-wave feminism was born out of a desire for unity that canceled out difference but also that, concomitantly, we find better ways to read the range of discourses that registered difference. Rethinking polemic, in offering one way of rethinking the midcentury moment, also allows us to rethink our own practice now. If in our desire to avoid grand moral claims (as signaled in our collective embrace of rhetorical contingency) we run the risk, as Anne Drury Hall suggests, of restricting conviction to what propriety will tolerate, it would seem we also run the risk of losing the generative possibilities of serious dialogue.

3
That Train Full of Poetry

And poetry—among all this—where is there a place for poetry?
—Muriel Rukeyser, *The Life of Poetry*

Maybe someday a young girl,
Will throw down my poem in disgust;
Thinking that such sensitivity
Is extravagantly vulgar
against the steel structure
that has become her body.
—Paula Stone, "A Quarter Century Retrospect"

It might be claimed, at the risk of some exaggeration, that poets *are* the movement.
—Jan Clausen, *A Movement of Poets*

ADRIENNE RICH HAS CALLED poetry at once "a criticism of language" and "a concentration of the *power* of language." By putting words together "in new configurations, in the mere, immense shift from male to female pronouns, in the relationships between words created through echo, repetition, rhythm, rhyme, [poetry] lets us hear and see our words in a new dimension" ("Power and Danger" 248). Poetry thus has the power to make sensuously present "our relationship to everything in the universe" (248). Feminist periodicals reflected this sense that poetry could have peculiar force and, in particular, that it could do work that prose could not do. In her 1971 *off our backs* review of an anthology of lesbian feminist poetry, Frances Chapman asserts that "poems are better than polemics any day" (35). Similarly, in making the case for community funding to support *Big Mama Rag*, Sandy Belgrade argued in 1974 that poetry is especially well suited to do the political work of women's liberation. "Men have had print since Gutenberg," but they only "sought in the word a reflection of themselves AND in 500 years have failed to make the world real, to give back to the earth sinew and life." In a brief time—only "six years of birthing"—the women's movement "realized the full capacity of media and sisterhood to be unifying. . . . by joining together with paper and bookstore . . . , women can renew the journey . . . that train full of poetry, not dialectic" (4). Rejecting any absolute dichotomy between the genres, Audre Lorde worries in her poem "Power" that unless she can "learn to use / the difference between poetry and rhetoric," her "power will run corrupt as poisonous mold / or lie limp and useless as an unconnected wire" (qtd. in Tanenhaus 31).[1] That poetry can do something other than rhetoric, dialectic, or polemic does not mean that it is not, or ought not to be, political. But what political poetry might entail, especially early in the movement, was not a settled question, in terms of either form, subject matter, or function.

The very proliferation of feminist poetry, produced outside what James Sullivan has called the "hierarchy of proper access," militated against aesthetic or political unanimity (J. Sullivan 3–4).[2] Like feminist polemic, feminist poetry makes clear the polyphonous, decentralized, and nonhierarchical nature of the women's liberation movement. Small presses and feminist periodicals could readily find space for poetry that was neither part of the mass media nor protected by those institutions that had traditionally controlled the publishing and consumption of poetry. In her early survey of feminist periodicals, Ann Mather noted the unusual emphasis given to poetry, suggesting that it was "rapidly emerging as a favorite form of expression for women" ("History Part III," 31, 19). The importance of the genre was reinforced in key women's liberation anthologies that included sections on the poetry of protest alongside plays, historical documents, "statistical or aphoristic ammunition" (Morgan 557), and various manifestos and essays (see Bambara; Stambler). Inexpensive pamphlets, often self-published, circulated through women's bookstores, coffeehouses, and centers. As Betty Peters Sutton, a member of the *Lavender Woman* collective, recalls: "Women encouraged other women to write more. When I think about it and look back on it, I remember the articles, but a lot of the poetry really took first place. It's strange to think about it right now, but I know that was true" (qtd. in Brody 28–29).

To the extent that such poetry operated with a "minimum of institutional mediation," readers felt that they were free to make whatever use they wanted of the poems that filled the pages of feminist publications (see J. Sullivan 3–4). Indeed, small presses and feminist periodicals understood poetry in populist terms: not only could readers make what they wanted of the poems, but they were strongly encouraged to compose their own poetry, to contribute to that "train full of poetry" that could do work that the prose polemics apparently could not (Belgrade 4). While feminist poetry workshops outside the academy did develop writing pedagogies, as will be discussed in chapter 5, I want to focus in this chapter on how the material availability of poetry was itself pedagogical in the sense of modeling formal possibilities and opening up a public space for a kind of poetic expression that had not seemed possible before.

Although in the nineteenth-century the mainstream press regularly featured poems, few twentieth-century commercial papers devoted much space to the genre (Codrescu), and in this sense reinforced the dominant cultural notion of poetry as an elite form, as Adrienne Rich suggests, that was "alienated from the sensibility of the general population . . . , a luxury, a decorative garnish on the buffet table of the university curriculum" ("Blood, Bread, and Poetry" 167). Despite poetry's traditional status as an elite form, however, feminists embraced what they saw to be the egalitarian potential in the genre. Thus most papers solicited poems from readers to extend collective ownership of the publication beyond the editorial group. The undated, first issue of Detroit's *Womankind* is fairly typical, inviting readers to contribute poetry as well as news reporting, fiction, and graphics ("Womankind" 1). Even for *off our backs,* which focused on news and cultural analysis, no other category in their index from the first five years of publication (1970–74) registers as many entries as poetry. The *off our backs* editorial group announced in the second issue that they "wanted at all times" not simply news stories or analytical articles but poetry ("Wanted" 11).

While some periodicals included only a single poem an issue, most provided more space, often designing a full page of poems and graphics. The first, undated issue of Boston's Cell 16 journal (later to be called *No More Fun and Games*) devoted part or all of twenty-nine of its eighty-one folio pages to poems.[3] One issue of *off our backs* designed the entire centerfold around Marge Piercy's poem "Burying Blues for Janis," in memory of Janis Joplin, a full folio sheet that could function as a pull-out poster. New York's *Woman's World* included few poems but placed those few prominently. Immediately below the masthead of the April 15, 1971, issue, a 1911 poem—the Japanese feminist Yosano Akiko's poem "The mountain moving day is coming"—serves as epigraph for the whole issue. In another issue, after a long reflection on the Women's Conference on Prostitution, the *Woman's World* editors placed "Roundelays," a poem, in English translation, from the seventeenth-century Mexican poet-nun Sor Juana Inés de la Cruz in which men are charged with inciting women to evil (Cruz 15).[4] The concision and force of the poem works to bring into sharper focus what is at the political center of prostitution. Other periodicals juxtaposed poems with a variety of items simply as part of the informational cacophony: the first issue of *Womankind*, for example, includes a single newspaper page of poetry, graphics, a boxed item on Title VII of the 1964 Civil Rights Act, and an advertisement for men's slacks and jeans, with the effect that reading poetry appeared as useful to readers as understanding the provisions of a federal statute or finding wearable clothing (17).

In understanding poems to be useful and belonging to ordinary women, midcentury feminists shared in the larger countercultural embrace of the genre. James Sullivan has suggested that "the proliferation of poetry in all formats during the sixties indicates the breadth of the population that considered writing and reading poems an appropriate way to explore their own relation to the historical moment" (2).[5] In 1982, reflecting back on more than a decade of feminist poetry, the poet Jan Clausen described "the relationship of poets to the American feminist movement" as "remarkable, crucial, and in one sense at least thoroughly astounding" (5). One might expect that feminism helped to nurture the development of women's poetry. Clausen asks parenthetically, "What term is, by the way, adequately descriptive of this phenomenon: renaissance? flowering? earthquake? volcanic eruption?" (5). But the process was more complex, less unidirectional, than one might expect. Feminism as "ideology, political movement, and cultural/material support network" clearly played an important part in enabling a "tremendous release of poetic energy," but poetry also functioned to galvanize participants by engaging them politically at the level of language (5). "Any serious investigation of contemporary feminism," Clausen asserts, "must take into account the catalytic role of poets and poetry; there is some sense in which it can be said that poets have made possible the movement" (5).

But what sort of poetry? By 1982 Clausen could offer "almost a caricature of feminist poetic practice": feminist poetry is supposed to be useful, accessible, "about" specific subject matter—"women's oppression, woman-identification, identity"; "it avoids both traditional forms and distancing techniques such as persona and third-person narration"; and it is a collective product or process (21, 22, 30, 31). That Clausen could identify such elements, if a bit wryly, suggests that at least by 1982, something like an identifiable feminist poetry movement had emerged. A bit later, in 1996, Kim Whitehead argued for an understanding of feminist poetry as a movement with identifiable characteristics similar to those that Clausen had identified: "Feminist poets wanted a poetry in which they could name the experiences that societal and poetic taboos had previously kept them from expressing, in which they could make the hidden known. As a result, they turned to more open poetic modes, seeking to strip language and form of excess flourish and meaning and to make it accessible to ordinary women" (xix).[6] Among the open poetic modes, Whitehead identifies prose poems in particular as in some sense demonstrating both the poetic in the everydayness of prose and also taking poetry down off the pedestal to make it look and sound more like the language of the everyday. Whitehead also notes the tendency among feminist poets to merge lyric and narrative strategies (xv, 29). Modifying Clausen's list a bit, she adds that feminist poets developed a "coalitional" voice "to address collective concerns while recognizing difference," employing poems as tools, "as useful" (xix, xxi).

But importantly both Whitehead and Clausen distinguish the later development of an identifiably feminist poetic movement from an earlier, unsettled period. Whitehead differentiates the initial "flowering" of feminist poetry in the "explosive 1960s" from the period she studies, the formative years (seventies) and the period of maturation (eighties). Clausen offers a more critical assessment of the shift when she notes a "trend toward increased professionalization of feminist poetry" in the midseventies that led to a "regrouping of hierarchy," in the sense of a return to a certain kind of elitism, and that meant that "the phase of initial exploration, of poems written, often enough, in the creative heat of the feminist 'conversion experience,' and necessarily in symbiosis with a dynamic, expanding political movement—that phase seems definitely over" (40–41, 43). Strikingly and, I think, appropriately, neither Clausen nor Whitehead attempts to read back onto the volatile earlier phase the relative coherence they identify as characteristic of the later seventies and eighties. One can find poems in the early period that exhibit the features Clausen and Whitehead identify, but the early poetry ranges more widely, making it difficult to impose a pattern without doing serious injustice to the "creative heat" Clausen recalls. I have thus found it more productive to read the poems—and the occasional review of a poetry anthology or the incorporation of poetry in prose—as negotiating what must have seemed then to be an almost infinite range of poetic possibilities modulated or intensified through a unifying commitment to radical populism. I have chosen to consider the poetry in terms of the questions that poets and readers were raising about form, subject matter, and purpose or function. It is rather rare to find in the periodicals, pamphlets, and anthologies anything approximating a feminist poetics in the sense of an articulated set of poetic precepts. The poems themselves, however, can be read as working out ways to address these questions about what feminist poetry can or ought to be.

In the early radical feminist publications, it was far more important that ordinary women write than that some set of either formal or political principles be observed. In fact, breaking with what were perceived to be the dominant poetic forms was itself understood to be a political act, even though feminist poets were not creating poetry out of nowhere but recombining available elements. As Clausen suggests, feminist poets may well have thought of feminist poetry as a "clean slate, an open field," but they were inevitably reacting against "what was perceived as the male poetic tradition" (21). That male poetic tradition was understood in part to entail what Robert Penn Warren called (approvingly) a "depersonalizing form" (78). One of the poets whom Cleanth Brooks anoints as forming the "third revolution in poetry" (75), Warren did not discount the poet's "personal feelings and convictions" altogether ("we all know [those feelings and convictions] enter somehow into [the] poem," he says), but we are also supposed to understand "that the strictly personal adequacy of the expression—the cathartic value for the poet, we might say—has nothing to do with the value of a poem" (78). The poem as "a thing made" must "stand apart from, though absorbing, even dramatizing, whatever human urgencies were involved in the making" (78). For Brooks, human urgencies are not merely personal concerns but serve as code for political or ideological affiliation. Thus, in his chapter "Metaphysical Poetry and Propaganda Art" Brooks damns politically aligned poetry as both sentimental and propagandistic. With these labels he "convicts" the poems of Genevieve Taggard, Langston Hughes, and others he calls "naive Marxists" for their "clumsy and inadequate account of poetry" (50–51). Whether or not the poets appearing in the pages of feminist newspapers, journals, and pamphlets had read Warren's 1962 reflection on his own practice as a poet (or Cleanth Brooks's earlier writings, for that matter), they were likely to have absorbed—thanks to the dominance of New Critical practices in schools, universities, and publishing houses—something of a high modernist aesthetic that privileged the observance of forms intended to signify a "depersonalizing objectivity."

That aesthetic was already being challenged, of course, most immediately—and probably for many radical feminists, most familiarly—through protest poetry (including protest songs) associated with the antiwar and civil rights movements. While it is true that throughout the twentieth century, poets had participated in various social and political movements, it is not at all clear how much of that longer activist literary history emerging feminist poets knew.[7] Nor is it clear how familiar these poets were with avant-garde poetry that challenged, at least formally, the dominance of high modernism.[8] The feminist movement itself fed the desire to rediscover forgotten women poets, and some established women poets appeared in the feminist periodicals. It is also clear that the proliferation of feminist poetry accelerated the rediscovery of a radical past: not just poets who happened to be women but also women poets from various cultures and moments in the past who saw poetry as a form of political activism and an expression of their experiences as women. But at least early on, many women contributing to feminist periodicals and small presses did not signal a familiarity with a longer feminist or activist tradition but performed as if they were working improvisationally, reveling in a new sense of creative freedom as they borrowed widely from the larger culture language, forms, and contents that establishment, elite, or school poetry had seemed to ignore or put off limits. The poems themselves are the primary evidence of this cultural borrowing. There are a few rare reviews of poetry anthologies, and a few prose essays that appropriate poetry in service of a particular argument, but there is little else that frames the poems in more typically literary terms, little about the poets themselves (many of whom used only a single name, a matrilineal, a pseudonym, or no name at all), and little about literary intentions or expectations beyond a very few poems that include some explicit reference to the process of composition or to expectations for readers. The poems are thus readable not as literary objects in isolation but as artifacts embedded in an explicitly feminist context, materially situated in relation to other visual and verbal expressions of feminism. Whatever the poets might have intended, because the poems were so situated materially, they were in fairly obvious ways preread as contributing to the work of the women's movement.

Finding Fit Form for the Matter

A few poets explicitly mark the formal choices they had available to them in order to posit alternatives. Karen Marsden begins a wry poem, "plastic wrinkle war," by reflecting on the act of composition: "I wanted to write a poem / about wrinkles, women's wrinkles, / but the words came to me not cleanly / nor fit themselves within the framework / of a nice, precise sonnet, / only a sprawling spill / of words about war" (11). Although the poem is clearly crafted, not literally a sprawling spill of words, it is also not a sonnet in the limited sense of a fourteen-line poem with formal rhyming pattern. Marsden shares with other twentieth-century poets a desire to achieve what Denise Levertov would call "organic form," a shape for words to fit the sense (11; see also Rukeyser 30).[9] In this case, Marsden wanted her words to do the work of making strange taken-for-granted cultural attitudes, to help her think through the cultural "ill-logic" evident in notions about women's looks.

Such a poem may seem to be at some remove from what Adrienne Rich defines as "true political poetry." In a late seventies essay on Judy Grahn's work, Rich distinguishes true political poetry from propaganda. Propaganda seeks to "persuade others 'out there' of some atrocity and injustice," whereas "true political poetry...can only come from the poet's need to identify her relationship to atrocities and injustice, the sources of her pain, fear, and anger, the meaning of her resistance" ("Power and Danger" 251). It might seem absurdly hyperbolic to read Marsden's focus on "wrinkles" as akin to identifying the poet's relationship to atrocity and injustice, but I understand Rich to be interested in the multiple microworkings of injustice and the ways in which the female body has served as a locus for such injustice. Reflecting particularly on the lesbian poet, but in terms that would encompass Marsden's poem and indeed much of the poetry printed in the periodicals, Rich sees that the poet has to "ask questions that did not occur to a Donne or a Yeats, or even to an Elizabeth Barrett Browning..., questions about taboo, integrity, the fetishization of the female body, the worldwide, historical violence against women by men, what it means to be 'true to one another' when we are women, what it means to love women when that love is denied reality, treated as perversion, or, even more insidiously, 'accepted' as a mirror-image or parallel to heterosexual romance" ("Power and Danger" 252).

Marsden's poem asks questions that she assumes to be outside the realm of the traditionally poetic, questions that do not seem possible within the confines of a tidy sonnet. While other twentieth-century poets had pushed against what was perceived to be the boundaries of traditional poetry, attempting to make more room for new definitions of the ordinary—in a sense, to make the prosaic poetic—Marsden and other feminist poets worked to ensure that the ordinary would be understood to include questions of gendering, and not as an isolated or trivial matter (Whitehead 4). In the "plastic wrinkle war" Marsden thus seeks her form in the matter, a shape through which to write about something as apparently trivial as "a plastic bottle battle against / women's wrinkles, / a subtle, sweetly perfumed, silken war / so honey soft it swallows women whole / to spit out uniformly plastic creatures / of design" (11). As if the sonnet in its regularity were akin to the desire for uniformly plastic creatures of design, she chooses instead irregular stanzas, plenty of white space, a mix of short and long lines, and simple language appropriate to the childlike stance of puzzling over a bit of cultural commonplace: "I do not know / what is so wrong / about a woman having wrinkles" (11).

Marsden risks playing with the apparently trivial by recollecting what the child learned about brains:

> I only recollect that as a child
>   I was told:
>   everytime you learn
>   something new or think
>   a difficult thought
>   another wrinkle is
>   added to your brain
>   the very wise have brains
>   like wizened, crinkled
>   wrinkled walnut meats
>   idiots have brains
>   like elegantly polished
>   plastic eggs (11)

Playing out the analogy, the poet asks, "What if a person's brain wrinkles / are echoed on her face?" This is not just a nice sentiment about wrinkled and therefore wise women but rather a critique of the smooth-faced woman more intent on looks than brains, who is by implication an idiot. Accompanied by Nancy Szabo's block-print image of three older women's wizened faces, as if to test the reader's transformed sensitivity, the penultimate lines of the poem conclude that "when you look into / an intensely wrinkled face / you look / O / God! / into the face of / mother natural wisdom" (12). The poem ends with what must be understood now by the reader as a rhetorical question: "What IS so wrong about / a woman having wrinkles?" (12).

Vernita Gray's title, "prose poem, a christmas card," announces an awareness of formal possibilities more particularly in relation to material medium. The poem itself questions both the straightforwardness of prose and the banal sentiments one might expect from a Christmas card. Appearing in the March 1974 issue of *Lavender Woman,* the poem tells a story of a childhood experience recalled in language close to ordinary speech but edgier, jazzed and syncopated enough to expose the inadequacy of ordinary language for conveying the weight of the experience. The poem's narrator remembers the "little ole black lady friend" of her grandmother who sent her family Christmas cards "until the christmas the card didn't come" (74). The narrator and her mother go looking for Miss Corine and find her "in the little ole crazy lady ward / at illinois state of mental institution" (74). Through the ordinariness of detail, Gray gives the reader a chilling sense of the inevitability of Miss Corine's ending up in a mental hospital where she has to be "hosed down with water until / she was calm / tired / or ready to stop" (75). This is a story not only about Miss Corine, and by extension all the women made crazy or deemed crazy by an out-of-whack society, but also about how mothers sometimes pass on reductively absurd, hopelessly inadequate gender instructions (or rationalizations):

> my mother said, miss corines mother had died and left corine
> in the care of an older brother who always called her Whore,
> (maybe he was so old he couldn't remember her name) but anyway
> he was generally into mistreating her until she grew up and
> went to work in uppermiddleclasswhite kitchens (75)

But according to the narrator's mother, it isn't this experience that sends Miss Corine to the mental institution: "my mother said, miss corine had gone crazy cause she never had a / man. and that when women don't have men they go crazy. The narrator and her mother visit Miss Corine only once, but, she says: "we never got to talk with her / never went back to see her / cause the visit gave my mother a headache / and me nightmares, / for days" (74–75). As in Marsden's poem, here too the recollected child's vision lets us see unvarnished the cruelty of cultural expectation and the inadequacy of a cultural formulation, not just the mother's explanation, but the gendering of mental illness or the hystericizing of femaleness. The poem suggests that the mother understands on some level the inadequacy of the explanation she gives her daughter to the extent that the mother's headache signals her own unease with Miss Corine's fate, her sense, perhaps, that such a fate is not Miss Corine's alone. The poem as poem in calling attention to form seems especially well suited to do the work of exposing the harm done through conventional forms and commonplace formulations.

Marge Piercy also makes reference to the question of form in her poem "Lies" when she addresses a "you" who turns out to be the "you / there in the mirror," a reflection of the narrator's own critical voice dismissing what the narrator does, how she acts: "You say I hate lying / because I want to be a child / holding my mother's hand / . . . You say, what is the truth then? / Does it come in a package? You say confession / is false orgasm. / You say feeding people part / of yourself is an attempt to bribe / them into love" (*Early Grrl* 59). In this poem from the early seventies, "confession" can stand for a version of feminist "honesty . . . a compulsion swinging a / heavy sword like loving / like poetry itself." At the same time, it can also refer to a kind of poetry, the confessional poetry associated with such poets as Robert Lowell, Sylvia Plath, and Anne Sexton, poetry marked, that is, by a psychoanalytic probing, an attempt to lift the veil to expose the poet's autobiographical self. Piercy's poem can be read as locating itself uneasily and defensively in relation to a part of the contemporary literary scene, to a fear of excess (is poetry always culturally excessive on some level?) and, at the same time, the fear of failing to be honest, akin to failing to love.

Marsden's, Gray's, and Piercy's poems are relatively unusual among the poems appearing in the dissident papers and limited-run pamphlets in calling explicit attention to the question of form and in tying form to subject matter and purpose. Rarer still are prose reflections on the question of the forms of feminist poetry. Although theories of the relationship of form to subject matter and purpose could be found in establishment or mainstream publications and would become increasingly available in feminist literary magazines that emerged later in the seventies, early radical feminist publications published little if any of such theoretical work. Frances Chapman's review of *Dykes for an Amerikan Revolution* is all the more striking because it provides an unusual glimpse at the reading practices of a practicing poet. In this 1971 *off our backs* review Chapman makes visible the various layers of her reading, from her attention to the physical appearance of the little pamphlet to her weighing the aesthetics in relation to the politics of the poems included in the anthology, and in the process she makes clear the difficulty of finding the right form to do the work of feminist cultural critique.[10]

Dykes for an Amerikan Revolution was available from Easter Day Press for fifty cents, and it promised to be "as diverse in sentiment and form as is the Lesbian Population." Chapman reads this collection as a physical object (with a slight nod to Marshall McLuhan's widely circulated mantra, the "medium is the massage"):

> The "booklet" is 8 1/2 by 11 blue, gold, and white mimeo bond, folded in half booklet-wise. At first, the reader doesn't see the title. It is spray painted on the pedestal of the statue which is the subject of the cover photo. My first response to the uneven reproduction, the pedestrian, mostly reprinted graphics: What the hell, the message is more important than the medium. Yet *Dykes* as a printed artifact says something about the eventually numbing effect of the glossy, eye appeal of the slick, stylish media of the Establishment and the Counter-Establishment. Whatever criteria of selection were used by the women who collected *Dykes,* what I read as individual pieces of writing and as a collection is as free of the appearance of preconceived literary "standards" as it is of stylistic uniformity or the conventional categories of genre. (35)

Reading the "uneven production" of the physical object as itself a political statement, Chapman admires the "different, but equivalent, accounts of valid experience" available in the poems. At the same time, as a practicing poet who has spent a number of "years analysing and building poems," Chapman is drawn to the "craft" of particular selections in the anthology. Working along the fault line evident in the periodicals' debate between egalitarian values on the one hand and quality of publication on the other, she realizes that although an uneven production looks unprofessional, potentially undermining the effectiveness and credibility of the work within, a too-slick professionalism can itself cancel out the message. Once inside the pamphlet, Chapman admires the collection because it is apparently free of "preconceived literary 'standards,'" and yet she prefers the poems that are more "carefully constructed." Although exactly what "carefully constructed" means (and how it can be named independent of preconceived literary standards) is not articulated, in naming that apparent binary Chapman identifies a key axis that feminist poets had to negotiate. As with Marsden's reference to the inadequacy of the sonnet to say what needs saying, Chapman registers what was a widespread suspicion of establishment or traditional poetic forms and expectations.

Such considerations of craft are not separate from Chapman's appreciation of the politics evident in the collection—in particular, the diversity of experience within a broadly conceived politics: "although radicalesbian, the collection speaks more of the liberating love that is Lesbian than it does of the political ideology that demands that all love be Lesbian" (35). Chapman makes clear that politics alone cannot make a poem work. She admires Cynthia Funk's poem "Collage" because it "describes the necessary soul-back-searching for what is gay in us, attractions, rejections, and betrayals," but at the same time, she thinks the poem spoiled by what she reads as the "obligatory Politically relevant ending" (35). Chapman does not elaborate on her criteria but offers instead examples of poems or parts of poems she admires. Crediting Rita Mae Brown with "some of the finest lines in the booklet," she quotes a few lines from Brown's "Epistle to Tasha":

> The dead are the only people
>   to have permanent dwellings
> We, nomads of revolution
> Wander over the desolation of many
>   many generations
> And are reborn in each other's lips . . . (35; ellipses in original)

I cannot say with certainty whether Chapman is drawn to the metaphoric work of these lines, but she does seem to be drawn to passages that are less evidently autobiographical, and in that sense she is perhaps rejecting elements of confessional poetry associated with some prominent women's work. She cites, for example, but does not quote a poem by Tami Kallen that she does not admire, describing it as a poem "child-printed about her mother," apparently conjoining her critique of the craft—"child-printed"—to her critique of the autobiographical subject matter.

Having quoted other passages for the benefit of those readers "who delight in the craft of poetry," Chapman concludes her review by returning to the politics of the pamphlet as a whole. Just as feminists engaged in political theater worried that propaganda defeated art (see chapter 4), so too Chapman worries about how to create politically charged poetry that is still poetry. "Although some of the writings assert the politics which says that Lesbianism is an obligatory preliminary to the liberation of society," she observes, "this is overshadowed by the language and emotions of alive and sensible women." Some of these emotions, she says "are lesbian" and "Lesbianism is still a political doctrine." But, she adds, "there is little of the strident and accusatory harangue with which the doctrine is usually argued" (35). It is thus possible to have political poetry that is something other than polemic, something that gets at the real emotions of alive and sensible women, recognizing that those emotions are never not political.

Chapman does not offer her review as a way to enforce a poetic or a political agenda. What forms feminist poetry should take is not a settled question for her any more than it is for Marsden, Gray, Piercy, or the hundreds of other women who were contributing poems to feminist periodicals or publishing through small presses. Feminist poetry encompassed a range of traditional and contemporary formal possibilities, from the epigrammatic and spare to the richly discursive, from the imagistic to the abstractly coded, and from the lyrical to the dramatic. The poems do not all eschew the third-person narrator, nor do they avoid persona altogether, yet when used, such techniques are rarely deployed to distance speaker from subject or speaker from reader in the sense that Jan Clausen means. Some of the poems work toward what Whitehead calls the "coalitional voice," in the sense of an identification with collective struggle, but far more poems work with the lyrical or narrative first person. Sometimes rhyming, more often blank verse, the poems borrow from literary, folk, and popular forms, bringing within the poetic space a wide range of cultural reference. Neither form nor technique thus can distinguish feminist poetry in the early radical feminist periodicals from other contemporary poetry. Finding fit form for the matter suggests that the forms were out there to be found, but what would constitute feminist subject matter?

When Women Paint the Naked Truth

A *Big Mama Rag* poem entitled "A Woman's Reflections on Seeing Her Painted Sisters Hanging on a Museum Wall!" sets out to consider female "objects of beauty / objectified," visible in a museum. On the walls can be found "goya's stoic spanish courtisan [*sic*] / renior's [*sic*] fleshy lovelies, in opera dress / toulouse's poster prostitutes / mona—what would she say if they let her speak" (6). The poet asks what these objects of the "man's brush," these women, would say were they to paint: "Would they paint penises / if they had unbound hands that could hold brushes / or would they paint / the pain of a thousand years which their hands hold / so beautifully?" the poet asks; "when will . . . the women paint the naked truth?" (6). If revealing the naked truth is the task of the feminist artist, what happens when feminist poets take up the pen? What sorts of truths do they reveal? In the early publications the naked truth could be about almost anything that touched in some way on women's experience, without particular regard for ideological conformity or consistency. In fact, it may well have been this sense of ideological free range that welcomed so many women to the genre. If feminist polemic on some level had the obligation to make the case for particular versions of feminism, to posit an ideological common ground, feminist poems evidence no such burden.

Poetry seems to have allowed women far freer rein than polemic to explore women's experience, without the necessity of claiming that all women or even most women experience the world in the same ways, thus accounting for the greater diversity of women contributing poems (rather than manifestos and treatises) to feminist publications and the greater diversity of contents. Feminist poems celebrated women's lives, critiqued heterosexist constrictions and misrepresentations, and imagined alternatives, without for the most part acknowledging an obligation to toe an aesthetic or political party line. Poems that long for men, poems that mourn the loss of the aborted child, poems that turn the tables and get their nasty revenge on male aggressors, poems that reveal a woman's weaknesses, that hold women accountable for their oppression, raunchy poems, silly poems, rabble-rousing poems—all find their way onto the pages of radical feminist publications. In individual poems, and more strikingly in the aggregate, poetry seems better able to hold dynamically together the complexity of human existence and to enact the interconnectedness of categories of identity than polemics, which must yield to the linear pressure of analytical clarity.

I do not intend to offer an exhaustive account of this unruly domain; rather, I will look at a few poems to consider how certain "contents" are addressed. I have tried to treat the poems as poems rather than as containers from which I could extract politically viable matter, to respect the fact that women contributed these as poems (not polemics) and that the assumption was that there was some work that the form of the poem could do that the polemical prose could not. The poems I consider here include not only critiques of the heterosexist regime—from gendering instructions, body image, and male predation to motherhood—but also personal alternatives, coalitional strategies, and calls to revolutionary action.

In one of a number of what might be called warning poems, "there was a young woman who swallowed a line," Meredith Tax identifies some of the commonplace means by which heterosexist mandates are enforced. This is a slight ditty, wittily parodic, that derives its "tune" from the child's verse, "there was an old woman who swallowed a fly" ("there was a young woman" 10). After swallowing rules, lines, rings, and some Dr. Spock, the young woman addressed in the poem is advised to "regurgitate" all that she has been fed, with the promise that she will thus (in contrast to the old woman of the original verse) "not die" (10). Such warning poems do not so much teach women what they do not already know but function as small acts of refusal of things as they are. Women do not have to be victims. They can throw up, throw over all the old lies.

In "Castle of Heterosexual," another, more elaborate warning poem that depends less on direct instruction to regurgitate cultural mandates and more on learning by example, Lynn Lonidier counterposes several scenes constituting not so much a minidrama but something more akin to the additive structure of dreamscape or psychic space that is also darkly comic.[11] In one scene, for example, there is "the boyfriend" who "refused to read Summerhill and said he'd put our six / unhappened children through boarding school" (*Female Freeway* 21).[12] In response to this betrayal—he has refused to read about an experiment in radical pedagogy, a kind of litmus test for a future parent—the narrator recognizes the inadequacy of this match and lets go of the material (and psychic) security he could afford, feeling, she says, "fingers / to my hairends come loose from his emerald estate" (21). This scene with the boyfriend is followed by another, more fractured scene titled "help meat," with the pun on *helpmeet* (*helpmate*) no doubt intended:

> the lady who folds herself in the sewing class Her classmates compete
> in pregnancies   their asthma souls pricked flamingo   The Lady
> sits spidering gold from her mouth her belly her nostrils   a wrinkle

full of children pulled tight plotting chesspiece movements over
bone carpets in a glazed mansion of unseen little people mincing
Midas' fantasies of female 'til the lady is shookwrungswept
out by the witch of no-such-thing on Man Street (21)

Putting these two scenes or moments side by side (with formal echoes of Emily Dickinson and Gerard Manley Hopkins), Lonidier's prose poem suggests that to have accepted the boyfriend's green estate would have been to make oneself his creature, a Midas fantasy of what it means to be female, the economic security of the green estate becoming the consuming greed of male fantasy. To be the Lady on Man Street is to be a consumable piece of meat.

If Tax and Lonidier imagine not only the necessity but also the possibility of pulling back from the oppressive cultural expectations before it is too late, a number of poems figure women as victims or near victims of male predation. In one of the first women's liberation journals, the untitled first issue of what would become *No More Fun and Games,* and surrounded by articles on women as an enslaved group, celibacy, the psychological castration of the female, and the need for a feminist vanguard, Ellen O'Donnell's "there are five senses" seems oddly passive, almost gothic in its illustration of the dominated woman. The poem, placed on an unnumbered page, sketches an intimate scene of sexual encounter. Like Lonidier's "help meat," O'Connell's female narrator is a sacrificial feast. While she is food for the man whose footsteps she dreads, she says she does not desire food herself and yet remains hungry. This man gives her nothing, in part because, although he feeds, he "savors nothing." This spare poem registers through its anachronistically decorous language the fear and destructiveness of a predatory sex:

I clothe myself in disarray
rather than be importuned
to disrobe.
No feast possible for
the eye alone.
He must touch
fingering to shreds.
Beauty to him
is only prelude.
He is full
and I am hungry.

Although the journal's opening prose polemic asserts, staccato fashion, that "women must liberate themselves" ("The ONLY way any human being can approach another on the basis of equality, or work for an egalitarian society, is if he or she is a WHOLE, and not seeking a body to leech off of" ["Slavery" n.p.]), the poem focuses on the other side of the polemical assertion, on the ravenous male from whom the woman needs to free herself.

An angrier poem, but nonetheless a poem about female victimage, "When My Dude Walked Out the Door / I Cursed Him with One Thousand and One Days and Nights of Hard Fuckin'," appeared in a 1972 issue of *Moving Out.* In the tradition of "my man done me wrong" ballads, Chris Lahey Dolega's poem borrows not from nursery rhyme or spiritual but from folk curse and blues or country lyrics. The female narrator does not seem to have much control over her situation beyond the curse of the title. She is acted on, subject to the man. The poem opens with a warped scene of intimacy: "with a black magic marker / you drew daisies on my knees / you said you needed midnight / bella donna desperately / only some times." Religion provides no safety but is part of the man's power when he calls in the "Bishop / to come exorcise the devil out of me." Even the gentle childhood recollection of the mother's healing ministrations simply reinforces the sense that this woman is not independent. The woman does not choose to leave, nor does she send the man away. Rather, the narrator says, still addressing the man, "you're leav'n now / and peelin' my skin / you find out / that I'm hollow / but intact" (82). The naked truth of this poem is that a woman cannot always extricate herself from harm, and the only lucky triumph may be that the woman remains "intact."

If O'Donnell's narrator offers herself as sacrificial feast, Cynthia EnDean-Conner's eponymous filing clerk gets her revenge against the adulterous male. Like blues lyrics that hinge on euphemism, this poem—printed ironically in script—visually mocks the mechanical and repetitive sexual act. The filing clerk is hardly free, but the poem does not seem to trouble the question of her complicity and instead takes a certain wicked (if incomplete) pleasure in the joke:

> She sprinkled wet green paint between
> Her thighs and laughed to think of what
> His wife would say. She became intoxicated
> On his beer breath.
> In-Out
> I'm sort of a filing clerk, she thought.

As if to compensate, she buys "herself flowers with his / loose change" and eats "a Hershey bar for quick energy" and repeats the refrain, "In-Out" (14).

This is no politically correct poem about the liberated mistress/file clerk who gets herself out of an exploitative relationship, nor is it playing on pathos or tragedy. Boss/lover and mistress/file clerk—economically this poem conjoins the commercial and private domains, offering almost as an emblem poem a flash of contemporary sexuality.

Juli Loesch's poem "Hitch," which like "Filing Clerk" appeared in Pittsburgh's *Woman Becoming,* is tougher in telling a story of gender disciplining, sharply exposing the relationship between systems of power and sexual violence. The story is told from the perspective of a female hitchhiker who is "stopped / By a cop," her apparently carefree "whistle cut short":

"Some nut
Could easily pick you up,"
he says,
"Chick."
He crushes the butt of his cigarette.
He checks his radio.
"White female, says she's 21,
Hair brown." He eyes
My tits. "About 135 pounds."
I bitch
Why pick ME up?
I don't attack . . .
He cuts
Me short. (Pushes
his fat finger
into my face.)
"You're bing smart. You're asking for it.
Bet that's how you get your kicks.
Likely wind up in a ditch."

The short, staccato lines dramatize through their clipped form how this woman has been "cut short," anatomized, and threatened into angry silence. The hitchhiker knows she cannot talk back and grits her teeth. She can only say to herself, "You wish, you wish," recognizing that the cop is projecting what he wishes for her (67). Hers is not a permanent silence, however, as the poem serves as angry testament.

Such poems about male threat raise the question of alternatives. Can a woman live in the world without a man? Do men necessarily have to be enemies? How else might women live in the world as other than victims? Poetry does not offer answers but suggests possibilities. Vernita Gray's poem about Miss Corine challenges powerfully, if indirectly, the assumption that a woman needs a man in order for her to be "normal": does Miss Corine go crazy because she never had a man or because she moves from the mistreatment at the hands of her brother to the demeaning job as help in an "uppermiddleclasswhite kitchen" (75)? Just as Gray conjoins gender, class, and race in her poem to diagnose Miss Corine's tragedy, Gloria Larry House's "Woman" challenges the assumption that every woman needs a man in terms that treat gender as part of a more complex and explicitly political matrix. This poem refuses the familiar terms of the female lament and exhorts women, particularly black women, to take greater responsibility:

Where is the revolution to be seen
Through all those tears?
Has the length of one man alone
So blurred your view
Can you leave the sons and daughters of Our time
Motherless?—no poems, no brown laughter, no acts of violence
For love squandered on one man? (60)

While some poems might (inelegantly) urge women to "cry, cry bitter tears / cause you've been screwed again" (Hamann 5), House has no patience with weeping:

Can you forget the hopes and longings
Pulling you into the dark unprecedented of Our Day?

This is not Malcolm's sister
Who sits sobbing for the love of one man
While the nation groans for birth! (60)

Such a poem wants none of the self-absorbed weeping of lovelorn adolescence, certainly not in the face of far greater needs.

Judy Grahn's poem "Carol, in the park, chewing on straws" appeared in the September 30, 1970, issue of *oob* accompanied by a line drawing of a female nude, big bellied, hair in curlers, with arms outstretched. The nude is superimposed on a phallus that is somewhat obscured by the foregrounded figure of the woman. The pose of the nude suggests the crucified Christ, as if the pregnant woman has been sacrificed to male sexual desire.[13] One might assume that the drawing is intended to illustrate the poem, that this will be yet another poem about how women are martyred to male lust, but the relationship between image and word is not so straightforward. Grahn's poem is not "about" pregnant women, nor is it "about" the relationship of women to men per se. Rather, the poem is about a woman who "has taken a woman lover." The poem begins with a four-line ditty that mimics, mockingly, a culturally mandated disapproval: "she has taken a woman lover / whatever shall we do / she has taken a woman lover / how lucky it wasn't you" (7). This woman, presumably "Carol" of the title, works hard to run beneath the cultural radar "all day through," smiling, lying, gritting her teeth, pretending to be shy, or weak, or busy. But once at home, she "pounds her own nails, makes her / bets, and fixes her own car, with her friend." Carol "goes as far / as women can go without protection / from men." And she dreams. Carol dreams "of becoming a tree that dreams it is ground up" to become a paper airplane that then rises

> on its currents; where it turns into a
> bird, a great coasting bird that dreams of becoming
> more free, even, than that—a feather, finally, or
> a piece of air with lightening in it.

Carol is, we learn, "angry energy inside a passive form." This "common woman is as common / as a thunderstorm," and thus her commonality cannot be dismissed but carries strain. She can in fact escape—albeit with difficulty—the sacrificial relationship suggested by the image of the crucified female of the illustration. This woman at least can dream of soaring (7).

Whether intended to be read as a commentary on male/female conflict it is not certain, but the Dayton Women's Liberation newsletter reprinted a series of three poems by Margaret Atwood under the heading of "Power Politics," thus inviting a gendered reading. In these poems Atwood urges the laying down of arms, the suspension of hostilities. Although no direct reference is made to gender, the poems locate power politics not in the world of international conflict but in the intimate space of touch. The poems suggest that the stakes are too high, that the world is too fragile to continue in conflict: "In view of the fading animals . . . , the sea clogging, the air / nearing extinction / we should be kind, we should / take warning, we should forgive / each other" (2). But "instead we are opposite, we / touch as though attacking, / the gifts we bring / even in good faith maybe / warp in our hands to implements, to maneuvers" (2). Might there be a cessation of conflict, whereby the mutual understanding of vulnerabilities is not used to cause more pain? The need for peaceful coexistence is most pressing not because such a peace will ensure survival but because the world is in such peril that we cannot afford not to comfort one another: "We need each other / breathing, warmth, surviving /

is the only war / we can afford, stay / walking with me, there is almost time / if we can only make it as far as / the (possibly) last summer" (2). Whereas much feminist poetry makes visible the dangers of too great a dependence on men, Atwood's poems—when read in the context of a women's liberation publication, at least—serve as a reminder of the need for human interdependence in the face of global destruction.

If one part of the heterosexist mandate is that a woman needs a man to be healthy and normal, another part is that it is natural and expected for women to become mothers. Ellen O'Donnell's "Sullen Cameo" begins familiarly enough as a poem about a failed love. In a first stanza disciplined through rhyme, the speaker muses: "There were words / better left unsaid / Silent gestures / easily read / I'd have preferred / a living anger / to love that's dead" (n.p.). But the poem veers away from the rhyme scheme in the second stanza as it veers away from a predictable plaint about lost love to express a maternal concern. This love that is now dead was not of value to the narrator alone but was "meant to be a gift / for the children." The speaker gets some distance from this sentiment—one might say a commonplace idea of staying together for the sake of the children—without abandoning it altogether. The idea is assigned to an earlier self, a "dreamy girl-woman" who hoped that love would be a gift for the children, who might then "know / Love's face / When they found their own / in their season / in their place" (n.p.). The poem begins with rhyme, loses the rhyme in the second stanza, and recuperates an off-rhyme in the final stanza, as if a gift of such a love were still possible.

Still other poems question the myth of mother love. An untitled prose poem published in a 1971 issue of *Women: A Journal of Liberation* suggests something of the inadequacy of the declarative statement. In this poem Brenda Coider gets out in compressed sentences what is supposed to go unsaid. She begins with the kind of assertion one could find in any number of polemics: "the oppression of women is absolute in the case of motherhood and that is why / mothers are angry" (32). But the momentum of the assertion rapidly unhinges what might otherwise serve as rather straightforward prose:

> the reason all of this happens is that mothers never get a chance to
> think about
> anything but that they are very angry
> because when they try to develop a peaceful thought say, one that
> would take
> minutes to come out whole and satisfying a kid comes in with a magic
> trick with

> a penny and then gives permission to the mother to watch it now even
>   when
> she says she is busy and by then of course that thought (of peace) is 10
>   minutes
> old and already dead before its time so she screams.

There is just the barest pause, a dash, and the scene turns to chaos: "the kid spits she gets up / and runs with raised fist to kill the killer of peace so by the time all of this ends / she has learned nothing about peace and has just sharpened up her / knowledge about anger." A period falls after anger, and the poem slows down, pulls back from the breathlessness of the scene to consider whether perhaps peace may not suffice to confront the oppression of women but may be absolutely necessary "in the case of motherhood" as "the only way to escape anger it's that simple / actually" (32). The sensible sentence very quickly becomes a run-on, words run together as if the poem is itself an enactment of how difficult it is for a peaceful thought to come out whole and satisfying, especially when the child enters the scene. The rush of words from "a kid comes in" to "her knowledge about anger" makes it difficult to rest easy with some simple notion of right action or victimage. The killer of peace is after all a kid who just wants his mother to watch his magic trick. The mother raises her fist "to kill the killer of peace," and in this act—a common enough scene, a common enough hyperbolic (is it only hyperbole?) language of violence—she learns nothing about peace, cannot restore peace, but only learns more about anger. The familiarity of the scene may push the reader toward comic recognition (of the sort one might find in TV sitcoms, where the spitting child and the ineffectual but raging mother could be found), but right behind that skim of the comically hyperbolic is the dark side of maternal care, the mother so pressed, even by an apparently innocent request, that she threatens harm to her child. The poem ends with an at-best paradoxical solution: the oppression of motherhood is absolute, but "a little peace" within the frame of this oppression can serve as escape from anger. Again, there is no tidy, politically sanctimonious resolution and no prettifying the anger to let the mother off the hook.

In Liz Brauer's "Letters from Mother," which is something like a list poem, the mother records in monotone her deadening routine. Using the most ordinary of language, this poem, too, does not try to erase political contradictions that risk distracting the reader from what seems to be the intended emotional purpose: "Saturday being beautiful / I washed all the bedding / And even aired pillows / Father played golf / That was good. However / He had a headache / Sunday but helped me / Finish cleaning your room"

(9). The poem depends on the reader's finding this housewife sympathetic, despite the fact that her husband has the time and the money to play golf. I cannot read this poem as an ironically self-conscious poem that could help the reader understand how the apparently middle-class wife is, despite her apparent economic security, nonetheless so downtrodden. The poem offers the reader little sense of tension between the woman whose husband can afford the leisure and money to play golf and the woman who faces a mind-numbing routine of cleaning rooms, who seems to have no way out. The final lines of the poem ask, "Where will you / Be on your / Birthday?" implicating the reader in the plight of the mother, whose birthday will be just like every other, "a full day's job / Doing it all alone" (9). Whether intentional or not, this is language "stripped of flourish and meaning," to borrow Jan Clausen's terminology. The prosaic flatness of this perhaps too accessible poem makes the routinized despair of the middle-class mother palpable, if not wholly sympathetic. Neither the language nor the form of the poem challenges the routine, echoing instead a kind of hollow inertia—and that itself may be its value.

Kay Lindsey's "Poem," in contrast, refuses such inertia. But it goes further still: Lindsey refuses not simply sentimentalized motherhood but more specifically the notion of revolutionary Motherhood, particularly as an ideal of black womanhood. The poet remarks that she is not "one of those who believes / That an act of valor, for a woman / Need take place inside her" (17). The revolution may need "numbers," may need new recruits, but she has packed her "womb...in mothballs," adding, "And I hear that winter will be mild." Although her body "deserves a medal" for giving birth twice, she notes that no such medal was forthcoming because they thought she was "just answering the call of nature." She is thus less than eager to answer the revolutionary call now: "But now that the revolution needs numbers / Motherhood got a new position / Five steps behind manhood. / And I thought sittin' in the back of the bus / Went out with Martin Luther King" (17). This bluesy poem rejects the cultural positioning of motherhood, particularly the version of it echoed in the notion of revolutionary motherhood, a positioning that makes of women merely bodies, creatures of nature (with gender and race together compounding the creatureliness of the designation).

If on the one hand, women's bodies are presumed to be designed by nature to serve, on the other hand, women's bodies are scrutinized for imperfections so that where Mother Nature has failed, the beauty industry can step in. Marsden's "wrinkle" poem is one critique of pernicious notions of beauty. Michele Clark's "Concerning Certain Sentiments" is another. The full-page poem in the April 11, 1970, issue of *oob* reflects on how various media reinforce limited and debilitating notions of female beauty. The poem gives us the thoughts of a woman while she is "in the heat of IT." The narrator disconnects herself from the sexual act in progress when the male lover cries out, "You're beautiful." Distracted by his cry, she is reminded that she is *not* beautiful, not by any cultural standard she knows: "I recount / (distracted) / (to myself) / (forgetting orgasm) / the long familiar list." She thus proceeds to catalogue the body parts that simply cannot measure up to socially defined beauty. She shifts from thinking that perhaps she was meant to be a warty old Grimm witch, "meant to frighten / little children / . . . rather than bearing them," to recalling how strangers on the subway have presumed to comment on her looks: "thinking about it later / there is murder in my heart." What doctors have said to her is not so far removed from what lovers have said, and their ideas of beauty and the natural are formed in part (as are the narrator's) by the "pristine women / I have seen . . . / in movies and magazines." Surprisingly, the hirsute women in Goya's paintings offer an alternative. A "beautiful woman" reflects: "I always thought Goya was mocking those ladies / with flecks of black hair / on pale, pale skin / above their lips, / but really / that was considered / a mark of great beauty. It's / hard to feel that way / about yourself / though . . ." (13).

But how is it possible to take such issues seriously, the poet seems to ask, when the apparent victim is an active participant in the process? How serious is the question of beauty in the face of so much else that is so deadly serious? Indeed, this question was raised against the women's movement more generally by many in the antiwar and civil rights movements. How pitifully ironic to worry about beauty in the face of war, massacre, genocide, and capitalist exploitation, and yet the form of the poem suggests, with its descending order of associational logics, an interconnectedness:

> Hard
> to blame
> the colusion of
> Vogue magazine and imperial capitalism.
> I do the best I can
>   tweezers
>   the vietnamese war
>   bleach
>   black panther massacre
>
> dandruff rinse

starvation
in the seventies
tweezers
my father weighed down
by the bill collector
and his own labor
bleach
my
brother beaten by cops
dandruff rinse
the Cuban revolution
tweezers
collective action
skin
softener
the massacre at My Lai
bleach
dead soldiers 19 years old
rinse
ben sook my lai eldridge cleaver song my lee
otis bobby seale jane alpert
VO_5 (13)

It may be difficult, but certainly not impossible, to see that the beauty industry is in cahoots with capitalism, that there might be some sinister purpose in reducing the female to mindless body, requiring that she be plastic-smooth and thought-less. But the narrator does not simply blame *Vogue* magazine but suggests the extent to which she is (and women more generally are) complicitous. There is thus both the personal and larger political parallel between what she does to her body on behalf of a culturally imposed notion of beauty and what is done to erase the traces of massacres, police beatings, and the incarceration of dissidents, all on behalf of capitalism.

Like Clark's poem, few feminist poems rest satisfied with things as they are. To expose through poetry the naked truth is a step forward, but other poems express an impatience with words alone. Such impatience is evident in a brief poem, "later, ferlinghetti," that appeared on the front page of the November 8, 1970, issue of *off our backs*. The poem is a takeoff on Lawrence Ferlinghetti's widely circulated "I Am Waiting," a series of seven poems, or "oral messages." The *oob* poet (identified only as "sandie") could count on at least some of the paper's readers to be familiar with Ferlinghetti, if not for his literary associations with an earlier generation of bohemian poets, then for his involvement in countercultural and antiwar activities (see Watson 205–9; J. Sullivan 74–75).[14] Ferlinghetti's poems literalize cultural catchphrases to call America to a "rebirth of wonder": "I am waiting for someone / to really discover America / and wail / . . . / and I am waiting / for the American Eagle / to really spread its wings / and straighten up and fly right / . . . and I am waiting / for the war to be fought / which will make the world safe / for anarchy / and I am waiting / for the final withering away of all governments / and I am perpetually awaiting / a rebirth of wonder" (48–53). In a far more compressed space, the *oob* poet replaces Ferlinghetti's literate anarchism with the assertion of radical feminism and substitutes his "awaiting perpetually and forever" with explicit impatience: "i am waiting / for the radical feminists / to seem / conservative / and i am waiting / for a little more education / for a lot of people / to become / a dangerous thing. / i am waiting / for the silent majority / to begin to speak / and most of all / i am beginning to find / i am not going to wait / much longer" (sandie 1).

Women's liberation is referenced in some poems as providing outlet and direction for such impatience. In the simplest form, such poems offer testimonial, as does Gabrielle Burton's "People Who Listen to Voices End Up in the Loony Bin (Written before WL)": "I found myself once / But then I got lost again. / I don't recall where it happened. / Someplace inbetween / Knowing all the answers. / And forgetting the question" (48). But other poems testify not only to the transformative potential in the women's movement but also to the danger it can pose and the reactions it can incite. Lynn Lonidier's "Female Freeway" records the seismic tremors that could be caused by the mere mention of "Women's Rights." The poem begins initially at a distance, with third-person narration:

> There are no markets for women's feelings   They asked was she
> a good lay   laughed before she could answer   To get her to
> cry strength   was an entertainment an amusement   They knew
> she never would (27)

But when "someone in the room mentioned Women's Rights," a small tremor is felt, disturbing the taken-for-granted: "if it weren't that / cobwebs were holding the cupboard china would've scattered and / Father Clock Face broke and quaint furniture creaked with the stir / of men's throat-clearings" (27). The force of habit gathers itself and the woman who spoke the words is dismissed because "her dress was short her hair long." In the guise of woman, she is the "ultimate female impersonator" (27). It is not until the fourth stanza, however, that the first-person narrator appears with an ugly violence of language, out of place among the quaint furniture and sedate male throat clearings, but in some sense a commensurate reaction to a culture that makes the woman's cry of strength an entertainment or an amusement. The crude reversal of violence, a literalizing of the sexual metaphor of eating, ends with an observation or threat; men and women "may murder each other," the narrator says, "now that I know where I'm going" (27).

The poem does not stop there, however, but exposes this stanza as no more than the woman's vengeful thinking, which comes to nothing. The last stanza shifts the scene to a car driven by a man. Women's rights are once again mentioned. This time the man is so "incensed he [doesn't] see the freeway," and the narrator decides that "We'd die unless I apologized / for mentioning Women's Rights[,] turn my talk to baby talk [and] heed his fantasies of The Cave." In this allusion to Plato's myth of the cave, the suggestion is that the man cannot stand the full force of truth but requires the illusion. The illusion of his power will be further reinforced as they head down the highway to Tijuana, where "shopkeepers bow and scrape and hate us" (27). For any reader of feminist polemics, the implied analogy would not be lost between the woman's baby talk and the shopkeeper's obsequiousness. Sexual dominance and imperialism are in these terms two sides of the same coin. Simply mentioning women's rights, the poem suggests, would not be enough to threaten such intertwined systems of power.

But what work were such poems expected to do? In an essay addressed to academic feminists, Rich considers poetry's relationship to action. She does not assume that poetry is the same as action but registers a certain "uneasiness about a movement infatuated with language to the neglect of action" and a wariness of a "ritual assent accorded to our poetic language" ("Toward a More Feminist Criticism" 90). At the same time, she does believe that "words can help us move or keep us paralyzed, and that our choices of language and verbal tone have something—a great deal—to do with how we live our lives and whom we end up speaking with and hearing; and that we can deflect words, by trivialization, of course, but also by ritualized respect, or we can let them enter our souls and mix with the juices of our minds" (90–91). In the early publications some poems register doubt about the power of words alone to make a difference. But it is clear from the proliferation of poems that the genre was assumed to have some special degree of revolutionary effectivity. No single form of poetry would do. Nor was any area of female experience inappropriate or off-limits as content for feminist poems. The primary defining feature was the sense that poetry was to be put to use, to strip bare the truth, but no poem was to be treated as reverenced object, as the exclusive province of those recognized in establishment terms as poets.

Putting Poetry to Use

Jill Johnston's 1971 *oob* poem "Priorities*," celebrating "certainty in action" and "ambiguity of thought," comes with instructions, as if to recognize that this poem may not do the necessary work for all readers (or put differently, that not all readers may be ready for this poem). The asterisk marking the title directs the reader to Zenlike italicized instructions following the poem itself: "**If you understand it, throw it in the garbage. / If you don't, cherish it*" (25). Johnston does not explain what the poem ought to mean. Indeed, the poem operates at the level of broad assertion, requiring each reader to invest it with a particularity or specificity that the words themselves do not provide: "I am for sisterhood / I am for certainty in action / . . . Lets make a mythology / How about women's liberation. / We can act on that" (25). The asterisked instructions signal that the reader is the one to decide the value of the poem. If the poem requires further thought—and only the individual reader can determine that—then the poem is worth saving. If it has yielded whatever it can yield for the reader, then the poem has done its work. This is not a poem to reverence unless it continues to pose a challenge, and it can do so only if the reader challenges herself.

James Sullivan argues that the question that should be asked of the sixties poetry broadside is not "Is it good?" but "Good for what and for whom?" (57). One can certainly extend that question to the poems appearing in the feminist periodicals and pamphlets. As Sullivan suggests, although many poets no doubt wish to "transmit their intentions with . . . clarity," the printed object passes through a number of hands in the making that alter how it will be understood, and it is likely to pass through many other hands to be used in ways that do not necessarily preserve the "purity of the poet's intention" (6). Johnston's asterisk seems to suggest that she expects precisely such a profusion of meaning, and the feminist periodicals would have given her some reason to expect as much. When the text is itself already outside established institutions, when it is made available in forms that announce its fleeting location in the here and now, Sullivan suggests that the very ephemeral form of such poems "demands an understanding of poetry not as a reified set of texts (whose ultimate frame of reference is the historical and biographical moment of composition), but as a malleable cultural practice that can involve a host of people, moments, intentions, and uses" (4). Just as the broadside presented the poem as a "contingent artifact" that was not simply tied to the occasion of its utterance but could be put to various uses, so too the ephemerality of cheap newsprint or inexpensive pamphlet could work to situate poetry materially in the context of women's liberation (33).

Sullivan borrows from Michel de Certeau in identifying "heresy-prone readers" who are "constantly constructing their own readings out of... texts... by using their own, uncertified frames of reference" (3–4). Although no text can fully dictate a reading, and all reading requires the reader to activate a text, I want to consider the idea of uncertified readings in a narrower sense, from two different perspectives: first, from the perspective of those poems whose level of abstraction or generality mandates that readers complete them to render them meaningful; second, from the perspective of readers who do not feel compelled to render a certified reading and are thus more clearly examples of Certeau's "heresy-prone reader." To take the first case, while many of the poems I have discussed thus far provide what John Berger might call a longer "quotation," in the sense that the reader does not have to do all the work of investing the poem with specificity (96), other poems (such as "later, ferlinghetti") operate as insider texts, constructed as transportable abstractions or generalities, removable slogans, emphasizing the "saying" rather than deep political analysis, and thus depend on the reader's willingness to do the transporting, to do more of the compositional work, to broaden and enrich them, and ideally to move from words to action.

Sally Hamann's "poem," for example, requires the reader to do more of the compositional work. As do many of the poems, especially those in the newspapers (rather than anthologies or pamphlets), Hamann's poem begins in a way reminiscent of pop or rock and roll lyrics, with the sort of generic direct address that allows the receptive reader, in the context of a women's liberation periodical, to see herself as the "you" of the poem: "sit on the back porch / and cry, cry bitter tears / cause you've been screwed again" (5). The generalized "you" appears to live in a world that has constricted in compass, because she does not seem to "have a choice left." We get no specific sense of a particular person or a particular kind of constriction of choice but only the general and therefore generally applicable lament. Hamann, however, does not end the poem in despair but builds from lament in order to transform "no choice" into a resisting, belligerent "only choice": "Your only choice is to fight them, not trust them / but it hurts to fight those you would like to be / . . . Then fight together / you have to fight now cause you haven't a choice left." The reader is not told who "them" might be, or in what way the "you" might want to be like them. The generic lines of the poem allow the reader to invest the lament with her own specifics, her own sense of injustice, of unfairness, and to be roused by the call to fight. Disconnected from its context, the poem seems rather hollow. But the poem reads differently in the context of the issue of *Ain't I a Woman* in which it appeared, an issue that opens with eleven demands to eliminate the oppression of all women and that includes critiques of America's rampant individualism, the American Medical Association, the pornographic content of a male-run underground paper, and "media stars" in the movement, as well as essays on women and self-defense, a visit to Christopher Street a year after the Stonewall riots, and collective living. This is not poetry that can be simply recollected in tranquility—or, for that matter, that could convince someone not already committed—but a work that requires the reader to connect it to its material location or some broader context so that it can signify.

The second perspective is most strikingly evident in the few rare glimpses of readers reading to be found in prose arguments where writers appropriate established poets for their own "unauthorized" uses. In an essay published in a 1971 issue of *Women,* Vivian Estellachild makes use of a poem by Edna St. Vincent Millay (1892–1950) to mount a critique of hippie communes and their destructive effects on women. Millay might seem an unlikely ally as a poet who by the late sixties and early seventies had been made unfortunately palatable and safe through the apparatuses of "proper access." But Estellachild has chosen from that part of Millay's work which Cary Nelson calls the "articulately antiromantic Millay that the culture has largely chosen to forget" ("Fate" 348). And she does so with little regard for some notion of a correct or respectful reading.[15] She initially inserts Millay into her argument literally as a parenthetical, without gloss, indeed as if Millay were herself offering gloss on the "hippie housewife's" experience. As Estellachild chronicles the ways in which communes simply parallel "the rest of Amerikan life" by encouraging a "pernicious form of bourgeoise individualism," she builds the case for women leaving the communes to create their own "tribes" (40, 43). Although it is difficult for the "hippie housewife to rebel," Estellachild remarks, "it is happening." Millay is deployed at this point to lend voice and motive to the argument.

Estellachild asserts that "men look around and wonder where have all the 'chicks' gone?" She then inserts as parenthetical a piece of Millay's poem:

I never again shall tell you what I think,
I shall be sweet and crafty, soft and sly.
You will not catch me reading anymore
I shall be a wife to pattern by.
And some day when you knock and push the door,
some day not too bright and not too stormy
I shall be gone
And you may whistle for me . . .
—E. St. V. Millay 1917 (43)

No title for the poem is given, no credit is given to a source, no sense of the context from which the passage of the poem comes, no explanation of how the writer sees the poem as connecting to the argument. This is no schooled or reverent use of the poet. It does not seem to matter whether or not Millay would have endorsed Estellachild's views or recognized her own intentions in this deployment of the poem. Estellachild exercises her readerly autonomy to make use of Millay in a new context distant from the circumstances of the poem's creation. In this sense, she offers the reader—whether intentionally or not—a way to read, a way to exercise readerly autonomy, and in the process jolts any reader to attention who is passingly familiar with an antiseptic Millay: why, one might ask, has this Millay been hidden from view?

A similar, if perhaps more predictable, use is made of Sylvia Plath's poem "Applicant" in Meredith Tax's essay "Woman and Her Mind: The Story of Everyday Life."[16] First published in 1970 in *Notes from the Second Year,* the essay deals with what the journal's editors term the "psychological aspects of consumerism" (10). A passage from Plath's poem serves as epigraph to a section titled "Assaults of Daily Life":

Open your hand.
Empty? Empty. Here is a hand
To fill it and willing
To bring teacups and roll away headaches
And do whatever you tell it.
Will you marry it?
It is guaranteed
To thumb shut your eyes at the end
And dissolve of sorrow.
We make new stock from the salt.
—Sylvia Plath, "Applicant" (Tax 10)

Immediately, without comment on the poem, Tax begins her analysis of consumerism: "In our society, where competitive individualism and the cash nexus are the dominant values, men are raised to see the world as a series of 'challenges.' They are taught to view everyone as a competitor for money, prestige, women, and the rest; and to be constantly on guard.... They are taught that to be masculine is to be physically and verbally aggressive, hyperactive sexually, authoritarian in manner, and capable of abstract thought" (10). Tax contrasts the ways in which masculinity has been socially defined with the ways in which femininity has been defined: women are expected to be passive, to serve as social mediators, conciliators to "keep unpleasant things from happening": "Since our awareness of others is considered our duty, our job, the price we pay when things go wrong is guilt, self-hatred. And things always go wrong. We respond with apologies; we continue to apologize long after the event is forgotten—and even if it had no causal relation to anything we did to begin with.... How willingly we suffer to prevent someone else a moment of discomfort!" (11).

As women learn to block out the mechanisms by which they are "emotionally deformed," Tax asserts, they begin to pay the high price of "false consciousness." In explaining what "false consciousness" entails, Tax again turns to Plath's poem. False consciousness, she argues, "is to think that you are miserable because you have a pimple, rather than because you have been taught to think of yourself, and always been treated, as an object for sale, and your market value (thus your only value) has been temporarily impaired by the pimple" (11). Tax then inserts another section of Plath's poem:

> First, are you our sort of person.
> Do you wear
> A glass eye, false teeth or a crutch,
> A brace or hook,
> Rubber breasts or a rubber crotch,
> Stitches to show something's missing? No, No?
>   Then
> How can we give you a thing?
> Stop crying. (11)

But this time, immediately following the passage, Tax offers something of a gloss on Plath's acid lines: "We have to face the fact that pieces have been cut out of us to make us fit into this society." This hardly exhausts what one might say about the passage, nor does it represent what might be called a proper schooled reading, but Tax is interested in using Plath for her own purposes.[17] Tax does not linger over the poem but moves to extend her own thinking, moving outward from the poem: "We have to try to imagine what we could have been if we hadn't been taught from birth that we are stupid, unable to analyze anything, 'intuitive,' passive, physically weak, hysterical, overemotional, dependent by nature, incapable of defending ourselves against any attack, fit only to be the housekeeper, sex object, and emotional service center for some man, or men, and children" (11).

Both poems—Millay's and Plath's—are deployed by the prose writers as useful language rather than as monuments to be held static in reverence to the "occasion of their utterance" (Sullivan 38). Estellachild and Tax enact readings relatively free of institutional control. Their readers in turn can then do what they choose with the parts of poems thus made available, to borrow them as fragments or to hunt down the whole poems to insert a bit of Millay or Plath into their own contexts for their own purposes. As I will show in chapter 4, with the skits and other performance modes from the period that made extensive use of various bits of cultural flotsam and jetsam, writers often borrowed from other writers' borrowings, so that excerpts moved further and further away from their "original" sources through a widespread process of irreverent appropriation. It is precisely the potential for readers to construct their own meanings that the feminist periodicals, pamphlets, and anthologies worked to actualize, providing, as James Sullivan puts it, "in concrete form a set of ideas, a language, a common cultural experience, and, in the actions of regularly buying and reading this material, a shared ritual" (28).

But feminist publications fostered more than active, unauthorized reading. They presumed that readers would become writers and, at least on one level, that to show how poems could be put to use served the pedagogical function of demonstrating what work poetry could do, and what work new poems needed to do, to fuel cultural and political change. The obvious fact that the periodicals and small presses gave women outlets to publish should not be underestimated. Feminist publications seldom paid women for the poems appearing in their pages, but they provided a too rare opportunity to go public with one's work. Once poems written by emerging poets were made public, publication provided further incentive for other women to try their hands at composing poems. Thus, to publish poems was to provide women with the incentive and opportunity to learn how to create poems.

All poems served as potential models, but some poems in particular urged women to take up the pen, directing them to work against the tide of literary history. Ruth Ikeler's "Note to William Wordsworth" imagines what might have been if Dorothy Wordsworth had been given the privileges afforded her brother, in particular, if William had had to tend to Dorothy's needs. The poem appeared in a special 1970 issue of *Women* devoted to the arts, in a section titled, "The Men Who Wrote about US." The poem, which the editors suggest "reveals the destiny of the aspiring poet caught in the maze of daily chores," is a set of instructions addressed to "Dear William." He is commanded to get up, dress properly, eat his breakfast, answer his mail, and call his dentist but not to write poems. He is reminded that he should not try to "catch / The essence / Of the morning" because this only "throws the household / Into chaos" (17). The editors preface Ikeler's poem with a bit of revisionary history: "A second look at the 'great classics' of literature reveals what we might have suspected. Most are written by men, and the women they portray are often distorted and stereotyped.... The response to our protests is often, 'well, why didn't *women* write more books?' But the limitations put on women up until the present century were stringent, and it is hard to imagine a woman trained from childhood to be a coquette, a gracious hostess, and an obedient wife, breaking out of that iron bubble with any ease" (17). The implication is that present-day Dorothys need to break out of the "iron bubble" and write.

While recognizing that it takes great courage to write, Winifred Convintree nonetheless warns that to fail to write is to risk destroying oneself. Songs by themselves could not save Janis Joplin or Bessie Smith, she acknowledges, but one still needs "to sing loud in the basement" for oneself, to hear even in the noise of the washing machine the beat of the rhythm, because to do otherwise, to "stop singing," means death (93). Also recognizing the need for courage in order to write, Rita Mae Brown invokes a more ancient female literary forebear in "Sappho's Reply," inhabiting that first women-identified poet to find and share strength: "My voice rings down / through thousands of years / To coil around your body / and give you strength / ... An army of lovers shall not fail" (2).[18]

A more complicated invocation of a literary forebear can be found in Lynn Lonidier's "Carry Me Back to Old Virginia." Playing on the song title, Lonidier is referencing not the Old South but rather Virginia Woolf's androgynous spirit. The poem begins with a series of revival meeting questions:

> When the sex changer comes
> to visit you, are you ready?
> Have you made your decision?
> Have you given yourself to your maker?

These questions serve as preamble to a compressed scene of girling and resistance:

> If I wear castles I must be a queen I folded out my silks from India
> my Turkish dyes my thread of animal gut   The women in sewing class
> nearly sewed their hands to their half-made dresses from looking at
> my realization of a garment of indistinguishable sex   They wanted to
> shape me   into the skins of their patterns: flaky brittle apparitions
> fastened down with pins   I'm another era   I wish to call Virginia
> Woolf back from the black sea trimmed in white   converse as two men
> (15)

Through such poems, women were urged to take up the pen, to carry forward the work of women before them, and to invent anew a genre that could lay bare the truths of women's lives. The poet Jan Clausen recalls the "intensive reading and gathering together of previously published poetry by women from Sappho to Sylvia Plath" that fed the creation of new poetry (13). As the poems evidence the negotiation with poetic possibility—whether explicitly or inevitably in the very forms of the poems themselves—they also suggest a range of functions and relationships with readers. And always, because these were poems that appeared within the interpretive frame of radical feminism, whatever their moment of creation, they operated preread as speaking to feminist concerns. It would be difficult to say that there were distinctively feminist forms that set these poems apart from other poetry produced at the time; rather, women were drawing from the available poetic resources to craft poems on behalf of feminist interests (or in such a way that the poems could be appropriated for those interests). In confronting the limitations of language and pushing against the constrictions of form, women learned how to read and write against the cultural grain. Poetry in this sense was practice, in the ancient sense of the word, that is, a "making," rather than an adherence to a set of political precepts or prescriptive forms. There were women poets in the mainstream, published by commercial presses and recognized by the poetry establishment, some of whom wrote out of feminist conviction. What set the poetry in the alternative feminist press apart was the wide spectrum of women who produced an anarchic outpouring of verse.

4

Locusts in the Nation's Cornfields: Feminist Performance Work

> Newsreel (New York). Newsreel #48, "She's Beautiful When She's Angry." A skit presented at the March 28th abortion rally in New York City by some very angry women, interrupted by a discussion among the women of their roles in the skit and in life. Newsreel #49, "Makeout" The oppressive experience of making-out in a car, from the woman's point of view—short and sweet. 4 1/2 minutes. Newsreel #126, "A Day of Plane Hunting" The women of Vietnam stand as examples of all revolutionaries in their complete participation in the struggle against U.S. impearialism. [*sic*]
>
> The Mod Donna & Scyklon Z: Plays of Women's Liberation by Myrna Lamb. A collection of six one-acts and a full length "musical soap opera." 200 pages, $2.25 paperback, Pathfinder Press, 873 Broadway, New York, N.Y. 10003.
>
> Women's Cranky: Women's street theater. A paper movie about women's history and their oppression, in cartoon form. 25c/each, 15c for 50 or more. People's Press, San Francisco, Calif. 94110
>
> Sweet 16 to Soggy 36: A Saga of American Womanhood. Cindy Abood, 1751 Bryn Mawr, Apt 1, E. Cleveland, Ohio 44112
>
> —*PM3*

THE 1971 *PM3*, a newsprint resource guide to the women's movement (see figure 7) devotes one of its eight folio pages to what they labeled "New Media Efforts," including notices for newsreel footage of feminist performances and copies of plays and street theater materials. This brief listing gives some sense of the kinds of performance work in which feminists were engaged from the late sixties through the early seventies. At the same time, the listing tells us relatively little about the dynamic processes that constituted

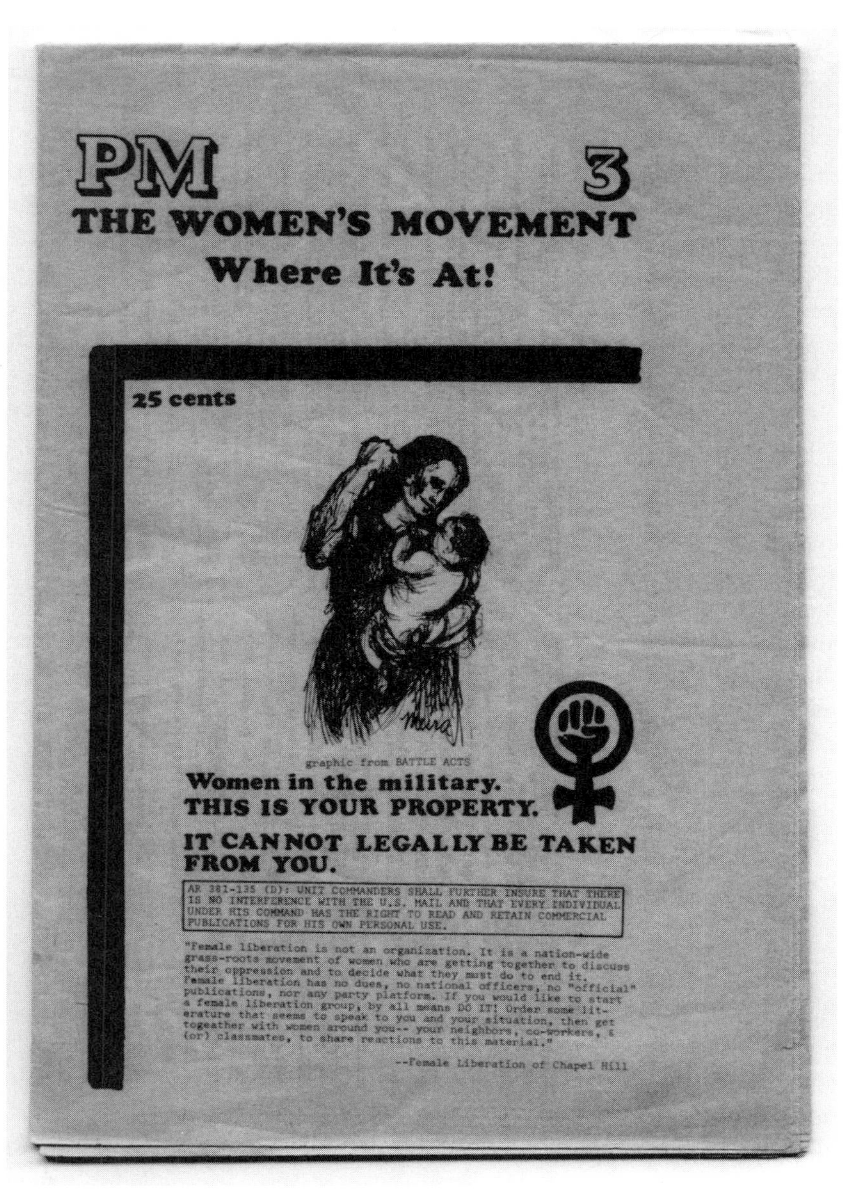

Figure 7. *PM3: A Research/Resource Guide (sort of) for the Movement* (*source:* author's collection).

performance events—the actors and audiences, the material circumstances, the performance techniques, the purposes, and the effects. As Lynda Hart reminds us, "the theatre's medium is the physical body" (5). Because "it is primarily women's bodies that have been politicized in systems of exchange," she argues, "the textualization of the female body poses special problems and potential" for women's theater (5). Feminist performance literalizes the risks of going public, of putting the female body on view. Such risk taking has the potential to call into question the ways in which women's bodies have been used as culturally loaded signifiers. Early feminist performance work explored which bodies had been traditionally absent from the scene, which bodies were traditionally represented, how such bodies were absented or represented, and to what ends. While feminist theater was not, of course, a utopian space that could somehow seal over cultural fissures, many groups nonetheless struggled to find ways to, in Charlotte Canning's words, "achieve actual integration that brings together women from different classes, races, and sexualities to produce theater while still acknowledging all their differences" (80). Feminist performance work was not exclusively or even predominantly white, heterosexual, and middle class in terms of the performers, the audience or the materials. Feminist performances in fact worked to make public what had been hidden, forbidden, or treated as shameful, creating not only theater that explored questions of class, race, and ethnicity but also, especially, performances centered on lesbian characters and lesbian issues, and they did so not only through the subject matter but also through the particular configurations and movements of actual bodies on the stage. It was not enough, in other words, to simply represent difference, but the theater was the place to make difference palpably and literally present.[1]

But for all the ways in which participants in feminist theater concentrated on the material body in motion, feminist performance events were nonetheless also literacy events. As discussed earlier, a literacy event, in Shirley Brice Heath's terms, "is any occasion in which a piece of writing is integral to the nature of participants' interactions and their interpretive processes" (350). Literacy was part of the feminist performance process not in the way that some traditional theater history would lead one to expect—not, that is, in the sense of the overriding importance of printed play or script—but as part of a temporally and spatially dynamic process. To read feminist performance work in terms of the concept of the literacy event is not, in other words, to lose sight of the central importance to theater of the simultaneity of bodies in motion, but it is to resist too easy an acceptance of the rhetoric that circulated in the period and that has dominated some accounts of the women's liberation movement since, that has it that radical women were rejecting books in favor of experience, that they were junking everything that had come before in order to start from scratch (Evans, *Personal Politics* 214). As is evident in feminist periodicals, the leaflet prose, and feminist poetry, the personal, political, and culturally radical elements of feminist performance grew out of the redeployment of available print materials and techniques that were transmitted not only through practice but also through reading. Performance underscores the extent to which midcentury feminism grew out of women's diverse experiences with radical movements for social justice and relied on literacy's potential not only to articulate the contours of oppression but also to point the way toward a transformed future.

Not all performances began with printed texts, but they nonetheless evolved into and through print. Some participants wrote in response to performances or as part of playwriting workshops (see Dell'Olio, "*In the Shadow*"). A performance in one setting for one set of purposes might be transformed over time, transmitted through print, to become a different performance for another setting and other purposes. Feminist newspapers ran advertisements for and reviews of performance events. Feminist journals printed play texts as part of their coverage of women and the arts (see Holden 120). Participants read a range of material—theater work as well as all kinds of cultural material, high and low—as part of their research to create performances.[2] While it is clear that reading and writing were not the whole of any performance event, nor can print convey what Roger Chartier has called the "irreducibly singular" experience of living performance (*Publishing Drama* 7), to ignore the role of literacy is to misunderstand how feminist performance worked culturally, politically, and pedagogically.

Many participants reported that they felt that they were creating something new. That perception is important in that it names part of their lived reality, but it requires some unpacking to understand more fully what constituted the "new"—in particular, what materials were at hand, how women went about recrafting those materials for their own uses, and how they taught themselves and others the skills—including literacy skills—necessary to create and perform. In crafting performance work consistent with feminism, women were not creating out of nothing and from nowhere. To think otherwise is to perpetuate politically and pedagogically unproductive commonplaces about the period. We either romanticize the iconoclasm of radicalism or dismiss it as simply naïve. It is more useful to see how women manipulated what they had available to them, how they recast material and practices in the service of an emerging feminism.

Some of the participants had formal, traditional theater training; others had worked in experimental theater. Still other women first participated in performance through their involvement in women's liberation groups where they had tried various kinds of theater gaming techniques as part of consciousness raising. Women learned to use various performance modes, some having already experienced the persuasive and galvanizing power of performance, of display, spectacle, and ritual, as part of their involvement in civil rights, antiwar, and student rights protests and demonstrations. Women adapted puppetry, mime, and melodrama, as well as elements of dance and yoga, and they borrowed from the visual arts and music. They drew on a wealth of sources, not only their own life experiences, but also the newly rediscovered lives of women in the past.[3] They borrowed bits from advertisement, television, and canonical high-culture texts, as well as from a newly emerging and rapidly distributed body of women's writings from various fields. Based on prior knowledge and skills, women were teaching themselves and others how to expand their performance repertoire. Much of the learning was hands-on, and it was fundamentally improvisational.

Improvisation has particular meanings for theater and performance art, of course, and I will consider the more specific uses of the term in the course of this chapter. But first I want to frame this discussion within a somewhat broader cultural and historical sense of the improvisatory. For the anthropologist Mary Catherine Bateson, improvisation is a metaphor for the ways especially women (but also men) must compose their lives in the modern world. I find her metaphor congenial for my purposes here. Bateson sees improvisation as "recombining partly familiar materials in new ways, often in ways especially sensitive to context, interaction and response" (2). Packed into Bateson's idea is a complex—and one might say, unashamed—notion of agency, of volition within the constraints of circumstance and history. In Bateson's terms, one has to discover the shape of one's creation "along the way, rather than pursuing a vision already defined" (1). Such improvisational work is especially necessary in times of social change. "In a stable society," Bateson contends, "composing a life is somewhat like throwing a pot or building a house in a traditional form: the materials are known, the hands move skillfully in tasks familiar from thousands of performances, the fit of the completed whole in the common life is understood." While the approach to pottery or building is not static and can "respond to chance and allow a certain scope for individual talent and innovation," "the traditional craftsperson does not face the task of solving every problem for the first time." In contrast, in our society, "the materials and skills from which a life is composed are no longer [so] clear." One cannot simply follow in the footsteps of earlier generations (1–2). When women who participated in feminist performance work remarked that they could not "use men's forms to express our content" (Lucy Winer, qtd. in Rea, "Women for Women" 87), they were registering something akin to what Bateson is noticing. Perhaps most acutely in such a time of social upheaval as the late sixties and early seventies, women experienced a lack of fit between the familiar cultural materials, forms, and practices and women's needs and circumstances. But importantly—and here Bateson's nuanced definition is especially apt—even as women were rejecting the familiar or traditional materials, forms, and practices, they could not reject them altogether but had to *re*make and *re*combine. As Bateson puts it, improvisatory art is "about the ways we combine familiar and unfamiliar components in response to new situations, following an underlying grammar and an evolving aesthetic" (3). Thus, even as Lucy Winer of the New York Feminist Theatre stated, "We can't use men's forms" (qtd. in Rea, "Women for Women" 87), she recognized that some of the theater work she was doing was related to work produced by such men as Marshal McLuhan and Andy Warhol, who—one might add—were themselves also borrowing and recombining. In this recognition, Winer gets at the paradox of the "new": the "new" resides in how one recombines, how one "bring[s] together all kinds of contradictory art forms, contents, feelings," and to what ends (ibid.). This improvisatory work was not haphazard or flying by the seat of one's pants but shaped in conversation with an emerging sense of both feminism (the underlying grammar, one might say) and performance art (the evolving aesthetic).

My interest in this chapter is in exploring how women crafted performance events in the service of feminism, in part through a redeploying of literacies already available to them. How did they teach themselves the necessary skills and knowledge, and how did they share what they learned with others? It is not news to say that political theater historically has had a didactic function, but I want to suggest that as women were improvising feminist performances, they were also improvising pedagogies partly to resist the kind of unidirectional transfer of knowledge that the term *didactic* implies (see Salvatori). Julie Malnig and Lisa Merrill have observed that there is "ample rationale" for linking the words *performance* and *pedagogy:* "Within both Western and non-Western traditions, our earliest known references to performance reflect a didactic impulse. People learn the values of their culture as spectators and participants in the reenactment of the culture's myths. We learn through performance" (5). They go on to say that to "consciously call definitions of performer/teacher into question, to reframe the role of 'spectator,' 'student,' 'participant,' and 'professor,' opens the door to a radical restructuring of meaning" (5–6). Women involved in feminist performance quite self-consciously called into question such terms and relationships but at the same time challenged—often quite explicitly—the label of didacticism, in part by attempting to craft an improvisatory, participatory pedagogy. In order to better understand this process, I turn first to the ground-breaking work of feminist theater historians who have focused their attention on feminist theater groups before moving to a closer look at specific theater events.

Feminist Theater Groups

Theater historians have discussed feminist performance primarily in terms of theater, thus tending to focus on more organized feminist theater groups rather than a wider range of feminist performance work. Nonetheless, their research provides a rich body of material for considering how women who were engaged in feminist performance attempted to craft alternatives to didacticism. Feminist theater groups emerged in the late sixties for the express purpose of creating and performing feminist work: not simply, as the theater activist Anselma Dell'Olio put it, "'to give women a chance' in the arts, though necessarily, feminist theatre will be composed mostly of women, but primarily to give a dramatic voice to the new feminist movement" ("Founding" 101). Even though some specifically identified themselves as "feminist theater groups," they constituted only a part of a wider range of feminist performance work. Still, an examination of some of their shared features is a useful starting place for considering the pedagogical practices and aims of feminist performance more generally. Three interconnecting features of the early groups are of particular interest here: organizational structure, relationship to the audience, and shifting locus of creative control.

Although some early feminist theater groups were organized around a well-defined leader, many operated as collectives.[4] Charlotte Canning suggests that theater can be seen as a microcosm of society "that did and could play out the individual's relation to society both actual, as in mainstream and conventional theaters, and potential, as in alternative and political theaters" (63). Like the editorial collectives discussed in chapter 1, feminist theater groups believed that "in order to work toward an end of the oppression of women they had to create organizations that would empower women both in the process of creation and in the product of performance" (Canning

63–64). The development of nonhierarchical performance collectives was for some groups a reaction against the male-dominated professional theater: "Since women for centuries have felt themselves to be less creative in the arts... feminists feel that to allow groups to evolve into the accepted power structure would be to perpetuate the thinking that has kept women from realizing their potentialities" (Rea, "Women's Theatre Groups" 79–80). From this perspective, it was thought "better to develop each member's ideas," if only "to a limited degree," rather than depend on the "genius" of individual stars (80). Some groups expected each group member to rotate through the various theater tasks, not only rotating roles within a performance, but also sharing responsibilities for creating and organizing performances (Leavitt 55). In Leavitt's terms, the nonhierarchical structure of the collective meant that "individuals [could] teach and learn, knowing that because there are not stars or leaders, their ideas will be heard and tested" (58).

That some theater groups became disenchanted with collective work is important to note. Although participants found the experience of working collectively to be exhilarating, even liberatory, over time some found that collective organization stymied creativity. Like some of the editorial collectives discussed earlier, they too found that the desire for consensus worked against a fuller expression of difference and could stifle the kind of risk taking necessary for the generation of powerful work. The sheer exhaustion of collective decision making also led some theater groups (as it led some of the editorial collectives) to move toward structures that, if not traditionally hierarchical, nonetheless distributed tasks according to differences in talents and interests.

Collective organizational structure was potentially important not only to theater group members but also to the audience. In Charlotte Rea's terms, "If every member must depend on her own creative output..., then the theatrical forms that the group produces must convey to women in the audience that they, too, possess untapped potential for artistic creativity" ("Women's Theatre Groups" 80). Even the bravest of audience members needs, in Cicely O'Neill's terms, "living proof that imagination will not destroy" her (62–63). But serving as living proof—modeling possibilities for courage and creativity—was only part of the pedagogical dynamic. Audience members did more than serve as spectators. They were also invited to participate in the creation of performances through workshops; to contribute to the performance itself through singing, chanting, call and response, and various kinds of body movement exercises; and to take part in discussions following performances (Natalle 6; Rea, "Women's Theatre Groups" 83). Feminist theater shared with other politically oriented theater a desire to overcome the "alienation of players from audience" in order to engage audience members not only in the "content" of the performance but also in the process of creating performance and building from it toward artistic and cultural change (Canning 178, 182; Leavitt 2).[5] As Canning puts it, "Through workshops, women, long denied training in many practical skills traditionally identified as male, could share with one another their acquired information" (185). Such information included not only knowledge of technical theater—of scenography, for example (Canning 186)—but also knowledge of how to develop performance pieces and how to perform through such techniques as improvisation, theater gaming, and physical theater.

Such techniques circulated among theater practitioners who had learned them from others by doing or who taught themselves by reading such widely available works as Viola Spolin's *Improvisation for the Theater* (1963) or Jerzy Grotowski's *Towards a Poor Theatre* (1968). Spolin's approach to improvisation and theater gaming was originally developed in the thirties and forties as part of New Deal programs for ordinary people with little or no theater training who were responsible for creating theater opportunities as part of community work in neighborhoods (Spolin vii; see also Flannery). Spolin understood that if participants could concentrate their "energies on playing [a] game," paradoxically they would lose their "self-consciousness and perform naturally and spontaneously." She designed games to help solve "theatre problems"—how to show grief, how to use the body rather than words to speak, what to do with one's hands, and so on—and to solve such problems "organically and uncoercively" (Sweet xvii). Theater gaming had been embraced more generally by activists, male and female, as a way to develop group interaction, cohesion, and trust, and Spolin's handbook had come to serve for many as "a bible for transformational training" (Keyssar 187n3). Spolin's emphasis on enabling ordinary people to feel comfortable performing in public was especially congenial for theater groups interested in developing not only their own theatrical and political abilities but also those of audience members.

Significantly, Spolin felt that in improvisatory theater, "no one teaches anyone anything" (392), not, that is, in the sense of direct or didactic instruction. Rather, one has to begin with the assumption that participants have multiple kinds of knowledge but often lack resources and opportunity to use their knowledge or to recognize such knowledge as useful in their own terms. Spolin's concern, then, is to assist participants in developing a stronger sense of their own agency in the world. The teacher/director has techniques—such as theater games—to enable meaning making, but she does not control the meanings that are made. The teacher/director's primary responsibility is to the participants as they produce a collective assemblage rather than to an already existing product (a stabilized text) that exists independent of and prior to the participants.

Jerzy Grotowski's *Towards a Poor Theatre* also circulated widely, serving as another source for theater exercises (Leavitt 26). In 1971 *The Last Whole Earth Catalog*, a counterculture resource guide, praised Grotowski for the "strongest work in theater lately" and described his book about that work as "social yoga, with balls" ("Towards" 347). While it is doubtful that many women would have been taken with the *Catalog*'s gendered reference, some involved in performance work found Grotowski's emphasis on a physical, committed theater useful, especially because it helped articulate a relationship with the audience. Some sense of what groups valued in Grotowski can be found in an *off our backs* feature article on the improvisational group Living Stage that includes a quotation from Grotowski concerning the purpose of art: "Why are we concerned about art? To cross our frontiers, exceed our limitations, fill our emptiness, fulfill ourselves. This is not a condition but a process in which what is dark in us slowly becomes transparent. In this struggle with one's own truth, this effort to peel off the life mask, the theatre, with its full fleshed perceptivity, has always seemed to me a place of provocation" ("Living Stage" 8–9). Grotowski believes that the "one absolute rule" of theater is that "bodily activity comes first, and [only] then vocal expression" (347). Such physicality is intended to be transformative not only of the actor but also of the audience. The actor, ideally, does not challenge only himself but "publicly challenges others, and through excess, profanation and outrageous sacrilege reveals himself by casting off his everyday mask[;] he makes it possible for the spectator to undertake a similar process of self-penetration. If he does not exhibit his body, but annihilates it, burns it, frees it from every resistance to any psychic impulse, then he does not sell his body but sacrifices it. He repeats the atonement; he is close to holiness" (347). One can recognize certain parallels between Grotowski's notion of theatrical confrontation and what Lucy Winer of the New York Feminist Theatre describes as woman's theater: "It would be a spectacle that totally surrounded one so that the audience couldn't relax, they couldn't be comfortable with what was happening up there, because they shouldn't be" (qtd. in Rea, "Women for Women" 87). In such theater, the "cloak of invisibility" that might otherwise protect the audience member is removed (Forte 263).

But the differences between Grotowski's vision and feminist theater are also instructive. Winer expresses some wariness of what she sees as a male-oriented theater that is "done artistically for effect" because it has "so little left to believe in or say" (qtd. in Rea, "Women for Women" 87). Because women have historically and culturally served as objects of male fantasy, feminist theater must first work to "thwart the illusion of distance" that makes such fantasizing safe, to make looking itself a theatrical subject, and to work to reassert female desire, female pleasure as controlled not by the male gaze (Forte 263). It appears that as women found in Grotowski useful techniques that demanded transformative participation from audience members, they had to at the same time revise Grotowski's terms: women in performance worked to reclaim their bodies, not to sell them or to sacrifice them, but to "embrace new, self-generated images" (Forte 263). While, in contemporary terms, one might say that there is no space free of either voyeurism or the fetishization of the female body, feminist performances nonetheless attempted to take back some degree of control over how women's bodies were represented.

Theodore Shank asserts that since the efficacy of political theater "depends on creating a sense of 'we' with the audience against 'them,' the Establishment, it is essential that the performer—the human being—remain visible under the character... [to show] the cracks in the illusion" (111). To this end, some players wore ordinary street clothes and mingled with the audience as a simple way to minimize the visual and spatial difference between audience and players. Engaging the audience in the process of creating a skit; improvising from life stories, some of which were provided by audience members; breaking frame by shifting roles; and engaging in ritualized activities with audience members—these various techniques worked to break down the traditional "fourth wall," that wall of illusion that divides stage from audience. Breaking down that wall of illusion, a characteristic goal of political and avant-garde theater more generally, was for feminist theater not simply a matter of aesthetics but a central component of the pedagogical process: if women in the audience participated in this public way, they would learn, through the action of their bodies and the actual sounds of their voices, that they could be heard and their presence felt. As Elizabeth Natalle points out, "just joining" was itself a potentially powerful experience (105). In a culture that has traditionally valued the passivity of (especially) female bodies and has marked class and racial differences in part by rewarding primarily privileged white women with the "gift" of inactivity, movement itself becomes a complex political act.

Collective organization and intense audience participation shift the locus of creative control away from a singular playwright and/or director and toward what might be called improvisatory composing. Canning asserts that traditional theater separates writing from performance: the playwright writes a play apart from the performers; the director then stages the play, expecting the players to perform the text as written. While such a view of traditional theater oversimplifies a more complex process—even for such canonically privileged moments in theater history as the English Renaissance—it does nonetheless capture what participants in feminist theater understood to be the case in mainstream contemporary theater (see Chartier, *Publishing Drama*). Thus, in reaction against a perceived hierarchical creative process, feminist theater tended to adopt the "one-method" process more typical of experimental theater: emphasizing the continuous act of creation by intertwining actors' improvisation with writing (Canning 65–66).

As O'Neill observes, improvisation is "not a matter of casting off all forms and limitations in order to be free and spontaneous" (151). Rather, improvisation requires finding ways to use available forms and working within the particular constraints of place, time, and body in order—in O'Neill's terms—paradoxically to "transcend" the limitations of conventions.[6] Importantly, feminist theater groups were testing such limitations through an alternative set of practices not simply of their own devising. Some of those practices, such as the Stanislavski method, were familiar to mainstream actors, while other techniques, such as Spolin's and Grotowski's, were borrowed from more populist or experimental forms of theater and dance or came from the visual arts and encounter group techniques.[7] Similar to the reciprocating literacies describing the dialogic interaction between poet and reader discussed earlier, these various techniques diffused creative, authorial control not only among writers and players but also among players and audience members. Improvisation depended on preparation and practice and evolved in the doing, through performing, writing, and reading.

Some groups improvised from the experiences of group members, tape-recording the sessions, writing from the tapes, and then revising the writing for performance (Canning 69). Other groups improvised from written materials. The New Feminist Theatre (formed in 1969), for example, created *Cabaret of Sexual Politics* by improvising from Jules Feiffer's *Marriage Manual,* a work by a man best known for his syndicated cartoons (Rea, "Women's Theatre Groups" 80; Leavitt 18). Borrowing from another group's performances was also common; for example, the players who would later form the Minneapolis-based Alive and Trucking Theatre Company in 1971 watched a Madison Street Theatre performance of the San Francisco Mime Troup's play *The Independent Female (or, A Man Has His Pride)* at a women's conference in

Madison, Wisconsin, and decided to put together a group to perform the play in Minneapolis.[8] The Alive and Trucking Theatre Company included players with various skills, some with formal theater training and others who had experience with gymnastics, mime, dance, music, writing, and technical theater (Leavitt 23). With their particular mix of skills, they improvised, in O'Neill's sense, by taking a ready-made play created by one group and seen in performance by yet another group and re-creating that play for a new setting.

The process of composing a feminist performance could include working with an already available, scripted, identifiably authored work; collaborating with individual playwrights so that playwrights and performers could work together on works-in-progress; or improvising from material that a performance group gathered through research. The Washington Area Feminist Theatre (WAFT) performed primarily written plays, not only by contemporary feminist playwrights, such as Myrna Lamb and Megan Terry, but also by previously neglected playwrights, such as Aphra Behn, Lillian Mortimer, Rachel Crothers, and Susan Glaspell (Leavitt 20).[9] The Westbeth players brought playwrights and players together to read works-in-progress (Rea, "Women's Theatre Groups" 88). Many groups began by researching a question, whether by asking ordinary women to report on their experiences or hunting through a variety of print sources. They then improvised from their findings through performance, later workshopping and revising together with audience members what they had performed. But even when working with an already-available script, players tended to read a script together and then put the script down to improvise around it (ibid. 80). As O'Neill notes, even "in conventional theatre the performance is always more than a simple recreation of the script" (18). Thus, when groups performed primarily written plays, they inevitably re-created those plays through the specificities and peculiarities of the performance context.

What the process of improvisatory composing makes clear is that no single person could have creative control, but rather, many hands shaped and reshaped performances. No single vision could dominate, and thus no single "message" could be conveyed through the work of an auteur. While participants sometimes worried that their "message" was too diffused, that they failed artistically and politically to offer a coherent performance, the desire to create collectively in solidarity with audience members tended to be stronger than the desire for a more traditional aesthetics defined in terms of unified vision. This overriding desire in fact made it far less likely that such theater could have been "didactic" even if it had wanted to be. While theater historians have tended to use the term *didactic* to describe feminist theater group performances, the three interconnecting features identified by those same historians as characteristic suggest resistance to either the singularity of vision or the unidirectional learning that didacticism implies.

Participatory Theater/Improvisatory Pedagogy

As evidenced through interviews, reflections and manifestos, participants made clear their awareness of the dangers of didacticism. One of the more prominent statements about feminist theater appeared in *Notes from the Second Year* in 1970. Anselma Dell'Olio was a founder and director of the New Feminist Repertory and Experimental Ensemble of New York City, begun in 1969 as a "first serious attempt to create a protest art based on the new feminism."[10] Dell'Olio addresses the question of didacticism directly. She asks whether feminists "see 'drama as a weapon'? And if so, aren't we just devoted to political propaganda?" Dell'Olio rejects this conclusion: "The most important qualification to be made about a theatre of commitment is that the playwright must at all times beware of simply illustrating acceptable dogmas. The pitfalls of didacticism can be overcome and art emerge only when the playwright continually develops his thinking, rather than presenting the audience with a re-hash of old conclusions" (102). The relationship with the audience is key here. It is not that the playwright goes off to ponder alone, only to return with finished truths to deliver to a waiting audience. Rather, "political theatre must set itself the task of learning *with* the audience" (102, emphasis added). Theater groups clearly learned from their audiences in the sense of taking ideas to serve as prompts for improvisation, but Dell'Olio is suggesting something more than that:

> The only sin, in my opinion, is the attitude on the part of either playwrights, directors, or cast, that one is out to "teach" the heathen rather than to share with the audience one's own learning process. I believe that guerilla theater has been a failure both artistically and politically precisely because it is guilty of this sin: talking only to the Believers and *preaching* to them at that. Perhaps it provides a (masturbatory) outlet for the rage of its participants, but it does not stimulate either them or their audience into developing new thinking. (102)

Dell'Olio is not counseling feminists to suppress their outrage—that would be a "parody of art of another kind," she says—but feminist theater has to recognize that "dogma makes for poor theatre and poor art." Feminist theater, then, has to create another kind of performance that is neither didactic nor apolitical; "outrage," she concludes, "can produce art in its highest form" (102).

Dell'Olio's counsel is echoed by the Washington, D.C., women's improvisational theater group Earth Onion, who were explicit in wanting to avoid didacticism, but they also make clear that avoiding didacticism does not ensure that audiences will be transformed by their experience. The eight women who formed Earth Onion in 1970 reflect a widespread sense that feminist theater should develop approaches that could actively engage women (and sympathetic men) in learning about feminism *and* theater. As they saw it, performance is an opportunity for knowledge making rather than knowledge delivery. Earth Onion was fairly typical: a group of women (and two children) with various skills and experiences—"dance, stanislavsky [*sic*] and improvisational theatre, puppets and music"—who expanded their abilities by watching others. Having seen a performance of Living Stage (a multiracial improvisational group based in Washington, D.C., that worked with children and youth), they were excited to learn how similar techniques could be put to new use ("Earth Onion Scrapbook" 2; "Living Stage" 8). As they were learning, they were also sharing their "discoveries" through their own performances. *Sharing* is the operative word: "*We don't try to be didactic.* . . . we don't feel we have answers to pass on! We want to present our honest, human responses, to develop our ability to do this, and to share what we learn with others" ("Earth Onion Scrapbook" 2; emphasis added). They express the sense, common in the early years of the movement, that they are in fact discovering ideas and techniques and that those ideas and techniques are tools with which to build.

To encourage women to participate in such a building process, Earth Onion announced their intentions to engage other women by advertising their performances as "Performance/Workshops" ("Earth Onion" 19). Such workshops were intended not only to show what the group had learned—"what we could do"—but also what others could do, how others could take "some positive energy" and put it to use (2). Recalling a workshop offered as part of a women's conference, one "onion" (as they called themselves) describes the experience:

> I'm directing. Seventy-five women come—all factions. Highest energy I've ever seen in our warm ups. Twenty-five women form a work machine, then a survival machine. I understand machines for the first time. These are total, uncontrived. People have really worked hard. I guide them into smaller groupings to form sound circles. Laying on backs with heads in center, breathing and letting out sounds. This is my favorite exercise; I want to share it. I am

> very loving with the group I direct.... I'm high on the spirit; feel proud that we brought people together for thirty minutes. I know it won't last, but believe these moments are valid. ("My Tour Notes" 4)

Some sense of how participants responded to a process the group conceptualized (in terms that echo Grotowski's) as peeling away the layers of societal constraint is evident in a poem addressed to Earth Onion published in the October issue of *off our backs.* The poem is constructed as a series of requests: "tell me more, i wish to learn," "sing to me and show me / your dance," "and help my body to relax/ from its heavy cast / which has not / yet melted." The poem concludes, "i grow ready" (Glixon 25). The question of readiness proved crucial. While the groups wanted to avoid didacticism, the openness of approach was predicated on the willingness—the readiness—of audiences to participate, to contribute to the building of performance work. The high energy evident among the participants at the women's conference was in contrast to the negative energy Earth Onion experienced when they brought their performance/workshop to Fort Bragg—an army town the group characterized as a "crystallization of America" ("My Tour Notes" 5). Performers wanted to share what they had discovered beyond the confines of those who were already sympathetic, but they found that without some degree of initial sympathy from audiences, the performances could not work. As they report, this could mean quite literally that the group would fail to perform; the "super shock" of finding themselves in an unwelcoming environment could paralyze the still-novice players ("My Tour Notes" 5). While other performance groups—the guerrilla elevator theater, for example—were intent on disrupting things-as-they-are, to offer social critique, Earth Onion emphasized their desire to produce celebratory theater to foster community cohesion (Hunter 334). It might seem axiomatic to say that all learning depends on a learner's willingness or readiness to learn, but at least for some of the theater groups feminist performance pedagogy did not develop the rhetorical tools to bring those who were not already "growing ready" into the performance process.

Performance Events as Literacy Events

I turn now to reconstructing a set of performance events that produced or were generated out of two artifacts advertised in the resource guide *PM3*, in order to consider in greater detail how particular women worked to improvise a nondidactic pedagogy through the dynamics of performance and to make visible the role of literacy in the development of that pedagogy. If the print record is never sufficient to reconstruct a performance event—if, in other words, performance work "exists purely in an ephemeral moment of praxis" (Callaghan 262)—that ephemerality is compounded in the case of early feminist performance because so little of the record has been preserved or preserved in ways familiar to theater historians and literary scholars (Fitzsimmons 114). Nonetheless, in the scattered ephemera of movement activism one can find traces of a range of performance work, occasionally a printed play, sometimes reviews or firsthand accounts by players or audience members, and bits and pieces of what might be called theater pedagogy—advice about resources, guides to performance techniques, and invitations to take part in workshops. Because no artifact is itself the performance, one cannot assume that any single artifact can capture fully that ephemeral moment of praxis, nor can it tell us about the ways in which performance work came into being, recirculated, or was transformed into another across "time, place and community" (Chartier, *Publishing Drama* 6).

Clearly, an artifact "speaks" never in isolation but always in relation to other sources. And no one form of or setting for performance art names all the theatrical practices engaged in by second-wave women. Rather, feminist performance included relatively "private" performances as part of women's consciousness-raising groups; planned street actions and guerrilla theater events; public performance of written scripts in nontraditional spaces, such as schools, women's centers, church basements, unwed mothers' homes, and women's prisons; public performances of forgotten plays by rediscovered women playwrights; and public performances of new plays, including some performances in "legitimate" theater spaces ("Denver Women's Theatre"; Canning 47; Leavitt 107). The set of performance events I have chosen to reconstruct here is not intended to be representative of such a rich and diverse range of work. Rather, the discussion of these performances in their material specificity is intended to be suggestive, to raise questions about the relationship between feminist performance and literacy, feminist performance and pedagogy.

Artifact 1: Crankies

> Street (or elevator) theater is . . . a statement in itself, an announcement of a counter-culture that makes art and surprise and joy a part of city life rather than a *divertissement* for the rich.
>
> —Sondra Lowell, "Art Comes to the Elevator"

If a reader of the *PM3* resource guide had sent twenty-five cents to the People's Press in San Francisco, she would have received what would be available a few years later in the *Guerilla Street Theater Handbook* (1973): that is, a brief explanation of the San Francisco Women's Street Theater "cranky" with instructions on how to build the device, along with a simple cartoon-like strip with accompanying script on the history of women's oppression and struggles. As the group explains, a cranky is "a paper movie or cartoon sequence inside a simple wooden frame. The moving paper roll unwinds (is cranked) onto a take-up reel, enabling you to tell a story with a minimum of words and a maximum number of strong images" (San Francisco Women's Street Theater 317; see figure 8). Many children no doubt have made a cranky out of a shoebox or milk carton with a window cut out of one side, using toilet paper tubes to scroll a continuous roll of paper on which they have drawn scenes. Crankies could be as small as the child's version or large enough for a street crowd to gather and watch. The San Francisco group was thinking large; they suggest building and mounting a forty-six-inch frame on a small stepladder equipped with wheels for mobility.

The physical object was only part of the performance, however: "Essential people to this cranky are a narrator to read the story; a cranker, to stand on

Figure 8. *Cranky on Wheels,* from San Francisco Women's Street Theater, "This is a Cranky," in *Guerilla Street Theater,* ed. Henry Lesnick.

a ladder behind the movie and turn the story; and two to six noisemakers as a chorus or orchestra" (San Francisco Women's Street Theater 318). As in earlier forms of street theater, the players wore costumes—"like red tunics or 'tatters'"—and they initiated the performance with some sort of "introductory flourish or song" to rouse themselves and the audience. Musical accompaniment was expected to "add focus and magic." Like the cranky itself, the instruments could be improvised from inexpensive materials—"rhythms set up on sticks and bottles"—or could include readily available instruments such as kazoos, slide whistles, and cricket noisemakers.

The San Francisco group reports that for this particular cranky performance on women's oppression, they had assembled a relatively elaborate orchestra including a tambourine, cymbals, drums, and a recorder or flute to accompany "a chorus of voices" (San Francisco Women's Street Theater 318). Reminiscent of medieval carnival or renaissance street theater, the cranky performance was intended to catch the eye and ear of the passerby, who was already a mobile part of a kaleidoscopic urban scene: the cranky "has been great at rallies, small meetings, in parks, on the back of flat-bed trucks, and on the marble steps of the Pacific Stock Exchange. People love it. They laugh, get involved, and have always been eager to discuss it afterward" (317). Inexpensive, relatively easy to construct, the cranky leant itself to populist, accessible—and in that sense, radical—street theater.

The history of women's oppression may not seem at first blush to be the subject for generating much laughter, but the San Francisco group, like other political performance groups, connected with a public in part through laughter generated out of political satire.[11] Such laughter was presumed to be both galvanizing and educative. Writing in the early seventies about political theater as popular entertainment, Theodore Shank observed that "in the exuberance of revolutionary zeal, it is natural that certain political theatre groups should turn to forms of entertainment associated with fun, with the common man, with people in general regardless of social, economic, or educational status, in contrast with the traditional aristocratic forms that have 'artistic' pretensions and tend to be more contemplative than energetic." These groups "use . . . techniques from *commedia dell'arte,* circus, puppet shows, music halls, vaudeville, parades, magicians, carnival side shows, buskers, brass bands, comic strips, striptease, melodrama, minstrel shows, and other means of exhilarating celebration" (Shank 110). In returning to older popular forms—some of which had been, ironically, already appropriated by the mass medium of television—groups like the San Francisco Women's Street Theater attempted to break with the *present,* to break with "an intellectualism that was seen as pretentious, a reliance on words that came to be considered the chief device of hypocrisy, and an estheticism that rejected political statement" (110). The past in this sense yielded more radical possibilities in providing performance techniques through which to improvise a political critique of the present.

The challenge such groups faced was to find an economical and popular form that could jumpstart politically generative conversation about important and complex matters. The San Francisco group articulates an understanding of what one might call materialist rhetoric—the way in which design, the arrangement of the page, and the conditions of production/performance shape the message. They suggest, for example, that "in writing your own cranky you might remember . . . to keep a strict economy between words and images;" but interestingly, they do not mean to dummy down (San Francisco Women's Street Theater 353). Rather, they connect aesthetic decisions with their political aims. The dialogue and pictures are expected to play off one another in such a way that the pictures do not simply illustrate the words—"the narration and the picture should always complete, not repeat" (ibid.). "Sometimes slow continuous pictures complement the narrative," the group explains, "or pictures can move to contradict the narrative; sometimes pictures punctuate a phrase or sentence, or interrupt a phrase; and sometimes the picture is a very funny surprise." They emphasize that "bringing the image with an impact to the people is the key to cranking, because running blather narrative is confusing and boring." They conclude with a rhetorical question: "All speeches should be crankies?" (ibid. 319). Thus, the form of the performance, the way word and moving image interacted, was presumed to be a fundamental part of the political engagement.

In the literally compressed space of the cranky, the group traces the history of women's oppression from hunter/gatherer cultures to the Vietnam War and rather remarkably refuses to collapse all women into Woman, in part through an economical attention to class, race, and ethnicity. The performance makes clear that women's oppression is rooted in notions of property:

> Some had more [Shake tambourine] and some had less. [Wood block—one hit] That's how the class structure began. A man needed a wife to give him legal heirs so he could pass on his property and name to the next generation. This was the beginning of [turn crank] monogamy. [Sing "love and marriage, love and marriage."] [turn crank] And it was enforced by law [Wood block—one hit] [begin turning crank] and religion [gong (drum or wood block mallet hitting one cymbal)]. From then on property was owned by the

> man. His wife and children became his servants. [All snap fingers and point to floor in a commanding manner . . . as to 'heel' or 'sit'] [begin turning crank] White men came to America looking for more property. [Hum "Oh beautiful, for spacious skies."] (San Francisco Women's Street Theater 324–27)

Neither the white men's wives nor indentured servants were numerous enough to supply the necessary labor, however, and so, "twenty million black people were torn from Africa. [Single drum beat] Those that survived the voyage to America [Drum beat] were sold as permanent slaves to the cotton and tobacco [turn crank] plantations. [Drum beat] ALL the slaves worked in the fields [Drum beat] but the female slave [turn crank] was used for breeding new slaves for her owner. [Drum beat]" (330–31). The cartoon that accompanies this narrative sequence shows a white hand ripping off a piece of the African continent, and that piece is attached to a chain. The chain links to and enslaves human figures appearing in silhouette (see figure 9). The next frame shows a white man lounging on blocks that could be read as representing bales of hay. His hat tilted forward; he seems to be contemplating a straw or stalk that he holds in his hand, as if he had just taken it out of his mouth; and his booted foot is propped casually on his knee. This white man, who seems to have nothing better to do than lounge, is at the same time the man who takes his "pleasure" from the female slaves and whose leisure is purchased through the slaves' labor.

The cranky offers a history that moves rapidly, compressed in tight frames, moving from slavery to Enlightenment notions of education (with quotations from Rousseau), from fair wages to child care. Throughout—despite the inevitable simplification of the form—the images and words remind the

Figure 9. *Africa in Chains,* from San Francisco Women's Street Theater, *In the Beginning,* in *Guerilla Street Theater,* ed. Henry Lesnick.

audience of the differences among women's experiences—making clear, for example, that the nineteenth-century effort to gain access to education for women primarily benefited white women, thus doubly necessitating the desegregation effort; showing the reprehensible treatment of immigrant labor; or linking patriarchal capitalism to the Vietnam War, in part by including images of Vietnamese women. The cranky performance ends with a call to "fight together" by giving a political and ironic edge to the cliché, "women's work is never done" (San Francisco Women's Street Theater 351). Remarkably, within the economical frame of the cranky, the San Francisco group achieves a level of complexity that has been assumed to have come only later in the progress of feminist thought, after feminists saw the errors of their essentializing ways. While the performance makes clear that there is a common enemy in patriarchal capitalism, the "we-saying" that comes at the end emerges out of multiplicity and radical difference and thus has the potential to act, as was seen earlier with the Women's Political Caucus workshop flyer, as a call for strategic coalition building rather than as an effort to erase difference.

Given that this was street theater, the performers could not count on an all-female audience. Photographs of street theater from the period show crowds with women standing closest to the stage and men standing further back, around the periphery of the crowd. While some of the men heckled, others could be expected to see that they were invited to become a part of a coalition of "all people" for change. The final paragraph of the performance script that calls for women to work together is extended idealistically outward through an image that shows a multiracial, multiethnic group of women carrying a banner that reads "All Power to the People" (San Francisco Women's Street Theater 351).

As noted earlier, the San Francisco group reported that audiences loved the cranky performances. Audiences laughed and were eager to discuss the issues afterward. One can imagine that the kind of laughter that such a performance invited was the laughter of recognition, the laughter that comes through disjuncture between the assertion that a man needed a wife to give him legal heirs and the happy-face image of the white matron whose image coincides with the singing of "love and marriage, love and marriage, [go together like a horse and carriage]" (San Francisco Women's Street Theater 324–25) or through the identification of the villains, including the pig-faced merchant with his pile of coins or the lolling plantation owner/rapist. To say that such theater was "popular" in Shank's terms requires that we appreciate the way in which such an apparently childlike form allowed the group to demand a fair amount from the audience in terms of political and historical knowledge. While the group refers to the cranky as a "newer form of propaganda—strongly visual, FUN, informal, and simple, a real turn-on to us and the people we brought it to," they make clear that they did not approach the performance didactically, if by that one means one-directional transmission of knowledge (317). Rather, they worked to create a multilayered pedagogy that invited participants to engage not merely as spectators but as discussants in a complex performance of words and images.

The cranky operated as a pedagogical tool in another way as well. Not only did the members of the San Francisco Women's Street Theater expect to engage a general public in a particular topic—in this case the history of women's oppression—but also, as is evident in much of feminist performance, they expected to educate themselves, not only through the preparation of the performance, but also through the engagement with the audience. They did not figure themselves as teachers disseminating conclusions but saw themselves as students educating themselves and inviting others into the process of learning. The group reports that they developed the cranky on the history of women's oppression by "researching, writing, drawing, gathering instruments, rehearsing" (San Francisco Women's Street Theater 317). Once they had created the cranky and performed with it "for many months," they felt that they had developed a set of techniques they wanted to share "with all our sisters" because they found the cranky to be such a valuable experience. In terms characteristic of other movement publications, the San Francisco women recommend that others use this particular version of a cranky only as a starting place. While they offer fairly specific performance instructions, they urge others not to "take us too literally": "make additions, subtractions, or change the colors, the texts, and any of the performing ideas as you want. IT'S YOURS TO PLAY WITH" (318). Because the cranky was intended as "a theatrical event," it required, by definition, improvisation, with the ultimate goal that other groups would create their own performances: "Enjoy it as we have and WRITE YOUR OWN" (318, 317).

Some sense of the improvisatory potential in the San Francisco Women's Street Theater idea—in particular, how the idea was circulated and how it was put to somewhat different uses—can be gained from an article published in *Ms* magazine in May 1973 and shortly thereafter excerpted in the *New Woman's Survival Catalog,* also published in 1973. In this article Sue Perlgut of the It's All Right to be Woman Theatre (founded in 1970) reports that she had become a "crankie crank" who had seen "crankies performing their magic in many situations" (66). She refers in particular to the San Francisco street theater group's "herstory" theme and includes the People's

Press address (as listed in *PM3*) for further information. But unlike the San Francisco group with its emphasis on the larger historical and political forces that have oppressed women, Perlgut and her theater group focused on the use of crankies for consciousness raising on a more personal level: "Women who are trying to share life experiences have used crankies to express individual feelings and also to express shared feelings when the whole group creates one together" (66). She observes that this "homemade storytelling device very much like a paper television" may sound simple, but "you cannot anticipate how effectively the most intense and personal stories are reduced to a simple clarity that gets right to the heart of the matter" (66).

It's All Right to be Woman Theatre included the use of crankies as part of a more complex revue format. Charlotte Rea, who attended their performances, reports that prior to going public, the performers worked for months at consciousness raising and that movement and acting exercises were part of their preparation. Like the San Francisco group, they first educated themselves not only about feminism but also about theater. But unlike the San Francisco group, who educated themselves through historical reading and political analysis, the It's All Right group drew more directly from their life experiences to improvise what would later evolve into a performance sequence. Part of the power of the performance, in fact, had to do with the "willingness of individual members to use their own lives as the basis of the material they perform" (Rea, "Women's Theatre Groups" 82). Such self-exposure may now seem so familiar a form of public (and exploitative) entertainment that it is difficult to recuperate the moment when such theater could have been experienced as revolutionary. To the extent that it was a new experience for performer and audience alike, however, the performances achieved a degree of political cohesiveness that was galvanizing. This was heady business, to join in as a body in motion, making a scene, making noise, and making trouble with other women who on some level shared one's political ideals.

In part because the group could reserve some performances for women only—something the San Francisco group could not do—they could expect that many in the audience would identify strongly with the performances, that they would not need to be persuaded but instead would be seeking confirmation, experiencing, as Rea saw it, "solidarity and lack of competition with other women" ("Women's Theatre Groups" 82). The audience's reaction to feminist theater was of course not uniformly positive. Many participants in feminist theater groups report how angry audience members could get if they felt that a performance failed to represent lesbian experience fairly, or when straight performers presumed to represent lesbian experience, or when primarily white groups presumed to present women's experience as if white, middle-class experience represented all women's experience (see Canning; Leavitt). Rea, however, does not report such responses to the It's All Right performance she attended. Rather, she focuses on the way in which participation seemed to happen "automatically" in the sense that "nobody prompts it; nobody insists on it" (83).

The performance began with music and chanting as the audience members arrived, and audience members joined in through clapping, singing, or humming (Rea, "Women's Theatre Groups" 83). Ritualized movement, mime, and brief plays improvised from dreams recalled by individual performers followed. And then came the cranky: in this case, "a long sheet of white paper with pictures on it, something like a paper television set on a long horizontal scroll," narrated by one performer to raise questions about cultural notions of acceptable body image and cultural taboos about women loving women. Chanting involving all participants, audience and players alike, served as the conclusion to the performance (84). As Rea describes it, the interior theater space, in contrast to the motility of street theater, fostered greater intimacy among participants. Throughout the performance audience members joined in physically and vocally, primarily through music and ritual movement. They were invited to take part in another sense, too, that of understanding the performance as a process to which they could contribute: after the first section of the performance sequence, and as a preface to the improvisatory dream plays, a performer explained to the audience the workings of the group. The audience was invited behind the curtain, in a sense, to see the workings of the illusion. In Shank's terms, this was a way for political theater to achieve solidarity, but it was also a way to let women in on a process so they could be active participants rather than mere consumers of spectacle. While the differences in emphasis between the San Francisco group and the It's All Right performers can stand for one of the ideological fissures that ran through the larger women's movement, evident in the poetry and the polemics as well, the two troupes nonetheless shared in common the sense that their theater work was fundamentally pedagogical, not only because players were teaching themselves and others about some aspect of feminism, but also because they were enabling others to join in theatrically and politically as full participants.

Artifact 2: Sweet 16 to Soggy 36

If a reader of *PM3* had written to Cindy Abood to request a copy of *Sweet 16 to Soggy 36: Saga of American Womanhood,* she would have received a small twenty-page folio pamphlet, approximately eight by five inches, the pale olive cover inscribed with the title in script and the work priced at fifteen cents (some copies hand marked up to twenty-five cents) (see figure 10).[12] The inside cover gives a brief history of the play. In 1969 the Cleveland Radical Women's Group—including the well-known activist Charlotte Bunch together with Barbara Toeppen, Julie Reinstein, Jane Adams, Carol McEldowney, and Sue Streeter—composed what they call a "review" as a "spur for discussion" at a political gathering.[13] When others at the gathering asked for copies of the play, the group decided to print it, making the resulting pamphlet available through the office of *The Voice of the Women's Liberation Movement Newsletter* in Chicago and eventually such resource guides as *PM3*. The revue was composed beforehand (rather than improvised on the spot) and performed as "reader's theater," so that no particular acting experience was necessary to read a part. According to the booklet's inside cover, two women alternated as "announcers," and four other women played various roles in the several skits that constituted the revue. Other than two stools for the announcers and four chairs for the players, no props were used.

A format common to many performance groups, the revue was borrowed from vaudeville via television variety shows such as *Ed Sullivan* and often included skits, dance sequences, songs, and comedy. Like the San Francisco group, which chose the cranky because it was "fun," feminist performers chose the revue in part because it allowed them to combine humor and theatricality to get audiences thinking about serious issues (Rea, "Women's Theatre Groups" 88). As a *Big Mama Rag* article puts it, with a "minimum of props and a maximum of energy," the revue could "barrage its audience with statements about women and women's roles" (Rev. of *Harper's Bizarre* 8). The relatively short segments also made the revue relatively easy to create. Another group explained that "a bunch of skits . . . are easier to write, easier to rehearse, and easier to make clear points with," especially when composed by a collective ("Witching the A.M.A." 4).[14] While the *Sweet 16* pamphlet does not include song-and-dance routines, it does include satiric bits, primarily quotations read by one of the announcers, that serve as interludes between skits. The skits together trace a loose narrative from a girl at "sweet 16" deciding what she wants to do when she grows up to a woman at thirty-six who is weighed down (soggy) with the sense that she has hit a dead end. But the revue offers neither an analysis of the origins of women's oppressions, of the sort to be found in the San Francisco group's cranky, nor a fully realized or complex character study. Rather, the skits work more like counterrealist allegories, brief scenarios that boldface the ways society hems in women. No player stays in character, so the very shifting of roles—as well as the shifting

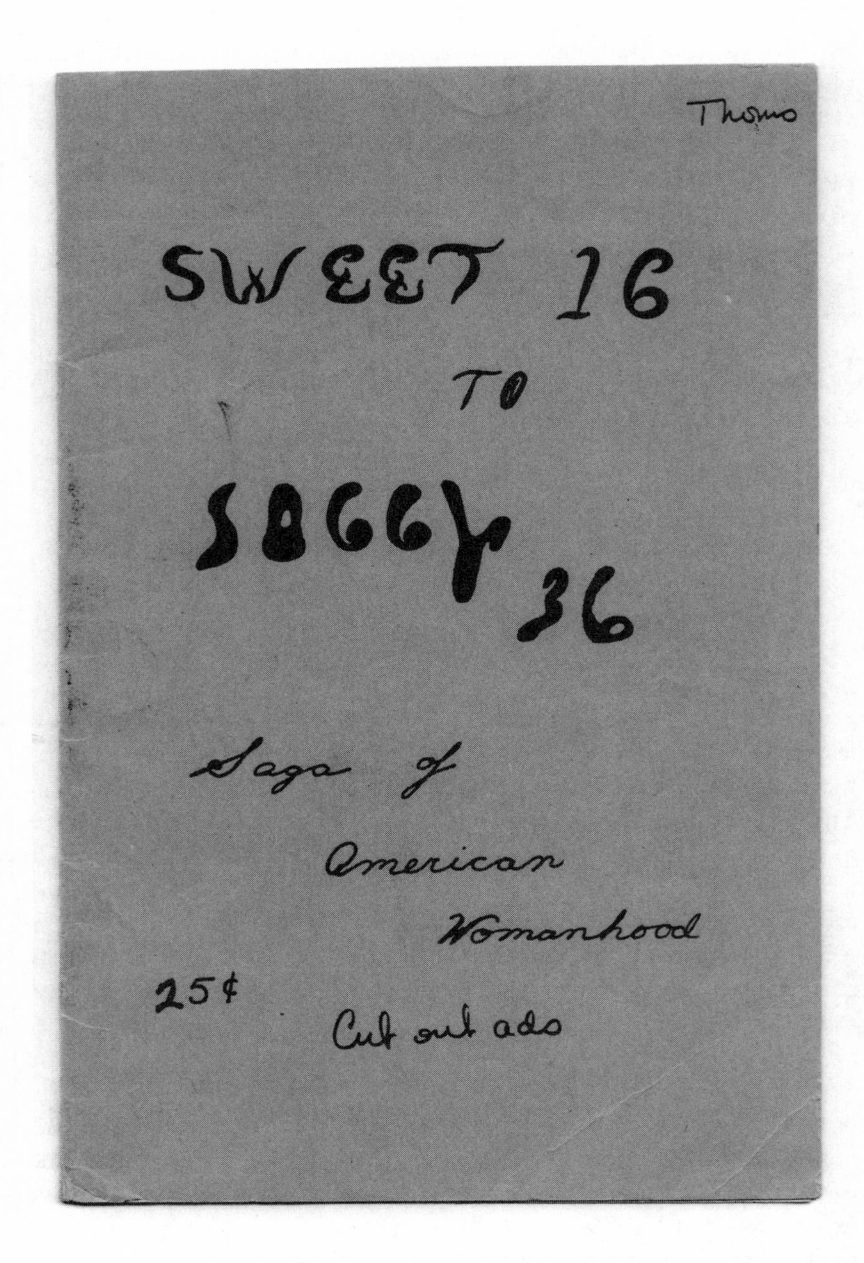

Figure 10. *Sweet 16 to Soggy 36,* Cleveland Radical Women's Group (*source:* author's collection).

between skit and satiric interlude—worked against any traditional linear notion of theatrical illusion or resolution. The revue requires that audience members do the work of investing the sequence of skits and satiric interludes with real-world significance and that they work—especially in discussion afterward—on possible resolutions.

Sweet 16 to Soggy 36 opens with one of the announcers reading a passage attributed to Nietzsche: "We men wish that women should not go on compromising herself [*sic*] through enlightenment—just as it was man's thoughtfulness and consideration for woman that found expression in the Church decree: Woman should be silent in church! It was for woman's good when Napoleon gave the all to [*sic*] eloquent Madame de Stael to understand: Woman should be silent when it comes to politics! And I think that it is a real friend of women that counsels them today: Woman should be silent about woman!" (1). The passage is followed immediately by "A Word from Our Sponsor," a Clairol ad for Wild Streak hair color: "Why hide the secret siren inside of you? Answer the call of the WILD STREAK. You're not the type to be timid. And this is no time to be tame." There is no commentary, no explicit linking of the quotations. Instead, another announcer reads a "public service announcement" from the "voice of the thinkers," in this case, a well-circulated quotation from Aristotle, who refers to women as "afflicted with a natural defectiveness."[15] Juxtaposed to Aristotle's pronouncement is an ad from a clothing store on "how to win and let him like it," which is followed by what appears to be a letter of the sort published in teenage girls' magazines, such as *Seventeen,* from a "teen-age girl" who wants to know how to love school and books and still be loved by boys. The quotations from great men and ad men sit side by side without comment, but the ironic resonance should be fairly obvious (and no doubt was for the first audience). Analyzing sexual stereotyping in advertisement has become something of a pedagogical cliché that may now blunt the political impact of bringing such disparate sources together. But the idea that, in current parlance, the subject position "woman" was a cultural construct multiply scripted from the ancients (the "thinkers") to the moderns (the Madison Avenue hype artists) had not yet become (if it is yet) old news.

In the course of the revue, the announcements and skits repeat the societal fear that women left to their own devices will run wild, in order to challenge women to think about what it might mean for themselves and the society as a whole if they were to actually claim independence. What would running wild make possible after all? Such questioning serves as backdrop for the first skit, "Under 21," set in a guidance counselor's office. A "high school girl"—addressed first not by name but by the identifying number on her folder, J31798-H—and a "female guidance counselor" discuss the "girl's" career aspirations, the guidance counselor advising against pursuing a medical career in cancer research or psychiatric medicine and suggesting nursing or medical illustration instead, because these career paths would be more compatible with marriage and family. The very brief skit—there are no more than seven "bits" of exchange—works to expose the rigidity of cultural gender scripting as the counselor asks (rhetorically): "You *do* want to be married and have children, *don't you?*" (Bunch et al. 3). The counselor gets the last word when she advises the girl to find some "nice woman's college" where she can learn to be "more realistic about what a woman can do, if she's really a woman" (4). In case there is any doubt what is meant by being a *real* woman, a Public Service Educational Announcement immediately follows, suggesting just the sort of place the counselor has in mind: "Texas Women's College: Planning menues [*sic*] for the week, making living rooms shine, and stirring up cookies for supper mean the approximation of the atmosphere of home as well as excellent professional preparation. Each girl spends an average of one hour per day doing her share of the cooking and other household duties.... No other school so fully recognizes the function of woman in this century or has so realistically advanced to prepare them for their place in home and nation" (4). As with the skit, this promotional blurb for an unnamed Texas college may now seem far-fetched, but most of the women in the audience could have offered examples from their own lives that would have rendered this blurb believable.

The skits and announcements trace the girl from her high school counselor's office to work with activist college students. A skit entitled "Inside the ~~Operating Room~~ Movement Office" registers the experiences of many women who had worked in antiwar, student rights, and civil rights organizations: it was common for activist men to expect the women to do the menial work, making the coffee and typing, leaving the important idea work to the men. When Mary says that she has a full schedule that won't allow her to type up stencils for the newsletter, she says to John, "You can type, can't you?" Although he *can* type, John has more important things to do: "I've got the research meeting, and three classes and the defense committee meeting.... I don't have time" (Bunch et al. 8). The skit is followed immediately by the Black Power activist Stokely Carmichael's frequently quoted remark that "the only position for a woman in [the Student Nonviolent Coordinating Committee] is prone" (9). As Alice Echols recalls, "among feminists Carmichael's comment came to symbolize Movement men's hostility toward women's liberation" (*Daring* 31). Carmichael made the comment in 1964 in the midst of the Freedom Summer voter registration drive, but by the time the Cleveland group includes it in their skit in 1969, the remark had become dislodged from its original context and stood for an attitude thought to be all too characteristic of activist men, white and black.[16] The Cleveland group reinforced the hypocrisy of a radical making such a comment by juxtaposing Carmichael's remark to a Hertz Rent-a-Car ad: "Should a Bride to be Work as a Hertz Girl Before Marriage? Yes, its gets her used to being taken for granted. And if that's not perfect training for marriage, we'd like to know what is. Go Hertz Rent-A-Car" (9).

More quotations follow that suggest how the dominant culture shapes middle-class—primarily white—women to become wives who only need to learn to shop and to care for men. The third skit, "Occupation: Homemaker," offers the briefest of scenes in which "a wife enters as if from work" only to find that her husband has done nothing to prepare for dinner; has failed to tend to their son, who has fallen and cut himself; and—the *coup de grâce*—has invited his buddies over for a game of cards. More quotations from advertisements, women's magazines, and newspapers sketch the limited path a middle-class woman is expected to follow, hemmed all around by high culture authorities and low. The final skit, "Where Did Everyone End Up? Frustration at Thirty-Six," focuses on a character identified simply as "Woman" who is in an empty house and yet has to contend with two voices: a female voice that seems to stand for the ways in which women are complicitous in their own oppression and a male voice that stands for the needy husband who requires Woman to "take proper care of" him (Bunch et al. 17). Woman imagines ways to change her life, "to start learning things again," but the female voice and the voice of the husband remind her of her proper role. In the final lines of this last skit, Woman asks "But what can I do? what can I offer? What am I?"

The quotations that follow the last skit do not seem at first to offer an adequate answer to Woman's questions. An ad for diamonds ("You're proud of her, right? . . . Diamonds make a gift of love") suggests how the woman's subservience can be bought, how her ability to "handle [the husband's] boss at dinner, 20 kids scrambling over a birthday cake, and [the husband] without [him] ever knowing it" can be purchased through a diamond. This bit of consumerist bribery is followed by a voice-of-the-thinkers quotation from someone identified only as "Political Leader Today": "Women are as vital to the nation's progress as its minerals, its rivers, and its agriculture. Harnessed and properly controlled but treated with respect, they present a great and powerful force which can be used for the benefit and progress of the nation. Left to run wild, however, or simply ignored, they will be as locusts in the nation's cornfield" (Bunch et al. 18). This passage picks up a thread that has run throughout the revue and midcentury feminism print production more generally: if left to run wild, women will be dangerous. There is both a threat and a promise in this notion of wild women who, if left unharnessed, will become locusts in the nations' cornfield, a threat underscored by the next passage, which links without commentary the political leader's warning to the now famous letter from Abigail Adams to John Adams—"Remember, all men would be tyrants if they could. If particular care and attention is not paid to the ladies, we are determined to foment a rebellion, and will not hold ourselves bound by any laws" (19). The Adams passage is followed by an excerpt from the WITCH (Women's International Terrorist Conspiracy from Hell) manifesto—"We are WITCH. We are LIBERATION. We are WE. . . . WITCH means breaking the bond of woman as a biologically and sexually defined creature. It implies the destruction of passivity, consumerism and commodity fetishism" (19).[17] The skit again raises the question, What might happen if women were left to run wild? What kind of power might they have to sweep across the cultural landscape like locusts in the cornfield? The concluding words of the play, however, are not the WITCH Manifesto but the Virginia Slims' slogan, "You've come a long way, Baby," and thus the revue ends by co-opting a co-opted bit of advertising schlock: women's "progress" has been commodified to sell cigarettes. But can women take back the phrase to resist passivity, consumerism, and commodity fetishism?

In the heady optimism characteristic of the early movement, women might well have answered with a resounding "yes!" In its first performance, *Sweet 16* operated as polemic in the sense that I used that term in chapter 3, in that it addressed women who already shared common concerns. As Canning puts it, political theater "worked to communicate values held in common and to induce actions based on those values" (114). As noted earlier, it was not unusual for the audience to be all-female. The Cleveland Radical Women's Group could count on their initial audience of women to recognize a familiar truth about women's lives (and to judge from the skit, more particularly, middle-class and primarily white women's lives) in the spare caricatures of the skits and the pastiche of limiting and limited cultural representations of women conveyed through the "Voice of the Thinkers" and "Words from Our Sponsors" quotations. Instead of involving the decorous audiences of traditional theater, feminist theater events counted on audience members' vocal (and sometimes physical, bodily) participation in the performance.

One can catch a glimpse of audience response in the occasional photograph running in a feminist newspaper or in the photographs accompanying Charlotte Rea's *Drama Review* articles from the early seventies. A Susan Opotow photograph of an It's All Right to be Woman performance shows audience members sitting on the floor, at the same level as the performers. Many of the audience members are laughing—full, open-mouthed laughter—some doubled over in laughter, using hand gestures to indicate their approval of the performance before them (Rea, "Women's Theatre Groups"). When the announcer reads Nietzsche's statement that "woman should be silent about woman!" audience members could be counted on to hiss, boo, or hoot in laughter. The skits were not created to be self-contained texts, because audience members were expected, in call-and-response as well as in postperformance discussion, to add their testimony to the bare outline of the skits, to extend examples of problematic cultural representations of women, and to consider how to work to counter such representations—how, in other words, to act out the WITCH Manifesto.

Sweet 16 makes evident that the Cleveland Radical Women's Group were involved in a complex pedagogical process that involved researching, writing, performing, discussing, revising, and publishing—but the process did not stop there. At the very least, making the text available in print form invited readerly appropriations.[18] While *Sweet 16* was initially intended to work as reader's theater—that is, it was read out loud as live performance by a group of people for an audience to watch and hear—the published text is set up with typeface changes and graphics that would be visible only to the person who was literally looking at the pamphlet. The look of this pamphlet is similar to much of movement literature in fact. Hand lettering intermixes with typeface and runs into line drawings and photographs. Like movement reprints, newspapers, and journals, this pamphlet celebrates the iconic possibilities of the handmade, the page crafted from found text, some of it readily available in the culture (akin to sampling in contemporary music or found poetry) and some of it available as part of a literate education (quotations from Aristotle and Rousseau, for example). A simple, unattributed graphic appears, for example, on the second page of the pamphlet between the clothing ad advising women that it is possible to "win and let him like it" and letter from "the teen-age girl" asking whether it is possible to love books and be loved by boys. This line drawing shows a woman on a subway with grotesquely leering men ogling her as she seems to tug at her miniskirt. Following the first skit, "Under 21," in which a girl's hopes and aspirations are distorted, Mark Bulwinkle's Potato Woman cartoon appears: familiar to readers of the Methodist magazine *MOTIVE,* the figure is a distorted female whose breasts on her potato-lumpish body are far larger than her head.[19]

A few grainy reprints of photographs include advertising photos showing a bride walking down an aisle lined with refrigerators and a news photo of women (all apparently white) protesting, carrying posters with such slogans as "Judge Women as people not as wives" (Bunch et al. n.p.). The pamphlet's final graphic, included on the inside back cover just before the "double double toil and trouble for the ruling class" chant, is a silhouette of three witches. These several images work together with the quotations for the reading eye as a pastiche of the cultural terms and signs by and through which Woman is defined. While the play was intended to initiate face-to-face discussion, the pamphlet could stand on its own, experienced as a text to be viewed and read, thus potentially extending the revue's use and impact beyond the relatively limited few who would either perform the review or experience it as an audience member. In crafting a visually appealing pamphlet, the Cleveland group clearly trusted to the efficacy of print to do much but not all of the work of political education.

Unlike the San Francisco group, the Cleveland group extended no explicit invitation to readers to take the play and make it their own, but the form of the pamphlet and its mode of distribution invite improvisation. One could add or subtract passages, omitting or remaking skits to suit local circumstances and purposes. The very spareness of the play and the relative simplicity of reader's theater as a performance process made *Sweet 16* transportable in the sense that it could be put to use by other groups for other configurations of players and audience. The play necessarily would be re-created through each new performance in each new setting with variations in audience members' and players' experiences. Once the Cleveland Radical Women's Group made the play available in print form, it could be performed by less politically homogeneous players and before less politically homogeneous audiences. Various individuals and groups from around the country could purchase the inexpensive play to adapt to their own settings and purposes.

In 1971 the Pullman Unitarian Universalist Church in upstate New York, as part of its efforts to increase gender sensitivity among members of the congregation, reproduced parts of the play, dropping the skit about the movement office and adding passages from the Bible to "Voices of the Thinkers." A typescript plan of service from the Pullman performance serves as a reminder that such materials circulated readily and widely, to be used up and made over by ordinary women and men.[20] Instead of using an all-female cast playing to an all-female audience, the Pullman performance included two women and two men who served as announcers and played roles in the several skits before a congregation of men and women who were not necessarily sympathetic or willing to accept the view offered in the revue of American culture. The physical setting was also not necessarily conducive to audience participation, with audience members sitting in the somber, historic church building (built by the Pullmans who established the railway car empire bearing that name and who were associated with the infamous Pullman Strike of 1894), occupying pews on a Sunday morning, and accustomed to listening to a service led by a minister. While the minister was one of the four players, his presence did not necessarily lend greater weight to the content of the play. Reflecting in 1974 on the work of feminist theater, the playwright Roberta Sklar said that feminist performance had to reach beyond audience members who were already persuaded by feminist principles to educate a larger public (Rea, "Women for Women" 81), but a play such as *Sweet 16*, designed to reinforce and extend commitment among women who were already so inclined rather than to mount a developed argument, could not easily do the work of political education among those who might well feel strong resistance. Not, that is, without the play's undergoing significant revision. While the Pullman congregation already thought of itself as a "we," as a group defined by denominational affiliation and membership in this particular historic church, the performance did not re-create this audience into a radicalized "we," especially not in Shank's terms, as a collectivity opposed to an establishment, if that meant an establishment gendered (negatively) as male. In fact, at least some members of the audience/congregation saw themselves as the target of the critique: they were the establishment by virtue of economic privilege, gender, or both.

As importantly, however, for my purposes here, the Pullman performance makes clear that the play, even a revised play made new for new circumstances, could not by itself do all the necessary pedagogical work. As feminists engaged in performance reiterated, the whole process of performance had to be reconceptualized to be pedagogically and politically transformative. Because the congregation as a whole had not chosen the revue, nor had members improvised from it a sequence more appropriate to their perceived needs, this performance of *Sweet 16* committed what Dell'Olio names as the only theatrical sin: the group performing the play chose it to "teach" the audience something rather than to "share its learning process with them." Perhaps not surprisingly given the church setting, Dell'Olio's term "preaching" describes this performance event better than does her preferred "learning *with* the audience" (102; emphasis added). The skit did produce the desired effect expressed originally by the Cleveland Radical women in that it served as a spur for conversation. But because the Pullman players could not count on audience sympathy or a shared horizon of expectation, and because they had not crafted a pedagogical experience that could have built either sympathy or the sharing of experience, the conversation tended to be merely adversarial. Such appropriations suggest the challenge women faced in attempting to take performances to audiences who were not already inclined toward feminism, and they can remind us (as will be discussed more fully in chapter 5) that there is nothing essentially transformative or liberatory about a pedagogy based on its content or its method, whatever its intentions.

Print/Performance/Pedagogy

> To think about theatre writing is to envision immediately a writing that "will do," that empowers speakers with vital words, incites bodies to move in space.
>
> —Elin Diamond, "(In)Visible Bodies in Churchill's Theater"

The two artifacts I have considered in this chapter show that print served as more than just a supplement to performance, more than mere residue or trace of the event "itself." Print, pedagogy, and performance were in dynamic relationship, reciprocally defining. But because print served such a remarkably ordinary role in the process by which performances were developed, the function of print—and thus the importance of literacy—has gone largely unrecognized in studies of feminist performance. Such studies have assumed that for feminists in the late sixties and early seventies, "reading was no longer the basis for thought, because it was superseded by the actual materiality of lived events" (Canning 45). Even as theater historians report that performers researched, read, and wrote in order to educate themselves about feminism and about theater, such literate practices were apparently so unremarkably a part of feminist performance work that theater historians have been able to focus almost exclusively on the ephemerality of the moment of performance—the bodies in motion—and overlook the more complex performance event that is also a literacy event.

Performers read and wrote to create performances, and they also used print to record performances. But the material forms—the inexpensive, low-production-value pamphlets and handbooks—suggest less the desire to memorialize a particular performance in time and more the desire to make material available for use. The material forms suggest not only the provisionality of performance but also the pedagogical aims of feminist performance work. The print artifact in this sense is not sacred text that requires respectful reproduction but a pedagogical text that invites others to participate in its re-creation by working on the particular text, cutting it up, rearranging it, stitching parts of it together with new material, figuring out how it can be made to work as prompt for performance, and improvising from it to create another performance altogether. The material forms are thus sign and substance of the pedagogical aims of feminist performance work, which sought to enable women, as fully literate agents, to learn how to go public with their politics and to effect significant social, cultural, and political change.

5

The Do-It-Yourself Classroom

> Women's Liberation is a model of education that works, and it is not surprising that we turn to social movements rather than to institutions in order to find some living educational process.
>
> —Donna Huse, "Women's Liberation and the Politics of Evolution"

> When much of the empowerment rhetoric pertains to practices which could or should take place within universities and schools, we must ask how much freedom can there be within the institutions and pedagogical exigencies of teaching? More attention to contexts would help shift the problem of empowerment from dualisms of power/powerlessness, and dominant/subordinate, that is, from purely oppositional stances, to a problem of multiplicity and contradiction.
>
> —Jennifer Gore, "What we can do for you!"

IN JUNE 1971, at a conference to consider alternatives for the future of higher education, Joseph Williamson concluded his talk with the assertion that "whatever 'teaching strategies for radical change' we can devise must be enacted outside the universities as they exist" (43). He had discussed three elements necessary for radical change: teaching methodologies that attempt to "democratize the classroom and break open the patterns of passivity and intimidation which characterize so much of education in the university"; radical content designed to introduce classroom material "intended to raise the critical consciousness of students" through "courses in United States imperialism, Black Studies, the role of women in society, [and] the recovery of a radical 'tradition' from Socrates to John Brown and W. E. B. Dubois"; and finally, contexts "in which radical education takes place" (40). Because academics had failed to take seriously this last element, Williamson contends, they had "deluded" themselves about their "effectiveness as radicals in the teaching profession" (41). New methodologies and new contents might give students "some breathing space within the old structures," but that would not be enough. Without changing the old structures—those "systems of order and legitimation"—changes in classroom practices offered no more than the "illusion of being radical" (41).

Williamson thus proposed that spaces outside the university must serve as seedbeds from which to grow radical alternatives. Among those spaces outside, women's liberation was seen as an especially fruitful source of alternative practices. As Paul Garver puts it, whereas much of the larger movement "was alien, sectarian, [and] harsh," making it difficult to integrate in oneself the roles of "persons, teachers, [and] political activists," the women's liberation movement offered a real alternative, "with its connection of the personal and the political and its innovative organizational methods" (25). Offering a "counterideal," Donna Huse identified "what we do in women's meetings" as a model of democratic and emotionally rich pedagogical practices (47).

That academics were looking to the outside for radical alternatives is perhaps not surprising. Although professional organizations, as well as the student power and New University movements, had urged reforms in higher education, it was not clear "where the reformers in the graduate schools [were] to come from to break the cycle" (Walsh 6).[1] Where, in other words, would one find those who would help to prepare the future professoriate in such a way that significant change could be sustained? The Columbia Women's Liberation group argued that the problem was especially acute for women because, while graduate faculty might be willing to work with women graduate students, they were less likely to want to hire them (DuPlessis et al., "Columbia").[2] For some of those attending the radical alternatives conference, the hope for change came in part from those who already had been politically active: out of "the political and social upheavals of the last few years . . . have emerged a motley amalgam of sights and sounds whose consciousness towards learning, politics, property, success, morality and religion differs profoundly from what had come to be expected of people called students" (Walsh 6). While some activists had found their way "to communes, monasteries, Canada, new media projects, [and] free schools," they were also finding their way back to colleges as faculty (Walsh 6). But what did these new faculty bring with them from the outside? And what would academics have found in the women's university-without-walls, in particular, that could help them transform institutions of higher learning? Could voluntarist, collectivist, and overtly political practices serve to transform classrooms that traditionally had been designed to rank order individual achievement in the service of objective knowledge?

In this chapter I consider the verge dividing the academy from the feminist "outside" in order to look more carefully at the osmotic relationship that developed. In this space on the margin, one could find women's liberation schools, free-university classrooms, continuing education courses, campus ministry groups, YWCA- and YMCA-sponsored groups, feminist workshops located on university property but not sponsored by a university, and women's centers that were staffed by and served both the university and community, as well as a wide variety of newly created women's studies courses with varying degrees of institutional status.[3] To help structure this discussion, I take Williamson's three intertwining elements—radical methodologies, radical contents, and contexts—as framing questions. While the methodology most typically associated with feminism was consciousness raising, it was neither a single practice nor the only pedagogical approach employed. Women disagreed not only about how consciousness raising should be conducted but also about the origin and history of the practice, its purposes, and its relative effectiveness. No single feminist pedagogical methodology or single agreed-upon version of a methodology was available for appropriation by the academy.[4] Thus, what was selected from the range of possibilities tells much more about the academy in the sense that it suggests what was found workable in that institutional context, but it does not exhaust the pedagogical potential that was there to be found in the movement. I begin, then, with the theories and practices of consciousness raising in relation to other pedagogical methods before turning to questions of content and context.

Consciousness Raising as One Form of Feminist Praxis

> We say that a small group of women can make mountains move. That was the lesson of [Chicago Women's Liberation Union] workgroups in health, education, employment, and gay rights, to name a few. There we created the ideas and actions that helped women liberate each other from oppressive beliefs and old social habits.
>
> —Chicago Women's Liberation Union, Herstory Web site homepage

> On campuses everywhere, right outside the classroom door, students form their own academic clubs for collaborative study.... In the women's liberation movement... people have begun to work collaboratively in support groups—sometimes called "rap groups" or consciousness raising groups—which subordinate figures of authority during the process of self-development.
>
> —Kenneth Bruffee, *College English*

In September 1974 Dayton Women's Liberation published in their newsletter a position paper from one of their affiliates, the Socialist-Feminist Consciousness Raising Group, that reflects on their first five years together. In the beginning Dayton Women's Liberation was a loosely knit group with "an open-ended definition of goals and politics" (Socialist-Feminist n.p.). Early on, it made sense that consciousness raising would be the primary activity because women were just beginning to react against "hierarchical structures that oppress women, and 'movement' organizations that were over structured and insensitive." Women needed to learn how to feel "equal, with no leaders, no 'stars,'" and this required flexibility in approach and "sensitivity to women's needs, fears, or feelings of inadequacy." As long as the group remained small and members continued to feel that they needed to better understand the extent to which they had been affected by sexism, consciousness raising met their needs. Ideally, women were able to begin the process of understanding how societal forces oppressed them as a group; they learned how to trust other women and how, by working together, they could effect real social change. The loose organizational structure and consciousness raising as the primary pedagogical method had proved remarkably successful to the extent that many new women were drawn into the Dayton group and the growing numbers enabled the creation of a women's center. But the very success made clear that consciousness raising alone was not enough. The proliferation of groups (at least forty groups in five years) without a clear sense of purpose or goals had led to "a very large, watered down and weak organization."[5] In particular, the failure to make clear the purpose of consciousness raising had left many participants with the perception that the women's movement was about "finding individual solutions to sexism" rather than developing ways to move toward collective social and political change. The group identified as the Socialist-Feminist argued that this constituted a serious misunderstanding, because consciousness raising had to be understood as a "means to an end and not the end itself." In fact, if not employed carefully, consciousness raising could close off the possibility of productive and open debate and derail activism. The Socialist-Feminists thus proposed that Dayton Women's Liberation recognize that they had outgrown consciousness raising and needed to move on.

In capsule, the history of the consortium of Dayton Women's Liberation groups is the history of many such groups across the country. While it has been commonplace among some academic feminists recently to see consciousness raising as the pedagogical method most definitive of feminism, the practice was never embraced by all midcentury participants in women's liberation.[6] Even among women who had found some version of the practice vitally important, differences arose about goals, the specifics of the method, and relative effectiveness. Through their words and their deeds, many feminists made clear that consciousness raising was, as the Dayton group asserted, a means to an end rather than an end itself, and that it was not sufficient to do all the pedagogical or political work of a radical movement. As earlier chapters suggest, feminists engaged in a variety of pedagogical practices, some of which involved elements of consciousness raising—as with some of the performance groups, for example—but more often than not, if engaged in at all, consciousness raising was seen primarily as a beginning, a first step.

While consciousness raising bears some resemblance to encounter movement techniques and sensitivity training, feminists generally located its roots in some combination of leadership-training methods developed as part of the southern civil rights movement, the "Guatemala guerrilla" approach as adapted by the SDS, and the Maoist process of "speaking bitterness."[7] Kathie Sarachild is frequently cited as the "originator of the concept," but it might be more accurate to say only that her's is the name attached to the well-circulated paper "A Program for Feminist 'Consciousness Raising,'" which was prepared for the First National Women's Liberation Conference, held outside Chicago in 1968. A member of the New York radical feminist group the Redstockings, Sarachild describes a technique women were already practicing for grounding the political in the personal. She asserts that the consciousness-raising program was planned "on the assumption that a mass liberation movement will develop as more and more women begin to perceive their situation correctly and that, therefore, our primary task right now is to awaken 'class' consciousness in ourselves and others on a mass scale" ("Program" 79). To perceive women's class situation "correctly," one must begin with personal recognition and testimony ("recalling and sharing our bitter experiences"). In Sarachild's formulation, women were expected to trust to their own experience over and above traditional forms of knowledge. Thus, they should recognize in themselves a "repository of real information about women." By studying "nature, not books," women would "put all theories to the test of living practice and action" (Sarachild, "Consciousness-Raising" 132). But even in this relatively severe approach, consciousness raising required women to move on to find in the collective body of individual testimonies the common roots of oppression. From there, one was to move to strategies for further organization and action.

Because many women had been taught not to trust their own experiences and to devalue the experiences of other women, "the bitch-session cell group" had to address itself to culturally induced forms of resisting consciousness. Sarachild asserts that because "male culture assumes that feelings are something that people should stay on top of and put women down for being led by their feelings," women have to reclaim feeling as a powerful source of knowledge: "We're saying that women have all along been generally in touch with their feelings... and that their being in touch with their feelings has been their greatest strength, historically and for the future" ("Program" 78). Part of the rhetoric of getting in touch with one's feelings, however, has more to do with guerrilla theater, with the discourse of rage, than with the now familiar mainstay of television talk shows and pop psychology.[8] "We have been so in touch with our feelings," Sarachild adds bitingly," that we have used our feelings as our best available weapon—hysterics, whining, bitching, etc." Such culturally devalued weapons, she suggests, were all women had to deploy, and women learned to do so strategically in response to specific instances of injustice (78). This is dangerous terrain, to embrace what has been despised, to take pride in characterizations that were intended as insults. And indeed, other movement women of various ideological affiliations feared even the hint that women—even in parodic outrage—would embrace any aspect of the stereotype of women as irrational beings. But Sarachild's purpose here is not to stall in useless rage but to recuperate women's strategic behaviors in order to learn from them and then—and this is critical—move on. To continue to whine, to wallow in self-pity, or to become mesmerized by the "wriggles of the psyche" (to borrow Marge Piercy's wonderful phrase from "Grand Coolie Damn" [422]) would lead to inaction.

Rage figures prominently in several accounts of consciousness raising. As suggested earlier in chapter 2, feminists recognized that women's rage needed to be harnessed in the service of revolutionary change, and consciousness raising was seen as one method for directing such energy. Pamela Allen recounts how women in her small group had to distinguish between productive anger and self-defeating resentment. Anger could be turned outward against "oppressive actions of individual men and social institutions," whereas resentment was more likely to be expressed by "striking out at other women for being weak (or strong)" (12). In an early paper from the Redstocking's literature list, Lynn O'Connor outlined the Blakean stages women almost inevitably went through, from rage to vision to a return to a transformed and purposeful rage. The first stage "demands a public admission of the individual's unhappiness in a society where unhappiness is viewed as a symptom of emotional illness" (35). The accumulation of stories lets loose "a lot of personal rage" (36). While these early sessions might seem like group therapy, O'Connor explains that the discovery of the common thread that women share helps them to move past self-blame and toward directing their rage outward. The second stage involves growing personal strength as women "liberate a vision of themselves as strong, serious people with inherent capacity for achievement and independence" (36). A vision of liberation, however, is not enough, because it inevitably comes up against the reality of cultural assumptions. When the strengthened woman comes face to face with her oppressor and her strength is met with violence or mockery, she discovers a new kind of rage. She realizes that she has not only to envision herself strong but also to act out of new strength. The third stage then requires that she join with other women to act collectively, combining strengths to change society: "The small group becomes a self-conscious collective defining its goal in terms of the violent overthrow of male supremacy—or anything which stands in the way of that goal" (37).

As with the editorial and performance collectives, women who were engaged in consciousness raising spent an enormous amount of time and energy in devising and refining processes. While some participants found the desire for rules of conduct to be unnecessary, artificial, and even offensive, others found articulating objectives and procedures to be a crucial part of the process. In 1972, reporting for *Woman's World* on a mass consciousness-raising meeting to be broadcast over New York's WBAI radio station, Collette Price reflects on the "dos and don'ts" sheet distributed at the beginning of the session: "I didn't remember any rules from my [prior] experience, only that you had to be honest and that wasn't exactly a rule, it was more like a necessary condition, and I didn't see that condition listed—so I put the rules away and got back to the demonstration" (10). Price had appreciated her early experiences with consciousness raising but objected to the increasing desire to codify behavior as the small groups proliferated. But many women found that without some agreed upon set of procedures, groups tended to unravel and little was accomplished.

One of the most fully developed approaches was published in 1970 in a small, inexpensive booklet from Times Change Press. *Free Space: A Perspective on the Small Group in Women's Liberation* was written by Pamela Allen, a former member of SNCC and cofounder of New York Radical Women who had moved to San Francisco and joined the women's liberation group Sudsofloppen (identified as the "oldest group in the city") in 1968 (Allen 5, 11; Echols, *Daring* 379). The title of the booklet suggests something of the paradox of consciousness raising: as a process or set of techniques defining a collective free space, it is intended to assist women in becoming "autonomous in . . . thinking and behavior" (Allen 6). Autonomy thus carries a double sense: on the one hand, the individual must work out for herself "what is correct for her as an individual," a process that involves "decisions that must be freely made by the individual woman herself, for she and not the movement must live her life" (44–45); on the other hand, women must find collective independence from patriarchal structures, which requires that women resist the temptation to drain their "energies from [their] own fight by constantly meeting [men's] needs" (40). The challenge, as the Dayton groups' experience suggested, was to find ways to keep hold of this double sense of autonomy, to resist submerging the individual within the group and at the same time to synthesize individuals' views on behalf of an understanding of their common cause (6).

To achieve this double sense of autonomy, Sudsofloppen developed four group processes: "opening up," or "keeping in touch with...emotions"; "sharing," or "giving one another information regarding experiences "; "analyzing," or "trying to understand the meaning of these events"; and "abstracting," or "finally fitting that understanding into an overview of [women's] potential as human beings and the reality of...society, i.e. of developing an ideology" (Allen 6–7). Over time, women working through these overlapping processes were expected to synthesize their collective views, but the process was not without conflict. Early on group members expected that simply getting together and recognizing the commonality of women's "burden" would alleviate the pain, but they soon discovered that it did not. To know that one is not alone can be a "freeing experience," engendering hope, but "this knowledge in no way changes objective reality" (12). Group members thus struggled to decide how to move past that stage of initial recognition of common grievance toward effective change.[9]

Allen recalls that the central tension in the group sprang from disagreement about "how liberation could be accomplished," whether "personally or politically" (12–13). Some who thought the best path was through personal change also felt that "politics were irrelevant if not detrimental to human liberation" based on their prior experiences in New Left groups, "where they saw people being inhuman to one another in the name of progress and humanity" (13). One criticism from the left had been that sharing personal experiences in women's groups was a bourgeois indulgence and a form of "escape from political struggle" (McAfee and Wood 1). Those who persisted in thinking that sexism and racism shared a common root thought that no real change in the lives of individuals could occur without larger societal change (13). Gradually group members came to realize that both approaches were necessary: they would have to build an effective political movement that also addressed individual women's intellectual and emotional understandings. Women would have to grow "both in the realm of personal relationships and in the realm of ideas and skills" (17). They would have to ground their learning in "concrete experience" but build upward and outward from that ground through "analysis and abstraction" (23). Abstraction is not an endpoint, not a place to stop, but it is a crucial part of the process because it is through abstraction that ideology emerges (30). To get to this point is a great pleasure: "It is a joy to learn to think, to begin to comprehend what is happening to us." "Ideas," Allen says, "are experiences in themselves, freeing, joyous experiences which give us the framework for formulating our actions" (30).

But for all this to happen, the group recognized, they could not just "let... things happen; they had to develop a procedure to insure room for all group members to grow" (Allen 23). In particular, they found that ecstasy of discussion was not enough, that literacy was a necessary component of political education. From the beginning, the group understood that they had to do more than "speak bitterness." As Allen recalls, "One very important step in the process of uniting the political and personal concerns of our group by defining the function of our group as Free Space, was the experience of writing our ideas about what we hoped the group could be, first individually and then collectively" (57). Committing themselves to writing was a difficult but significant step because they had been afraid to express their ideas, afraid especially to express their ideas in writing.[10] They thus had to confront their "weaknesses in conceptualization, writing, theorizing, and taking [themselves] seriously" (62). But the act of writing marked a level of commitment and served as a "concrete example" of what they were "discovering about meaningful work" (58). Recognizing that personal experience was not enough, the group members decided that they needed a study plan to extend their thinking beyond the confines of the single small group. The plan involved sharing reading materials among several small groups.[11] All the small groups were to read a text; after that they would meet collectively to discuss what they had learned. Allen explains that the first reading was Juliet Mitchell's "Women: The Longest Revolution," a reprint from a 1966 issue of *New Left Review* distributed among the network of feminist groups through the New England Free Press and the San Francisco Radical Education Project. Each small group planned to spend a month discussing each of Mitchell's four analytical categories for naming women's condition: production, socialization, sexuality, and reproduction (49–50). For each category, the group was expected to move through its own process of opening up, sharing experiences, analyzing, and abstracting. In the final week of the month, the various groups would then convene to compare their analyses and "evolving theory" (50). Allen anticipated cycling through the categories yet again, this time using them to develop ideas for liberation, moving outward from ideology toward a framework for radical action (50). Thus, while Allen's group continued to value experiential knowledge, "nature" for them was to be put in critical dialogue with "books."

Importantly, Allen emphasizes the extent to which the participants' socioeconomic backgrounds would shape the trajectory of the study plan. Although she grants that the individual women would all share their status as female, she stresses the extent to which ways of thinking, job opportunities, and psychology, among various other factors, could differ along class lines. Each collective of women thus would be necessarily limited by the class profiles of its membership.[12] Reading and joining together with other groups would then function to extend consciousness beyond the limitations of any single group. At this point in her discussion Allen is building toward a warning not only against the limitations of examining just the "wriggles of the psyche" but also against the arrogance of assuming that "what benefits white women automatically benefits all women" (52). In a familiar formulation, she argues that "our first duty is to understand our own predicament," because "then we will be clear about our motives for joining with other women in a mass movement" (51). But that first duty is not a place to rest. Each group in its particularity has to identify indigenous concerns, but they each also have to scrutinize their concerns in relation to the concerns of other women.

Her early experience with the study plan taught Allen that the most divisive question facing groups was how the "enemy" was to be defined. Instead of having to agree on a single response to the question, however, she suggests that the answer should be "multifaceted": "Rather than defining one enemy we may find that we have many fronts and many levels on which to battle. Some of these are internal, within us, and regardless of their origin in society's values and institutions, they can cripple us and destroy us just as easily as can our enemies from without" (52). Allen first names four enemies—capitalism, men, ourselves, and the state—corresponding roughly to Mitchell's four categories (production, sexuality, socialization, and reproduction). But she finds these categories insufficient. Also needed is a fifth category that recognizes racism as "all pervasive and . . . probably our most dangerous enemy for it has historically separated women from each other allowing white women to seek privileges for themselves rather than making their cause with all women" (52). A racist society such as ours requires that all who benefit from white privilege "must learn to give up privileges we have at the expense of others at the same time as we fight for the rights which have been denied us as women" (52).

Importantly, even as Allen is outlining a utopian ideal, she is also articulating an important pedagogical principle. Relatively few feminists who theorized consciousness raising said much about the extent to which differences among women shaped how the process would play out or about the differing ways women would draw from their varied experiences to move from words to action.[13] Some white women did worry about the relative absence of black women from consciousness raising groups, but they did not necessarily consider the possibility that consciousness raising was not a universally useful process, that it might not address the concerns of all women, or that having the time to participate in small-group bitch sessions was itself a sign of relative economic privilege. The small group in isolation, in other words, could not carry the whole burden of consciousness raising, much less the burden of political activism, if the women's movement was to include women across a range of difference. Because "ideology does not develop separate from action and programs," part of the purpose of the small group, as Allen understands it, is to make room for the evaluation of political activity. Ideally, group members would involve themselves in a variety of political actions and programs, allowing for multiple affiliations and thereby broadening the political perspective of any given small group. Allen sees differences in political perspective to be "natural and healthy" to the extent that such differences generate better theory, which in turn generates better political action (42). The burden is thus not on the consciousness-raising group per se to organize political action—in fact, Allen anticipates that more "action organizations" would soon develop, involving many of the women already participating in small groups—but rather, the consciousness-raising group, in this version at least, serves as a reflective space for consolidating understandings and making needs visible.

While Allen and her group approached consciousness raising primarily as education preparatory to action, others expected not only that women would rethink their own lives in relation to other women and to the larger society but also that, through the group process, they would learn how to organize other women as a step toward activism. Paradoxically, the leaderless group was "designed to eliminate preexisting habits of passivity, dominance, the need for outside instruction, or a hierarchy." If one or several women in the group dominated, the others were expected to take the responsibility to "set the balance straight." Consciousness raising, from this perspective, was intended to develop the leadership qualities in all women by eliminating the possibility of any one woman or group of women leading the group. Various techniques were tried to ensure what was referred to as "internal democracy," which meant that all women should be able to speak without interruption, that no woman would be allowed to dominate, and that the quieter women would be protected (see O'Connor 38; Leon 13).[14] Such techniques were viewed by some as patronizing in presuming to protect women from one another and in assuming that to be quiet was necessarily a sign of silencing rather than a strategic choice (see Leon 13; Price 11). If women could not learn to disagree, to challenge one another, how, it was asked, could they learn to effectively assert themselves in other, less protected arenas? How would women learn to be leaders? If women could not learn to disagree productively, how would change in consciousness lead to change in concrete reality?

Reformulating Feminist Method

At least a partial answer to these questions can be found in the actual practices of radical feminists, practices that constituted the women's university-without-walls. As I suggest in earlier chapters, radical feminists did not rely on consciousness raising alone to teach themselves how to enter into the public sphere to effect social change. They were learning by doing as they built a decentralized network of counterinstitutions. They experimented with a variety of organizational structures to enable women to learn various skills. As Carol Downer, one of the founders of the self-health movement, put it, "as feminists, we are careful to have an OPEN structure, maximal participation in policy making activities, and we have a profound commitment to struggle to achieve not only the ideals of equalitarianism [*sic*], but we are also determined to make the structure work for us, not us for the structure" (qtd. in "Feminist Women's Health Centers" 71). Such structure was intended to get work done—in Downer's case, to ensure appropriate health care for women—but also to educate women in the process by making information available and providing multiple opportunities for women to read and discuss (and sometimes write) together. The women's university-without-walls was dedicated to political education (even as the various component elements focused on particular issues, such as health care, welfare rights, child care, and the like), and such an education had to mean something other than the inculcation of political content if women were to become politically active. While they struggled—not always successfully—to find ways to foster democratic processes without denying individual women's talents and expertise, the evidence in feminist print production and the alternative spaces they created makes clear that feminists were quite capable of radical disagreement. Such disagreements were often painful, even on occasion destructive, but it is also clear that disagreement generated multiple and competing versions of a feminist revolutionary ideal and concrete practices that pushed establishment institutions toward change.

In the middle space between the university and the "outside," one can find evidence of how feminists took something of the spirit of consciousness raising but developed other practices to better do the necessary pedagogical work. Beverly Tanenhaus provides a revealing record of how one such approach to feminist teaching evolved. Motherroot Press calls Tanenhaus's account of her experience a "document of community and a primer for establishing writing workshops." Tanenhaus organized a series of women's writing workshops that met on the Hartwick College campus in Oneonta, New York, from 1975 until 1982. Famous and soon-to-be famous writers participated as guest teachers, including Adrienne Rich, Toni Morrison, Audre Lorde, June Arnold, Alice Walker, and Judy Grahn. Talent, expertise, and authority were thus acknowledged as these guests read their work and interacted with the workshop participants. But the greater emphasis for Tanenhaus was on the ordinary workshop participants. If the writer's workshop concept associated with prominent university programs was established by men for men, Tanenhaus's workshops evolved instead to address the particular concerns and needs of women learning to write. Because women could be too ready "to sabotage their writing by trivializing their efforts through apology or boast" and thereby "dilute the intense confrontation demanded between the writer and her words," Tanenhaus felt it vitally important to organize writing workshops to give ordinary women an opportunity to learn how to take their own work and the work of other women seriously (13).

From the smallest details, the workshops were structured so that women learned to respond to one another "with generosity as well as shrewd, critical judgment" (Tanenhaus 8). Workshop participants were expected to respect class time: "Anyone who sauntered in late [was viewed] as breaking our contract and disrupting the class" (6). Papers were expected to be "legible" and "accurately typed," because if a "workshop leader allows a woman to present, for example, a poem with numerous scrawled revisions toppling into the margins, she is reinforcing the writer's lack of respect for her work and for her audience" (6). "Unfocused technical discussions" were discouraged (9), and "no one was allowed to state a one-dimensional pejorative reaction to work, since 'I hate it,' or even 'I love it,' would leave the writer helpless to evaluate the response" (11). The critic needed to put herself on the line, to share in the writer's vulnerability, and thus critical comments had to be supported by specific reasoning. These various strategies were intended to ensure "a friendly but professional atmosphere," one in which participants would learn how to "disagree with each other's analyses, including statements by the teacher" (6, 11).

For participants to learn how to disagree with the teacher, Tanenhaus decided she had to be a presence, not simply one writer among many. She thus offered herself as a point of professional resistance, but not in traditional academic terms. Outside the structured classroom, in personal conferences, Tanenhaus learned that the "hierarchical distances between teacher and students" could (and needed to) be broken down (12). But inside the classroom, she worked to create an environment in which students could learn to disagree with someone who occupied that hierarchically defined version of the teacher. While participants were expected in each workshop session to read and respond to their peers' work, Tanenhaus made clear that she was the discussion leader, but not in the sense that she controlled the floor or that she was the gurulike force of creative energy in the room. Rather, she made herself visible as the discussion leader by assuming "the burden of careful listening, of keeping track of comments, of making sure that everyone had a chance to speak, and that feedback was consistently constructive" (7). She describes the delicate balance that was required and in the process distinguishes the writer's workshop from the authoritarian classroom on the one hand and those versions of consciousness raising that could be read as patronizing on the other:

> A workshop leader must be attuned to people who are just beginning to sail into the discussion and make space for their comments. At the same time, the more self-confident, verbal women must not be made to feel that they are crowding the shyer types by their eloquence and perceptiveness. In the classroom, we still battle sexist stereotypes that praise the inhibited, insecure woman as beguilingly demure, and condemn a self-assured, articulate woman as overpowering. Ideally, each woman in the room is thoughtfully, comfortably contributing her comments. Then each of us will feel her individual importance in articulating her insight, not only for the benefit of the writer but for the creation of community among us. (8)

The sense of community will not develop, she observes, if the discussion leader dominates by speaking first or offering grand pronouncements about the quality of the work. Tanenhaus thus sees her role in part to involve holding back at least part of what she knows, providing "focused critical feedback without overwhelming the piece with [her] own impressions or dominating the discussion" (9). She designs her remarks instead to elicit discussion from workshop participants by making "a careful presentation of contradictory points of view" (9).[15]

One of the greatest hurdles was for participants to understand that they were not showing lack of support for another writer when they offered constructive criticism. On the one hand, the writer had to learn to "trust the critic's good will"; on the other hand, the critic had to learn that "shrewd negative comment is at the very least constructive and often exhilarating." Tanenhaus adds that "to censor one's criticism [shows] a lack of generosity and [is] a gesture of contempt that will keep the writer from developing her finest potential" (11). The stakes are high, as she sees it: "Under patriarchy, all women pay a price for challenging the company line, whether it's specific retaliation in a personal relationship, trivialization or ridicule..., or simply the loneliness of being an outsider" (16). If, however, within the relative safety of the workshop, women could learn how to give and accept criticism, they would have a greater likelihood of strengthening themselves as writers and political beings. If they could learn how to disagree with one another and with someone in a position of relative authority, they might then have greater courage to write what would be threatening to the status quo or culturally unacceptable.

Tanenhaus's workshop offered a useful transitional space between the women's liberation's consciousness-raising groups and the academy because Tanenhaus explicitly situated herself within a feminist arena, and she articulated many of the concerns about authority, responsibility, and expertise that women within the academy had to negotiate. When women within the academy began to carve out space for courses in women's studies, they drew from multiple feminist pedagogical practices.[16] It may be that the emphasis placed on consciousness raising in reports from the time and in retrospective accounts has more to do with the fact that such small-group practices seemed to represent a more dramatic change from traditional pedagogies and thus took on relatively greater importance. In 1973 Florence Howe and Carol Ahlum reported their impression that especially those graduate students and junior women faculty who were teaching women's studies courses came to view their disciplines differently and to change their teaching styles and "their *ability* to teach." While Howe and Ahlum concede the necessity of lectures in large classes, they contend that women teaching women's studies courses were more likely to include small-group discussion, "often quite deliberately intended as consciousness-raising experiences." They assert: "Indeed, if one generalization were called for, we would say that the trend is to substitute, wherever possible, groups and group processes and cooperative ('collective') projects for the individual competitive ones so familiar to us in academe." Such a shift should not be surprising if one takes into account the "emphasis in the women's movement on *sisterhood,* antielitism, leaderless consciousness-raising groups, and the power of collective decision-making and activity." What is striking, however, is the "speed with which the movement's priorities and principles have been extended into the classroom" (403–4). Even in this qualified account, Howe and Ahlum are attempting to name that which distinguishes feminist pedagogy from other forms of teaching. But the evidence from actual course materials suggests a more variable set of practices than Howe and Ahlum describe. The materials, of course, are not the whole of the pedagogical experience, and students may well have experienced small-group work as a more prominent part of a course than the materials themselves evidence. Nevertheless, the course materials add an important dimension to a reconstruction of midcentury feminist teaching practices.

The *Female Studies* booklets published by KNOW, Inc., for the National Organization for Women in the early seventies constitute an important source of information on early women's studies courses.[17] Including course syllabi from various disciplines and institutions, bibliographies, and reflections on classroom dynamics, as well as discussions of institutional politics and the conditions of female students and teachers, the booklets provide a remarkable record of formative pedagogical work in women's studies from preschool to the university. Among the university courses, one can find a range of pedagogical methods. Some instructors planned time outside of class for consciousness raising, opening the groups to students or community members who were not enrolled in the courses themselves (see Tripp 55). Some reserved one class meeting a week or alternated class periods to make room for "rap sessions" or discussion groups and to ensure that there would be time to address more systematically the course readings (see Munday 71; Roberts 98–101). Others treated consciousness raising as the topic for a single class meeting, as one method to examine alongside others, such as simulation games (Schramm 5). And some courses seemed to make no use of small-group process. Among those classes that incorporated collaborative groups, I do not find any groups that were leaderless, to the extent that the instructor set the syllabus and assigned topics for discussion. And of equal importance, although many, if not most, of the instructors indicate their desire to engage in "the process of mutual *learning*" (Roberts 94), such mutuality did not preclude the recognition of differential levels of knowledge and relative expertise.

In one especially revealing account, Joan Roberts describes the "restructuring of authority" that has to take place for women's studies courses to have real impact. She explains that "questioning the *validity of societal reality*" requires that "each woman's experiences must be heard," but the process requires a reciprocity of talent and knowledge. On the one hand, "women students go for help to women faculty whose training and awareness have *earned* them a reputation for authority, not from status, but from knowledge and experience" (94). On the other hand, "faculty have begun to recognize the tremendous talents and maturity of younger women students, whose support is needed in critical periods of change" (94). In Roberts's terms, this restructuring of authority entailed not doing away with the teacher's authority or expertise but building pedagogies that made possible "cognitive-affective" learning among teachers and students alike (94).

Like Tanenhaus, academic feminists learned that they did their students no favors in creating classrooms that obscured the workings of power and authority or that devalued expertise (Ryan 41). The female teacher has historically had to establish her right to be in the academy and to make her professorial authority legible. The challenge, then, for the feminist teacher has been not only to establish her intellectual authority but at the same time to make her expertise available so that her students can make use of that expertise to further develop their own intellectual authority. While a model of consciousness raising that deemphasizes disagreement and conflict and that focuses on ensuring that each individual feels valued has come to define feminist pedagogy, it is well to look at the early practitioners who did not construct their classes either to abnegate their own authority or to refuse to recognize relative levels of and incommensurate kinds of expertise. It is understandable, given how embattled many women in the academy felt, that they would have envisioned an academic space that provided a safe space in which disagreements would be muted. Recognizing that "self criticism is one staff of the scholarly life," Jane Roland Martin recalls that in the early years of women's studies, "in a world in which women's words had for so long been discredited, the last thing we thought we needed was criticism from one another" (9). But it may be that what Martin recalls as an "acritical policy"—to the extent that it was in fact enacted—had as much to do with the relative homogeneity of the student body as it did with "policy" or with pedagogical methods designed to nurture supportive rather than agonistic intellectual exchange.

Some hint of a different kind of dynamic is evident in some of the *Female Studies* accounts. In her discussion of the creation of women's studies courses at the University of Wisconsin at Madison, Joan Roberts explains how different constituents brought different knowledges and concerns to the table. Just as Allen found that the differences among group members would necessarily shape how the process played out, Roberts explains how the participants in women's studies brought a variety of concerns that shaped the processes and goals of the early courses: faculty women from various disciplines tended to devalue their own knowledge; women students were sometimes better read in feminist literature than the faculty; male students experienced for the first time what it felt like to be in the minority; some women preferred to be in groups without men; community women, demographically more diverse than the student population, did not always sympathize with the younger college women; unmarried students were not always sympathetic with married women, in particular with what were perceived to be heterosexist presumptions; and many participants wanted more rather than less organizational structure in the courses (88–90). Such multilayered conflict could be paralyzing, especially when Roberts herself was under fire from the university administration and the women's studies courses were threatened with termination (95). Roberts, however, draws from the experience a model for "a multi-pronged approach to women's studies" (94). The course involved extensive readings, lectures by women faculty, presentations by community organizations, and group discussions.

The course, however, did not stand in isolation but was part of a larger network that included evening lectures open to the public, a weekend conference, small discussion groups outside class, and radio broadcasts (95–106, 131–69). Roberts concludes, "From a single course, I believe a number of objectives have been, at least, partially achieved. Clearly, the *interdisciplinary* dream of male academicians, which often bogs down in bickering about dominance, has, with women, taken on a sustained reality. So, too, has the partnership of university and *community* begun its move beyond rhetorical words to realistic action. In the dialogue, searching thought has replaced *unspoken taboos* as women of all ages from all circumstances have met together" (94). Having participated in this first successful interdisciplinary course, Roberts's colleagues went on to create new courses within their specific disciplines. Other signs of success were to be found in the number of participants who published ideas generated from the work on the courses and in the reports from both students and community members who testified that their lives had changed because of their involvement in some aspect of the network that spoked out from the single course.[18]

It is clear from Roberts's account of the Wisconsin experience, as with accounts of other programs around the country, that no single method could do the necessary pedagogical work of women's studies. As radical feminists outside the academy also found out, the success of any method depended on the productive friction created through the interplay between the multiple knowledges a variety of women brought to the table and the reading and writing that challenged and extended what any individual or group of women could know. Further, although much emphasis has been placed on feminist methodology, the course materials demonstrate that the "how" of teaching was understood to be in reciprocal relationship to the "what." Making new or newly recovered knowledge available to women was at the core of the women's university-without-walls as it was at the core of early women's studies courses.

Feminism's Responsibility to Content Knowledge

> First, women's studies means learning more about women and bringing this knowledge to the classroom or publishing it in scholarly journals. Second, work is being done to develop new ways of analyzing, approaching, and arranging both new and old bodies of knowledge from a feminist perspective. The development of a feminist theoretical orientation, however, is still in the preliminary stages. Third, women's studies proponents are sharing their work with men and women students in the hope of fostering changes in their attitudes and behaviors.
>
> —Lora Robinson, *Women's Studies*

> I was avidly reading everything tha[t] came to hand about feminism, from Mary Wollstonecraft to Germaine Greer; from the Seneca Falls Declaration to the SCUM Manifesto; from Sappho to Adrienne Rich. . . . I became conscious of what, for teachers of my generation particularly, constitutes a set of ethical questions: Is one justified in abandoning one's "field" and one's degree-defined "subject matter"?
>
> —Mildred Brand Munday, "Women, Literature, and the Dynamics of the Classroom"

Feminists working to transform the academy approached the question of content knowledge in two ways. As Jane Roland Martin has suggested, feminist scholars worked not only toward epistemological equality but also toward curricular equality. It was not enough, in other words, that "researchers and scholars devoted equal time and attention to women and women-related phenomena as their objects of study" if the knowledge produced did not find its way into the curriculum (103). But where would the pedagogical materials come from? In an account of the Feminist Press's first decade, the editors recall:

> Only ten years ago, in 1970, the second wave of feminism had just begun to make its way onto campuses and bookshelves. Kate Millett's *Sexual Politics* was published that year, as was Toni Cade Bambara's *The Black Woman,* and Robin Morgan's *Sisterhood is Powerful.* Still, Rebecca Harding Davis, Zora Neale Hurston, Agnes Medley, Charlotte Perkins Gilman, Margaret Fuller, and many others long out of print were unknown to the new mass of feminist readers who were preparing to teach or study in the several hundred Women's Studies courses the movement had spawned. Where were the necessary texts to come from? Who would begin to publish the lost women writers, and the instructional materials needed to reeducate a generation of teachers?" ("A Decade" 1)

The Feminist Press, the editors assert, was founded to publish materials that would "change the male centered curriculum and to help teachers envision and create nonsexist classrooms" ("A Decade" 1). Significantly, however, the founders of the press, in "wanting to provide materials for the new education of women" (*NewsNotes* [1972]: n.p.), saw their efforts as extending the published work that was emerging from the women's movement outside the academy. Such texts as Millett's, Bambara's, and Morgan's were in this sense treated as having helped to underscore the need for more instructional materials by renewing interest in neglected women writers and creating a demand for contemporary feminist work.

More recently, Sheila Tobias has argued that in the newly emerging field of women's studies, "scholars provided the data, the analysis, and the documentation; popularizers laid out the consequences of patriarchy in delimiting women's social and political roles" (205). The Feminist Press account suggests, however, that this dichotomizing formulation of feminist "content" does not adequately reflect the critically reciprocal relationship between the academy and the "outside." Syllabi from the early seventies provide further evidence that as academics struggled to make room within the traditional curriculum for women's studies, they were not only generating and publishing new or reclaimed knowledge, but they were also drawing on the print production of the women's movement for course materials. If, as Charlotte Bunch argued, the mimeographed articles that passed from hand to hand had spread the ideas of women's liberation with greater clarity than the mass media could manage ("Feminism and Education" 15), so, too, had the reprints of those articles and the enormous outpouring of print available through feminist newspapers and journals opened up lines of inquiry that academic publications had for the most part failed to consider. The publications of the women's movement were not sufficient, of course, but it is quite evident that those nontraditional materials were treated not simply as "popularizing." Rather, especially early on, such materials served as sources of legitimate—if historically and institutionally disenfranchised—knowledge and thus proved especially useful for putting pressure on more traditional academic approaches to the production of knowledge about women.[19]

A syllabus from Alison Jaggar's course in the philosophy of women's rights, taught at Miami University of Ohio in the spring of 1971, offers a striking example of how radical feminist content found its way into the academy (see figure 11). Like other universities around the country, Miami was under pressure from faculty and students to change both the content of curriculum and the context for teaching and learning. The Miami chapter of the New University Conference produced *The Gentle Revolution,* a pamphlet calling for radical educational reform. While the pamphlet includes a discussion of working conditions for professors, no mention is made of the status of female faculty. In calling for interdisciplinary studies, the group names "Afro-American Studies, Comparative Literature Studies, Victorian Studies, Studies in the Theory of Mind, Russian Studies, Asian Studies, Aesthetic Studies, [and] Studies in Advocacy Planning," but no mention is made of Women's Studies. Included in the pamphlet are proposals concerning the "Greek" system, the university and racism, the ROTC, the draft and teacher disclosure, and the university's relationship to the community—all clearly important questions—but no proposals appear concerning inequities in admission standards for women students or in the rules governing women's living conditions on campus. That the traditional curriculum and structure of the university failed to recognize questions about the status and treatment of women is not surprising. But it is important to notice as well how the prevailing radical discourse on campus also failed to notice feminist concerns.[20] While women clearly drew from the radical discourses circulating at the time, they were appropriating materials not necessarily intended for them, and they were having to do the groundwork to remake those materials for their own needs.[21] Like many other women's studies courses across the country, Jaggar's emerged

University room

Tues—1:30
317 Clokey

317 Clokey
3:00
Friday

Bibliography for

PHILOSOPHY OF WOMEN'S RIGHTS

Philosophy 310

The following books (all paperbacks) are required:
- Betty Friedan The Feminine Mystique, Dell, 95¢ (FM)
- Robin Morgan (ed.) Sisterhood is Powerful, Vintage, $2.45 (SIP)
- Toni Cade (ed.) The Black Woman, Signet, 95¢ (BW)
- Albert Memmi The Colonizer and the Colonized, Beacon, $1.95 (CC)
- Frederick Engels The Origin of the Family, Private Property and the State, New World, $1.85 (FPPS)

You will also be asked to buy: these journals and pamphlets:
- Shulamith Firestone (ed.) Notes from the Second Year, $1.50 (2Y)
- Leviathan (issueoon women) Vol. 2, No.1, May 1970, 50¢ (Lev)
- Marlene Dixon Why Women's Liberation? Glad Day Press, 10¢
- Beverly Jones and Judith Brown Toward a Female Liberation Movement, New England Free Press, 20¢
- Evelyn Reed The Myth of Women's Inferiority New England Free Press 15
- Joan Jordon The Place of American Women, New England Free Press, 15¢
- Kathy McAfee & Myrna Wood Bread and Roses, Glad Day Press, 15¢
- Laurel Limpus Liberation of Women: Sexual Repression and the Family, New England Free Press, 10¢

The following books are suggested additional reading:
- Simone de Beauvoir The Second Sex
- Virginia Woolf A Room of One's Own
- Kate Millett Sexual Politics
- Sylvia Plath The Bell Jar
- Mirra Komarovsky Blue Collar Marriage
- Ruth & Edward Brecher An Analysis of Human Sexual Response
- Mary Lou Thompson (ed.) Voices of the New Feminism
- Doris Lessing The Golden Notebook
- Margaret Mead Sex and Temperament in Three Primitive Societies
  Male and Female
- Caroline Bird Born Female

Other suggestions will be welcomed.

Any other material which is on the required list but not mentioned on the list of books and pamphlets to be bought will be reproduced and distributed. Material on the suggested list will be put on reserve in the Alumni Library.

The Philosophy Department contributes to the following journals. They will be available for reading in Room 320, Clokey Hall
- Everywoman
- Off Our Backs
- It Ain't Me Babe
- Woman: A Journal of Liberation

Figure 11. Alison Jaggar's philosophy of women's rights syllabus (*source:* author's collection).

113 Laws

I (Jan.6th) Introduction
~~Marlene Dixon Why Women's Liberation?~~
→ Meredith Tax "Woman and her Mind: the Story of Everyday Life", 2Y p.
Marilyn Salzmann Webb "Woman's Roles"- handout
FM, Ch.1

Suggested:
Beverly Jones and Judith Brown Towards a Female Liberation Movement

2 (Jan 13th) Female Nature
Bad → ✓ Evelyn Reed The Myth of Women's Inferiority
Naomi Weisstein "'Kinde, Kuche, Kirche' as Scientific Law: Psychology Constructs the Female", SIP p.205
Excellent ✓ Sandra L. & Daryl J. Bem "Training the woman to know her place: the power of a nonconscious ideology" - handout
✓ Louis Feldhammer "Sex, the liberal ethic and the zoological perspective in the social sciences" - handout
FM, chs. 6 & 7
✓ Matina S. Horner "Woman's Will to Fail" - handout

Suggested:
Dee Ann Pappas "On Being Natural" - handout
M. Mead Sex & Temperament in Three Primitive Societies
Erik H. Erikson "Inner & Outer Space: Reflections on Womanhood" - handout

3 (Jan 20th) Sexuality Linda & Patti
FM, Chs. 5 & 11
✓ Anne Koedt "The Myth of the Vaginal Orgasm", 2Y, p.37
Dana Densmore "Sex and the Single Girl", "On the Temptation to be a Beautiful Object"✓, "On Celibacy"✓- handouts
✓ Gene Damon "The Least of These", SIP, p. 297
✓ Martha Shelley "Notes of a Radical Lesbian", SIP, p.306

Suggested:
Zoe Moss "It Hurts to be Alive and Obsolete", SIP, p.170
✓ Susan Lydon "The Politics of Orgasm", SIP, p.197
Mary Jane Sherfey "A Theory on Female Sexuality", SIP, 220
✓ Kate Millett "Sexual Politics (in Literature)", SIP, p.311
Ti-Grace Atkinson "The Institution of Sexual Intercourse", 2Y, p.42
Roxanne Dunbar "Sexual Liberation: More of the Same Thing" - handout

Chapter B Sullivan

4 (Jan 27th) Class & Ethnic Differences between Women
"Reena" ✓(p.20) "Motherhood" ✓(p.63) "Double Jeopardy"✓(p.90) "On the Issue of Roles"✓(p101) "Is the Black Male Castrated?"✓(p.113) "The Pill, Genocide or Liberation?" (p.162) "From the Family Notebook" (p.232) SIP
Enriqueta Longauex y Vasquez "The Mexican American Woman"✓ SIP, p.379
"Women in the Professions: Five Testimonies", SIP, pp. 62-86 ✓
Judith Ann "The Secretarial Proletariat" SIP, p.86 ✓
Women's Caucus "The Halls of Academe" SIP, p.101✓
Carol Glassman "Women and the Welfare System" SIP, p.102 ✓
Jean Tepperman "Two Jobs: Women who Work in Factories" SIP, p.115

Suggested:
Mirra Komarovsky Blue Collar Marriage, esp. Chs. 2,3,4 &10

Channel 17 Black Journal advertisements overpowering Black woman myth

5 (Feb 3rd) Sexism & Racism Adrienne
Albert Memmi The Colonizer and the Colonized
Marlene Dixon "The Secondary Social Status of Women: Class and Caste Applied to Women's Position" - handout
Jo-Ann Gardiner "The Face Across the Breakfast Table" - handout
Myrdal The American Dilemma, Appendix 5: "A Parallel to the Negro Problem" _handout
Spock spoof - handout

Suggested:
Caroline Bird Born Female, Ch.6
Albert Memmi Dominated Man, Chs. 14 & 15
Interview "Different Strokes for Different Folks" - handout
Pauli Murray "The Liberation of Black Women" - handout
Helen Hacker "Women as a Minority Group" Social Forces, Vol.30, Oct, 1951
Everett C. Hughes "Social Change and Status Protest: An Essay on the Marginal Man" Phylon, Vol X, 1949

6 (Feb.10th) The Image of Woman in the Media Marlene Fran
FM, Chs. 2 & 9
✓ Donna Keck "The Art of Maiming Women" -Handout
Todd Gitlin "Fourteen Notes on Television and the Media" - handout
Jo-Ann Gardner "Sesame Street & Sex-Role Stereotypes" - handout

Any T.V. or radio programme, movies, newspapers, magazines (especially women's magazines), advertising, etc.

→ read

7 (Feb. 17th) Women in the Economy Diane Sprague
Ellen Willis "'Consumerism' and Women" 2Y, p.72
Joan Jordon The Place of American Women: the economic exploitation of women
Margaret Benston The Political Economy of Women's Liberation - handout
M. & J. Rowntree More on the Political Economy of Women's Liberation - handout
Kathy McAfee & Myrna Wood Bread and Roses
Karen Sacks "Social Bases for Sexual Equality" SIP, p.455

Suggested:
Martin Nicolaus "The Contemporary Relevance of Marx" - handout
Elinor Langer "The Women of the Telephone Company" - handout

8 (Feb 24th) Women and the Family Barb Wanamaker & Sandy Schwallie
Frederick Engels The Origins of the Family, Private Property and the State
Beverly Jones "The Dynamics of Marriage and Motherhood", SIP, p.46
Laurel Limpus The Liberation of Women, Sexual Repression and the Family
Pat Mainardi "The Politics of Housework", SIP, p.447
Roxanne Dunbar "Female Liberation as the Basis for Social Revolution" SIP, p.477

Suggested:
Peggy Morton "A Woman's Work is Never Done" Lev, p.32
Aeschylus Eumenides

9 (Mar 3rd) Child Care and Communes Shirley

Vicki Breitbart "Day Care, Who Cares?" Lev, p.26
L. Gross & P. MacEwan "On Day Care" - handout
Leslie Y. & Karen Rabkin "Kibbutz Children" - handout
Other articles will be assigned.

Suggested:
Bruno Bettelheim Children of the Dream

10 (Mar 10th) Women Internationally Shirley Fran & Marlene

"The Status of Women in Sweden" Report to the United Nations, 1968 - handout
Charlotte Bonny Cohen "Experiment in Freedom: Women of China" SIP, p.385
Chris Camarano "On Cuban Women" Lev, p.39

Other articles to be assigned.

in the midst of this political ferment and against the institutional backdrop of at best indifference and at worst open hostility.

Like the University of Wisconsin course that Joan Robinson described, Jaggar's course did not operate in isolation. On the one hand, many of the students were active in the community or extracurricular political activities. Some students belonged to the local women's liberation group, which included students and community members; some met outside the class as a consciousness-raising group; some helped create free university courses as part of International Women's Day; and others volunteered to speak with other groups on campus and in the community about women's liberation. On the other hand, within the university itself, students could find other courses from which they could draw knowledge of use to them politically, whatever the intentions of the particular professor. To the extent that there was flexibility in course requirements, students could develop projects for regularly offered courses that focused on women's issues. On an individual basis, in other words, students could do what they have always done: they could appropriate the available course materials for their own interests.

The creation of women's studies courses took what students and faculty were doing extracurricularly or in isolated fashion within the curriculum and provided collective and concentrated space for feminist work. Because students were coming with a fair amount of interest and prior knowledge, it made perfect sense for a class to be designed to take advantage of that energy and knowledge. Although Jaggar's course focused intensely on the course readings rather than on students' sharing their personal experiences, this was not a traditional, knowledge-delivery or -transmission model course. Instead, students had responsibility for organizing and presenting course materials. Jaggar had designed the syllabus, but the students were expected to draw from an extensive list of recommended materials to augment assigned readings—and they could bring their experiences outside the classroom to bear on their readings.

Likely the first of its kind in the United States, this philosophy course was ambitious in providing a broad overview of women's rights (Jaggar and Bordo, *Gender/Body/Knowledge* 361). The course addressed questions of female nature, sexuality, class and ethnic differences among women, the interconnections between sexism and racism, media images of women, women in the economy, women and the family, child care and communes, and women internationally. No overarching theory was imposed on the disparate materials; rather, students were expected to negotiate competing perspectives. They were expected to read Betty Friedan's *Feminine Mystique*, Robin Morgan's

Sisterhood is Powerful, Toni Cade Bambara's *Black Woman,* Albert Memmi's *Colonizer and the Colonized,* and Frederick Engels's *Origin of the Family, Private Property, and the State,* as well as selections from feminist journals, pamphlets, and reprints. Copies of such feminist periodicals as *Everywoman, off our backs, It Ain't Me Babe,* and *Woman* were available for students to consult through the philosophy department. For each class meeting, handouts and suggested readings extended the discursive range. Required readings on female nature, for example, included a New England Free Press reprint of Evelyn Reed's "Myth of Women's Inferiority" taken from a 1954 issue of *The Fourth International* (later to be *The International Socialist Review*); Naomi Weisstein's "Kinder, Kuche, Kirche," first delivered at an American studies conference and later reprinted in *Sisterhood is Powerful;* a mimeographed copy of Sandra and Daryl Bem's "Training the Woman to Know her Place: The Power of a Nonconscious Ideology"; and other handouts with titles such as "Sex, the Liberal Ethic and the Zoological Perspective in the Social Sciences" and "Woman's Will to Fail." Students were encouraged to read Margaret Mead's *Sex and Temperament in Three Primitive Societies,* Erik Erikson's "Inner and Outer Space: Reflections on Womanhood," and Dee Ann Pappas's "On Being Natural." For a class on sexism and racism, Albert Memmi joined Marlene Dixon, Gunnar Myrdal, Jo-Ann Gardiner, and Pauli Murray. Frederick Engels was to be read alongside Beverly Jones, Roxanne Dunbar, and Sophocles. Enriqueta Longauex y Vasques rubbed shoulders with Aeschylus, Simone de Beauvoir, and Virginia Woolf.

Cultural studies curricula in the eighties may have made more common such anticanonical groupings, but in 1971 courses such as Jaggar's were remarkable in challenging intellectual hierarchies by refusing to privilege one kind of text or source of materials over another. As with feminist newspapers and journals, early courses in women's studies were intent not only on uncovering knowledge about women that had been ignored or neglected but also on critically evaluating dominant perspectives and making room for the production of new knowledge. But there was considerable risk involved in challenging traditional systems of legitimation. Courses needed to be approved so that students could receive credit and teachers could get paid. Feminist academics had to demonstrate that they could do the work the academy valued even as they were challenging the structures of valuation. For programs to remain viable, they had to measure up to traditional scholarly expectations. Thus, by 1975 the University of Maryland faculty proposing a women's studies program felt the need to address questions of legitimacy in part by pointing out the willingness of respectable academic journals to publish articles relevant to women's studies, including "many journals (e.g., *Trans-action, Journal of Marriage and the Family, American Journal of Sociology, Student Lawyer*) [that] devoted whole issues to women's topics" (University of Maryland 186). Thanks to what they identify as a "women's studies movement," new journals "devoted solely to women's studies issues, such as *Women's Studies: An Interdisciplinary Journal*," were appearing (186). The Women's Studies Committee at the Bloomington campus of Indiana University offered a list not only of "leading journals" that devoted special issues to research on women but also of newly established journals in various disciplines that published current work in women's studies (Bunnell 196). As feminist academics sought approval from their institutions for courses and programs, they had to demonstrate that women's studies was an intellectually and scholarly enterprise, with prominent scholars and legitimate journals. Questions of value and legitimacy are of course always political, but in the case of women's studies (as with black studies), in which scholarship challenged the status quo, faculty work could be labeled as "too political" and thus in the terms of the academy, ipso facto insufficiently academic. Feminist academics thus risked (and sometimes lost) their jobs by making their feminism visible.

Given these circumstances, I cannot argue that seeking institutional legitimation for women's studies was inevitably some sort of political sell-out, or that the radicalism of the women's university-without-walls was inevitably thwarted when it moved inside the academy's walls. Greater legitimacy for the emerging field was needed to gain the power necessary to influence who was admitted into universities, who taught courses, and how courses were taught. The fact that legitimation continues to be an issue speaks to the considerable inertial resistance to change characteristic of universities.[22] Seeking legitimation did require, however, acts of forgetting in the very process of distinguishing recognizable academic knowledge production from the print production of the women's movement. Forgetting no doubt enabled the proliferation of programs and the generation of a considerable body of feminist scholarship, but it also made it more likely that parts of the story of midcentury feminism would drop from view, that some of the participants would disappear from the story, and that feminism would be disciplined if not wholly domesticated. Ironically, forgetting also necessitated the current critique of midcentury feminism, in the sense of noticing absences, both ideological and bodily. The problem as I see it comes when academic feminism's omissions are treated as reflecting actual absences within the larger women's movement at midcentury. Paying closer attention to how some of the early courses depended on a commerce of ideas between the academy and the "outside" makes visible not only the potential in such commerce for transforming academic business as usual but also the extent to which the academy worked to stabilize and regularize the cacophony of knowledges from the decentralized social movement "outside."

Contexts for Transformative Pedagogy

> "What we don't know we must learn; what we do know, we should teach each other." Women in Chicago are learning to tell a distributor from a carburetor, the clitoris from the vulva, good healthy food for survival from the plastic, often poisonous variety being sold off the shelves in supermarkets. Women are learning—and relearning—the theories of Marxism from a feminist perspective, how to get a divorce without a lawyer, how we can move with freedom and joy—together. And we're learning why we never learned any or all of these things in the course of our lives.
>
> —Chicago Liberation School for Women, *New Woman's Survival Catalog*

> Women's courses are the rarities in that they, unlike most other university courses, evidence real involvement of community people. Women came with their babies plumped on their backs, with toddlers clutching their mothers' hands. Some came from integrating neighborhoods, from working with clients all day long, or from overworked typewriters.
>
> —Joan Roberts, "A Multi-faceted Approach to a Women's Studies Course"

The women's university-without-walls arose in part out of the belief that available institutions and structures could not or would not meet the needs of a diversity of women. Some sense of what propelled women to create alternatives to the university with walls can be gained from a 1971 Modern Language Association study of 595 academic departments. The study found that women were

69% of all seniors planning graduate study in foreign languages
65% of all seniors planning graduate study in English
55% of all graduate students in modern languages
55% of the M.A.'s who received degrees in the last five years
31% of the PhD's who received degrees in the last five years
33% of the faculty full-time appointments
32% of full-time assistant professors
28% of full-time associate professors
18% of full-time professors

18% of faculty members teaching at least one graduate course
10% of faculty members teaching graduate studies in Masters' programs
8% of faculty teaching in departments with PhD programs. (Chmaj 136)

Similarly, in a review of some thirty studies conducted between 1969 and 1972 on the status of women in fourteen academic disciplines (including English), Laura Morlock concluded that women were more likely than men "to receive initial appointments at lower ranks or in nonrank positions," and they were more likely to be promoted and receive tenure at a later age, "if at all." Further, women were "less involved in administration or in decisionmaking at either the departmental or national professional association level" (299). She accounts for "some portion of these differences" by noting that women were less likely to have completed their doctoral degrees and were "more heavily involved in teaching responsibilities to the exclusion of research" and thus were less likely to publish at the same rate as men (299). She concludes, however, that even controlling for such variables, men were more likely to occupy higher ranks and command higher salaries (299). Women had been let in the front door, but once in, they were less likely than men to thrive. The relatively few women faculty who did survive appeared to be the product of "abnormal criteria of excellence" designed "to limit artificially the number of qualified people with access to the profession" (DuPlessis et al., "Columbia" 32).

Reacting against these artificial limits, some midcentury feminists turned away from the academy altogether to create alternative spaces in which to educate themselves, as women had done in earlier periods of American history.[23] According to Lauren Kessler, many women felt that "only through separate organizations could they be assured an outlet for their ideas" (74). No one kind of counterinstitution could do the work, as earlier chapters suggest. Women's clinics developed courses on women and health care because, as a Madison, Wisconsin, group put it, "We have not learned enough about our bodies, and often what we have been taught has not been true" (Grimstad and Rennie 125). The Sojourner Truth School for Women in Washington, D.C., was created to provide a place where professional and nonprofessional women could share skills and knowledge, because "women have long been denied recognition of the importance of what they are capable of doing [and have become] dependent on authority figures, be they car mechanics, plumbers, professors, or realtors" (125). Some feminist counterinstitutions arose in part because consciousness raising alone was not enough. As the organizers of the free school Breakaway explain, they began as a group of individuals within the San Francisco women's movement "who wanted to take their learning about themselves, their oppression as women, and women's history, further than the small consciousness-raising group would allow." Because most of the Breakaway women had "been through the oppressive environment of male-dominated schools or colleges," they had no interest in "getting entangled in a women's studies program in a conventional campus setting." They wanted the "freedom to innovate . . . outside established institutions," and that meant breaking away not only from "sexist education" but also from "the orthodox modes of learning which have alienated so many women from conventional institutions—intellectual one-upping, ego-tripping, teacher/pupil dichotomies, smart/dumb labels" (Grimstad and Rennie 123).

Women's centers, YWCA- and YMCA-sponsored workshops, and women's liberation schools offered a range of courses and attempted to accommodate the needs of a diverse constituency. Basic home repair, self-health, women and the law, lesbianism, women in Indochina, creative writing, the works of Chairman Mao, female mythology, women in prison and on parole, white feminism and racism, car repair, nonsexist child rearing, job hunting, and the image of women in literature—all were among the courses offered in alternative spaces across the country. Some groups provided child care and transportation, and all tried to involve participants in the running of the organizations, from recruiting new members into the collectives to helping teach classes. Akin to labor colleges in the earlier part of the twentieth century, these alternative schools sought to integrate education into the lives of the participants and to provide, as the Breakaway group puts it, "a warm, supportive atmosphere to share experiences and knowledge" (Grimstad and Rennie 123; see also Kates).

As earlier chapters suggest, central to the women's university-without-walls was the idea that women needed to educate themselves and, equally important, that they have the intellectual capacity to do so. Women were learning how to ask questions, to develop lines of inquiry, to critically evaluate different sources of knowledge, and to share their findings with others. They were deciding what was useful knowledge—not only what was analytically powerful, or what helped make sense of women's roles in the current social world and across time, but also what could produce change in women's real, material lives. Thus, akin to earlier progressivist movements, the women's university-without-walls emphasized learning by doing, with the expectation that theories would arise in dialectical relation to action. Ideally, as one worked to remake the world, one would necessarily improvise requisite knowledges from the materials at hand; through practice one would further refine available knowledge, and that increased store of refined knowledge would further enable transformative, revolutionary work. Although feminist publications occasionally register frustration with "incorrect thinking," far more of the print production registers a worry that feminist knowledge would calcify into dogma, and thus readers are frequently urged to treat knowledge as provisional, as open to critique and revision.

But what happened when pedagogies that were developed through a process of self-directed learning, and knowledges that were intended not as revered texts but as intellectual and political compost, found their way into the context of the academy? While there were, no doubt, some who thought the academy would be revolutionized through the importation of radical practices and knowledges from the outside, still others understood that the disciplining function of academic bureaucracies would resist any wholesale challenge. If change was going to happen, women and sympathetic men would need to work on multiple fronts, increasing the numbers of women faculty, creating innovative and flexible courses and programs, creating structures to encourage women to pursue careers in higher education, and developing equitable systems to ensure that women students could compete academically in all fields. They would, in short, have to change the academic context so that radical methodologies and contents would provide more than temporary breathing space. The paradoxical challenge was to transform the processes of higher learning without simply replacing one static bureaucratic structure with another.

If change came in part because activist women sought academic careers, as participants in the Conference on Teaching Strategies for Radical Change optimistically hoped, another essential factor was the pressure that came from students themselves. It was not unusual for students to begin the process of change by proposing independent study projects, petitioning departments to offer courses, convening caucuses within particular disciplines, or holding public meetings to raise awareness (Bjorkland 181). Once begun, the success of early courses and programs depended in part on the willingness of students to take responsibility for their own learning and, most important, to act as if they were in a space of relative freedom where self-directed learning was not only possible but necessary. In many cases, because students had a greater familiarity with feminist writings than did some faculty, mutual learning was almost an inevitability (Roberts 88). Although the university was not voluntarist of course in the same sense as, for example, the Boston

Women's Health Collective, faculty and students nonetheless tried to organize themselves in as nonhierarchical and democratic a way as possible in order to recognize (rather than create) the crucial involvement of students (Bunnell 202). Courses depended on a critical mass of students having a more than ordinary stake in the work and a commitment to ensuring that the classes would succeed. One might say, in this sense, that Alison Jaggar's course worked in part because students sought out such a course and took responsibility for its materials for more than credentialing, careerist, or grading purposes.[24] Whether students collaborated with faculty to create courses, to develop bibliographies, to organize panels and conferences, or simply to read and think seriously together about the course materials, they had to sort through competing discourses and to work without a ready-made map of the intellectual terrain. Such conditions of freshness and newness, as well as a relative parity between students and faculty in terms of feminist knowledge, were difficult to sustain. That subsequent cohorts of students would experience feminism as already critiqued is thus not surprising (Rosga and Satterthwaite 469). Later students could be made to feel belated to the extent that the multiple beginnings of midcentury feminism were consolidated into a single originary moment that necessarily excluded those who "weren't there" or did not fit the limited profile of women presumed to constitute the movement. Progressively more of the knowledge that students and teachers brought to the table would seem "secondhand" and about someone else. No rehearsal of what had been situationally effective pedagogies could recuperate the increasingly mythologized origin.

After teaching an early women's studies course, Mildred Munday was surprised to find that "education, in the best sense of that much-abused word, can happen in a community cohesive in its mutual respect and concern and its active curiosity about sex-determined myth and reality" (73). What strikes me in Munday's reflections is that it was not some distinctly feminist pedagogy per se—it was not methodology or content, in other words—that made such a course work; rather, it was the desire and intellectual commitment of students and teacher that propelled the learning experience. Munday refers not to a community of like-minded or like-bodied individuals but to a community that coheres, remarkably I would say, out of mutual respect, concern, and curiosity. The challenge for women's studies courses, it would seem, was how to make space for and build from a coalition of students and teachers that was in many ways the result of historical accident rather than pedagogical design, to build in such a way that some presumed originary and defining moment could not hold canonical sway.

Ironically, I would argue, it is a lack of historical knowledge that allows the perpetuation of too narrow a notion of origin. Just as "second-wave" women had to learn more about the differences among the "first wave" of suffragists so that they were neither in thrall to that past nor too quick to dismiss what women had actually achieved, so, too, current feminism may need to engage in a more complex reading of the sixties and early seventies to order to see in earlier feminists' pedagogical practices inside and outside the academy an improvisatory alertness that allowed them to seize the opportunities afforded by so much intellectual and political energy. For those early courses to work—and they did not always work—teachers had to be willing to work with students' energy and their knowledge, to match the students' curiosity, their willingness to inquire broadly and generously, and they had to tune in to the differences that students brought with them. That did not mean that teachers had to sacrifice their own expertise or bestow power upon students: both are versions of feminist pedagogy that circulate now, but neither is desirable or in fact possible. To pretend that one can hand students power is to fail to understand the workings of power. Rather, feminist teachers at their best worked to share their earned expertise with students in part because students sought out the expertise. At the same time, students had to push beyond mere enthusiasm in order to challenge the institutions to make room for women's work and to challenge themselves to develop greater expertise and authority through writing, reading, and dialogue. Because (as Beverly Tanenhaus puts it) participants had to value the collective work and the collective's time (6), improvisatory pedagogy was demanding on all participants, requiring planning, intense intellectual labor, and an openness to revise not only one's thinking but oneself.

It is clear that academic feminists—faculty and students together—did in fact forge new spaces within the academy where women could re-create themselves in Adrienne Rich's terms. They were able to import into the academy both radical methodologies and radical contents from the women's university-without-walls, and they used the borrowed practices and materials to revise (rather than revolutionize) the educational context. Feminism helped to fuel a larger (and ongoing) critique of objectivist epistemologies and, perhaps more than other intellectual movements of the time, made room for a diversity of literacy practices that worked against traditional scholarly hierarchies. A range of print materials used as texts for the new courses worked to legitimize nontraditional, noncanonical sources of knowledge and simultaneously to challenge traditional knowledge-producing monopolies. What such materials lacked in theoretical or ideological consistency they made up for in requiring that readers exercise a high degree of critical and intellectual autonomy. I do not find that there was a privileging of personal, experiential writing over analytical modes. Nor do I find that more traditional academic modes were the only forms assigned students. Rather, a range of forms of writing made clear that how one used language shaped what one could know, inviting a linguistic self-consciousness that exploded into a still-ongoing critique of the politics of language. Because the early women's studies courses were permeable to the outside, there was commerce between the kinds of literacies women exercised within the university and the kinds of literacies they engaged in as part of their activism in the larger community. Writing a herstory of the women's movement for a women's studies class could lead to an outline for a free university class that might generate a public document—a flyer, a pamphlet, a letter to the editor—and that might lead in turn to a skit performed in the local women's center or YWCA. Readings on health care might lead to a petition to improve health care for women on campus, and that in turn might lead to the creation of a local women's self-health center. The materials generated outside might then return to the classroom, adding resources for future classes. Perhaps most strikingly, because women's studies was not yet a recognized discipline—it was still frontier—it was in no position to impose discipline either in terms of ideology or literacy. And for a brief time, a generative because unruly literacy flourished.

Appendix: 1972 New York State Women's Political Caucus List of Conveners

CONVENERS

ORGANIZING CONFERENCE OF THE NEW YORK STATE WOMEN'S POLITICAL CAUCUS
(organizational affiliation for identification purposes only)

Bella Abzug	National Policy Council, U. S. Congresswoman (D.NY) National Woman's Political Caucus
Joyce Chaikin Ahrens	Women's Rights and Political Action, Chairwoman Ripon Society, Committee
Shana Alexander	National Policy Council, NWPC: Vice President, Norton Simon Communications, Inc., Journalist
Evelina Antonetty	National Policy Council, NWPC, Council Against Poverty
Eleanor G. Bailey	Manhattan-Bronx Postal Union
Nancy Banning	"Women: A Political Force", Conference Coordinator
Virginia Baron	Church Women United, Citizens Action
Carol Bellamy	Brooklyn Women's Political Caucus, Attorney
Laurie Beers	National Youth Caucus, Co-Chairwoman
Wyoma Best	Former City School Board Commissioner, Rochester
Amalia Betanzos	N. Y. City Commissioner of Housing Relocation
Carol Harp-Biernacki	Journalist
Peggy Billings	United Methodist Church, Board of Missions
Denise Bouche	Committee Against the A.B.M.
Karen Burstein	Nassau Law Services; Former Congressional Candidate
Virginia Cairns	Interstate Association of Commissions on the Status of Women, Executive Secretary
Sally Catlin	Young Women's Christian Association, National Board
Jacqueline Ceballos	National Organization for Women (N.O.W.), Eastern Regional Director
Cathy Chance	Coalition of 100 Black Women, Inc., Co-Chairwoman
Shirley Chisholm	National Policy Council, U. S. Congresswoman (D.Kings) National Women's Political Caucus
Cindy Cisler	Abortion repeal activist
Nola Claire	National Organization for Women, Central New York
Felicia Clark	N. Y. S. Educational Development, Coordinator Urban Development Corp.
Tess Cohen	B'nai B'rith Women Public Affairs
Constance Cook	N. Y. State Assemblywoman (R. Ithaca)
Margaret Cox	Democratic District #71 (N.Y.C.), Leader
Dorothy Crouch	National Organization for Women, New York Chapter, President
Mathilda Miller Cuneo	New York Women's Bar Association, President Former Assistant Corporation Council of the City of N.Y.
Evelyn Cunningham	N. Y. State Women's Unit, Director, Office of the Governor
Irene Davall	Chelsea Committee for Family Planning
Evelyn Davis	Coalition of 100 Black Women, Inc., Co-Chairwoman
Karen DeCrow	Former Candidate for Mayor, Syracuse
Kathy DeFieore	Monroe County Y Reps., President
Irma Diamond	National Organization for Women, Bronx Chapter
Peggi Drum	American Association of University Women Business and Professional Women
Etheline Dubin	Neighborhood Action Program, Better Government Democratic Association, Day Care Committee

The organizational affiliations are shown as provided by the Organizing Conference of the New York State Women's Political Caucus. This list of conveners reproduces the form and content of the original four-page list distributed at the first New York State Women's Political Caucus. I have not edited or annotated the list in an effort to preserve as much as possible the quality of the original source.

Nancy Dubner	Monroe County Women's Political Caucus, President Democratic State Committeewoman (132 A.D.)
Ronnie Eldridge	National Campaign Coordinator of Major Presidential Candidate; Former Special Assistant to Mayor
Bea Epstein	Planned Parenthood, National Board
Julie Everitt	Rochester Journal, Editor
Brenda Feigen Fasteau	National Policy Council, NWPC
Jill Ferguson	Women's Caucus, SUNY (New Paltz)
Ronnie Feit	National Policy Council, NWPC
Marguerite J. Fisher	N. Y. State Business and Professional Women's Clubs, Past President; Syracuse University, Professor
Camilla Flemming	Young Women's Christian Association, National Board(YW(
Muriel Fox	National Organization for Women, National Chairwoman
Eleanor Clark French	N. Y. City Commission on Human Rights, Member Former N. Y. City Commissioner to U. N.
Betty Friedan	National Policy Council, NWPC; Founder of N. O. W.; Author
Betty Furness	N. Y. State Department of Consumer Affairs, Former Director
Jane Glassbrook	Former Democratic Executive Committeewoman (Brighton)
Judith Glazer	SUNY at Purchase, Coordinator of Special Projects
Ilene Goldman	Consumer Action Now (C.A.N.), Co-Chairwoman
Lois Gray	N. Y. State School of Industrial and Labor Relations (Cornell University) Metropolitan Director
Carol Greitzer	N. Y. City Councilwoman
Elinor Guggenheimer	National Policy Council, NWPC; Founder and Honorary President, Day Care Council
Barbara Gelobter	Leader Democratic District #67
Elizabeth Hardwick	"New York Review of Books", Advisory Editor, Literary Critic
Ann Hansen	Assistant to the City Manager (Rochester)
Rita Hauser	Prominent Republican, Attorney
Carol Haussamen	Haussamen Foundation, President(Instant Housing Rehabilitation Project)
Dorothy Height	National Policy Council, NWPC National Council of Negro Women, President
Sherrye Henry	WCBS "Woman!"
Elizabeth Holtzman	Democratic State Committeewoman, District #44 (Kings)
Phyllis Holzer	N. Y. State Campaign of a Major Presidential Candidate, Executive Director
Julia Rodriguez Huertas	East Harlem Community Corporation
Dorothy Pitman Hughes	Committee for Community Control Child Care
Elizabeth Janeway	Trustee of Barnard College, Author
Jonni Jones	Lower Eastside Service Center, Board of Directors
Sarah Kovner	Democratic District Leader #65; New Democratic Coalition, Vice Chairwoman
Geri Kenyon	Former Candidate for Sheriff, Onondaga County
Mary Ann Krupsak	N. Y. State Assemblywoman (D. Montgomery)
Linda Lamel	National Organization for Women, Long Island Chapter, President; American Federation of Teachers, AFL-CIO
Jane Bagley Lehman	ARCA Foundation, President
Ruth J. Levine	Sheepshead Bay Task Force, E.D.A.
Esther Levitt	Distributive Workers Union Vice President

Bonnie Lobell	N. Y. New Democratic Coalition, Former Executive Director
Marilyn Marcosson	Women's Political Caucus, Queens County, Chairwoman
Alice Tepper Marlin	Council on Economic Priorities, Executive Director
Dorothy McHugh	Republican National Committeewoman
Tanya Melich	National Board Ripon Society, Member, Political Writer
Ruth Meyers	Women's Political Caucus, Manhattan, Coordinating Committee; Women's Strike for Peace
Gloria W. Milliken	Presidents Council of the School of Education N.Y.U.
Joan Monroe	Political Scientist and Teacher
Emily Moore	Sociologist and Demographer
Bess Myerson	Consumer Affairs, Commissioner (N.Y.C.)
Cornelia A. Netter	N. Y. State Office of Planning Services
Eleanor Holmes Norton	N. Y. City Commissioner of Human Rights Executive Assistant to the Mayor
Lee Oliver	Women's Political Caucus, Inc., New York County, Chairwoman
Dorothy Orr	N. Y. State Human Rights Commission, Member
Jan Peterson	National Polish Community Development Council; Williamsburg Greenpoint Comprehensive Health Planning Board, Co-Chairwoman; Education Action Center, Director
Corine Petty	Leader Democratic District #67A
Helen Power	State of New York Regent, Rochester
Sylvia F. Pines	Pulse of Women (POW); Hofstra University, Professor
Letty Cottin Pogrebin	"Ladies' Home Journal", Columnist, Author
Yolanda Quitman	Pulse of Women (POW), Founder
Lola Redford	Consumer Action Now (C.A.N.), Co-Chairwoman
Lillian Reiner	Liberal Party (Onondaga County), Chairwoman
Mary Ella Reutershan	N. Y. State Legislative Chairwoman, American Association of University Women
Mildred Pafundi Rosen	State Labor Board, Commissioner
Esseye Ross	Nassau County Women's Bar Association; Former Committeewoman, Republican Party; Board of Directors, Nassau Business and Professional Women's Clubs
Lucille Rose	Salvation Army; Deputy Commissioner; Chairwoman, Advisory Board Bedford Corporation; Manpower and Development Agency (N.Y.C.)
Beulah Sanders	National Policy Council, NWPC; National Welfare Rights Organization
Jane Small Sanford	League of Women Voters, Treasurer (Capitol District Peace Center)
Mary Sansone	Congress of Italian-American Organizations (CIAO), Executive Director
Irma Santaella	National Caucus of Spanish-Speaking Women, Chairwoman; N. Y. City Human Rights Commission, Member
Doris Sassower	Professional Women's Caucus, Special Consultant; Women's Rights Lawyer
Eleanore Schnurr	American Baptist Convention Division of Christian Social Concern
Phyllis M. Silber	National Federation of Temple Sisterhoods, President, District #3

Althea Simmons	National Association for the Advancement of Colored People (NAACP), Secretary for Training
Gloria Steinem	National Policy Council, NWPC; "MS. Magazine", Editor
Catharine R. Stimpson	Barnard Women's Center, Acting Director
Ellen S. Straus	WMCA "Call For Action", Chairwoman
Carol Stumer	NWPC, State Liaison, Research and Public Contacts
Geraldine Stutz	Henri Bendel, President
Amy Swerdlow	Women's Strike For Peace; "Memo", Editor
Carole Ann Taylor	National Policy Council, NWPC; Women's Unit, Office of the Governor
Judy Tobias	N. Y. State Council on Continuing Education
Beverly Barr Vaughan	Susan B. Anthony Republican Club, Rochester, Vice President
Clara E. Wade	Bedford-Stuyvesant Neighborhood Council; Black Caucus Delegate; Board of Directors Model Cities Site #36
Flo Wade	National Organization for Women, Rochester Chapter
Joanne Ward, S. C.	Leadership Conference of Women Religious
Jeanette Washington	Welfare Rights Organizer
Grace White	League of Women Voters, Spring Valley

Notes

Preface

1. I owe this formulation to a conversation with my colleague Steven Leo Carr.

2. In this construction I am drawing on the work of the Personal Narratives Group as well as Linda Brodkey's concept of autoethnography. Any speaking "I" is necessarily partial, but autoethnography is concerned with the multiple affiliations that compose the speaking subject. My identity is multiple and shifting. The "I" is never fully captured by a single designation, although at any given moment a single designation may operate to offer some semblance of stability. Autoethnography, in recognizing the multiplicity of the "I," works against unitary narratives. It does "not attempt to replace one version of history with another, but tr[ies] instead to make an official history accountable to differences among people that communitarian narratives typically ignore" (Brodkey 28). In its multiply valenced specificity, autoethnography works to raise questions about master narratives, not to typify, but to interrupt generalizations through particularity. *Autoethnography, autobiographics, autography,* and *personal criticism* are all terms used to designate work that focuses on local and specific histories, challenging master narratives and at the same time problematizing the status of the subject, the "self" (see also Gilmore; McDonald; Perreault).

3. VISTA (Volunteers in Service to America) was intended to function as a domestic Peace Corps.

4. The underground press coverage tended to be dismissive, failing to acknowledge the range of positions and the remarkable group of women assembled for the New York State Women's Political Caucus. A 1973 issue of *Big Mama Rag* is fairly typical: it reported that the NWPC that year was a "dull affair... strong armed by a presiding officer and a parliamentarian" ("Women's Political" 9). See also an earlier editorial in *Woman's World* that charges the NWPC with "spreading the lie that 'there are no such things as women's issues" (Sarachild, "Women and the Elections" 11).

Introduction

I take the title of the chapter from a passage in Howard Zinn's *People's History of the United States:* "Could women liberating themselves, children freeing themselves, men and women beginning to understand one another, find the source of their common oppression outside rather than in one another? Perhaps then they could create nuggets of strength in their own relationships, millions of pockets of insurrection. . . . And together, instead of at odds—male, female, parents, children—they could undertake the changing of society itself" (504).

1. The Derridean critique of such privileging is by now familiar, of course. But the critique is also a reminder of how deeply ingrained in Western thought is the notion that the spoken word is primary, more real than the written. One might say that it was not the spoken word that was radical but women interacting with other women and valuing their ideas.

2. Consciousness raising has come to stand for feminist pedagogy in a number of accounts. MacKinnon, for example, defines feminism as "the theory of women's point of view" and "consciousness raising" as "its quintessential expression" (qtd. in Kenway and Modra 156), but as will be discussed more fully in later chapters, the term applies to a variety of practices, and it was not the only pedagogy articulated or practiced by second-wave feminists.

3. I read hooks's signature choice to drop the definite article before "women's movement" as a way to emphasize women in motion, doing rather than simply belonging to an organization.

4. One might add "along sexual orientation lines as well," but hooks at this point does not mention this axis of difference. I don't want to minimize the fact that middle- and upper-class white women constituted the majority of participants in the women's movement, just as they constituted the majority of women in the larger population (see hooks, *Ain't I a Woman,* 148–149). Some white women in the movement continue to be unapologetic about the need for a white women's movement distinct from the civil rights and antiwar movements and independent of leftist political theorizing. In her recent memoir, Susan Brownmiller quotes Anne Koedt as saying that it was "thrilling" to be "cleanly feminist": "We didn't feel we had to apologize all the time when the leftists talked about Vietnamese women or black women or poor women" (33). In my reading of the movement literature, however, I found many women among all identity groupings who were deeply worried or profoundly angry about race, class, and sexual blindness. I am thus interested in following hooks's suggestion that there was in the early movement a potential radicalism that was all too quickly undermined (*Ain't I a Woman* 188). I have found that when I look beyond the most prominent women and pause a bit longer on what the heterogeneous rank and file were doing, such radicalism is more vividly evident.

5. Echols notes that "the one thing that feminists could peddle were their ideas, and as a consequence, women writers were especially mistrusted," because they

were perceived as selling out to the system. Indeed, "media women" were sometimes "vilified" ("Radical Feminist" 220–23).

6. As Pamela Kearon commented, "It is not for any well-educated woman to declare that education is unnecessary or undesirable. It is essential for all women to be politically educated" (qtd. in Echols, "Radical Feminist" 148).

7. In Toni Cade Bambara's preface to her 1970 anthology *Black Woman*, there is, in the midst of a celebration of a distinctly black women's university-without-walls, a passing sentence that traces the origins of the works anthologized in the collection to "an impatience with the half-hearted go-along attempts of Black women caught up in the white women's liberation groups around the country" (10). Citing a Louis Harris–Virginia Slims poll conducted in 1972, bell hooks notes that "sixty-two percent of black women supported efforts to change woman's status in society compared to forty-five percent of white women, and that sixty-seven percent of black women were sympathetic to women's liberation groups compared with only thirty-five percent of white women" (*Ain't I a Woman* 148). Although women might well have supported feminist efforts without participating actively in the movement, hooks nonetheless goes on to discuss those black women who did participate in "women's groups, lectures and meetings" (149). She argues that "as concerned black and white individuals tried to stress the importance to the women's movement of confronting and changing racist attitudes because sentiments threatened to undermine the movement, they met with resistance from those white women who saw feminism solely as a vehicle to enhance their own individual, opportunistic ends" (150). The emergence of separate black feminist groups, in hooks' analysis, was not an entirely positive occurrence to the extent that it allowed white women to ignore the interconnectedness of race and gender as categories of oppression.

8. DuPlessis and Snitow see a very brief moment of solidarity early on that then "exploded into a mass movement" made up of "all kinds of protagonists with their multiple identities, allegiances, and needs complicat[ing] the assumption that there was one universal identity for all women" (8). While there were clearly calls for solidarity, I have found very little evidence of a general assumption that solidarity was ever achieved and quite a bit of evidence from the outset that solidarity did not mean that women were all the same.

9. Important and useful book-length studies have been written about the women's movement, but they have tended to concentrate on the large-scale political workings of second-wave feminism or the lives of women prominent in the movement. Alice Echols's *Daring to Be Bad*, Sara Evans's *Personal Politics*, and Jo Freeman's *Politics of Women's Liberation* have had considerable influence in shaping understanding of the women's movement from the perspective of sociopolitical history. Recent memoirs include Susan Brownmiller's *In Our Time*. Both the large-scale histories and the memoirs tend to reinforce the common view that women in the movement were turning away from traditional sources of knowledge and learning to rely more on experience as a basis for knowing. An important exception is Rachel Blau DuPlessis and Ann Snitow's especially rich collection *The Feminist Memoir Project*.

10. Histories of the development of women's studies and accounts of the history of intellectual women remind us that women were engaged on a remarkable scale with educational reform and remind us too that heady interpersonal encounters among women did not preclude active involvement in print. See, for example, Jane Roland Martin's *Coming of Age in Academe,* Marilyn Jacoby Boxer's *When Women Ask the Questions,* Sheila Tobias's *Faces of Feminism,* and the concluding chapter of Barbara Miller Solomon's *In the Company of Educated Women.* While the best of this work acknowledges the extent to which academic women were drawing on knowledges and practices generated outside the university, no study thus far explores lay pedagogies and lay literacies as a vital part of the women's movement.

11. Kathleen Weiler suggests that "if the consciousness of all individuals in society is, as Gramsci says, 'strangely composite,' it is clear that the ideological development of personality is the result of learning and experiences in all sorts of settings—the family, church, school, work, informal associations" (15). But because it is often presumed that the primary force in the creation of intellectuals is "the formal apparatus for the transmission of ideology—that is through the schools" (Weiler 15), the importance of informal settings too often has been ignored.

12. Lisa Hogeland argues that feminism is a kind of literacy, by which she means a "way of reading both texts and everyday life from a particular stance" (1). She contends that the "importance that many feminists accorded literary endeavors derived from an overinvestment in literacy, from the belief that literacy was feminism, rather than its precondition" (1). While Hogeland's approach enables her useful analysis of the feminist consciousness-raising novel, I want to distinguish the material practices that women engaged in to produce, distribute, and make use of print, from a theory of interpretation—from, that is, feminism as a way of reading.

13. As Terry Anderson has noticed, most studies of sixties' activism draw almost exclusively on the establishment press as a primary source of information and too rarely use print sources produced by activists themselves ("New American Revolution" 201). This oversight allows for a relatively easy dismissal of different "phases" of feminism. So, for example, Frances Bartkowski can compare "contemporary feminist theory" with "early feminist texts" to argue that more recent theory treats the question of power in "much more subtle" ways (55). In an endnote she contends that the first phase of feminist studies "might best be represented by... *Sisterhood is Powerful*... and *Voices from Women's Liberation*" (57n10). Alice Echols's work is a striking exception in its much more detailed attention not only to the materials produced but the contexts in which such materials circulated. Otherwise useful exceptions, such as James Sullivan's *On the Walls and in the Streets,* pay insufficient attention to the women's movement. Janet Lyon's *Manifestoes* includes only a brief reference to two documents produced by radical feminists in the sixties and seventies. M. Bahati Kuumba's *Gender and Social Movements,* while providing a useful international perspective, nonetheless cannot, given its scope, deal in any detail with a single movement such as midcentury radical feminism in the United States.

14. Jessie Bernard introduces Maren Carden's 1974 study, *The New Feminist Movement*, with the observation that she did not think movement women would cooperate with such a study because they did not want themselves defined by outsiders (ix). Carden herself comments that "active social movements in general cannot be studied by conventional social-scientific methods. The women's movement in particular is too fluid and its members too hostile to the impersonal approaches of highly quantitative sociology, which they feel loses sight of the total picture" (178). Given the largely negative, trivializing mainstream media coverage especially in the early days of the movement, it is not surprising that women were wary of talking with outsiders. Further, I recall a real fear that any social movement was vulnerable to government infiltration and that to talk to outsiders was to weaken movement defenses. There has been enough evidence of such government involvement in various movement groups at the time to be wary of dismissing such fears as paranoia.

15. The Women's History Research Center was begun in 1968 by Laura X, who maintained the collection in her small house, depending on donations and eventually federal grant money ("Women's History Research Center" 140–41).

16. I have found Rachel Blau DuPlessis's articulation of "social philology" especially congenial for my purposes here. She defines social philology as a "method—itself poised febrilely between the social and the aesthetic—[that] would want to seek precisely the way poetic forms (and not simply the statements in poetry) become sources of knowledge, the way poems become acts of cognition" (*Genders* 14).

17. Professor Jaggar suggested in personal correspondence that the course was probably the first of its kind (see also the contributors note in Jaggar and Bordo, *Gender/Body/Knowledge* 295).

Chapter 1. Going Public with Pandora's Box

1. The interaction of technological change and social change is not insignificant: the widespread availability of mimeo machines, the development of Thermo-Fax copying, and the relative ease of operating offset printing equipment made publishing relatively inexpensive and accessible for novices (see McDermott 38–39nn5, 18). Robert McClaughlin contends that "the underground press . . . , consisting of little more than a typewriter and a mimeograph machine, provided outlets for the political and artistic expressions of thousands whose subject matter, stylistic innovations, youth, gender, or ethnic background would have been a basis for rejection by commercial publishers" (183).

2. This phrase draws on John Guillory's contention in *Cultural Capital* that women are not represented in older literatures because, "with few exceptions before the eighteenth century, women were routinely excluded from *access to literacy*, or were proscribed from composition or publication in genres considered to be serious rather than ephemeral" (15).

3. While some women were in the process of rediscovering an earlier suffragist

press, those periodicals were not the primary influence on second-wave publications because the material history of that earlier phase of women's publishing, the practical legacy, was not readily available (see Hole and Levine 10). There were also some contemporary periodicals that, while not devoted exclusively to feminism, nonetheless addressed feminist concerns. *The Jeannette Rankin Brigade Newsletter* (1968), *Memo* (1962), and *Cassandra* (1967) had each linked feminism to the peace movement, and *The Ladder* (1957–1972), produced by the Daughters of Bilitis, was a groundbreaking lesbian magazine that after 1970 identified itself as lesbian/feminist. For a brief insider's account of *The Ladder*'s evolution, see Gene Damon's essay "The Least of These."

4. Terry Anderson notes that movement news became so popular that underground news services were established—such as the Liberation News Service and the Underground Press Syndicate—with some three hundred underground papers subscribing by 1968 ("New American Revolution" 193).

5. Susan Brownmiller recalls an "easy takeover" in which the "*Rat* men walked out" and simply "gave [the women] the paper" (76).

6. Although Jo Freeman, who helped found one of the earliest publications, *Voice of the Women's Liberation Movement* (1968), overstates—with a fair dose of sprezzatura—the ease with which women took what they had learned, she nonetheless registers the extent to which women's liberation periodicals recognized their indebtedness to the underground press: "What took the black and student movements so long to get off the ground was all that time spent figuring out how to communicate nationally. They had decided early on against using the mass media, and it was a long time before a network of underground papers emerged. But by 1967–8, when women began organizing for themselves, putting out newspapers and knowing where to distribute them was second nature" (qtd. in Hole and Levine 270). In 1964 there were only 4 underground newspapers, but by 1968 there were 150, with an estimated combined circulation of between 1 and 2 million (270n6). It should also be noted that while activists expressed considerable wariness about mainstream media, they nonetheless staged events to attract media coverage.

7. McDermott notes that feminist periodicals, like the underground press more generally, "rejected the use of copyright" (22). But the approach to copyright was less uniform than that. While some periodicals made no mention of copyright expectations, *Notes* ran a copyright warning on its editorial page, as did *Women: A Journal of Liberation.* Some of the periodicals included copyright symbols on individual poems or articles (see *Moving Out* 2, no. 1). Similarly, the January 1971 issue of *Mother Lode* informed its readers that if they wanted to reprint Judy Syfers's "Why I Want a Wife"—a piece that also appeared in *Notes from the Third Year* (1971)—they should contact Syfers about copyright (2).

8. "Usually such periodicals are written by a small collective of six to twelve people whose views, as they themselves declare, do not necessarily correspond to those of other local movement members" (Carden 178). What I interpret as a necessary caution

on the part of editorial collectives, their unwillingness to speak in
reads as a sign that the collectives were not representative and
unimportant to the women's movement.

9. See David Nord's "Reading the Newspaper" and "Religious
in Antebellum America" for careful discussions of the difficu
readers do with newspapers and books.

10. Certain articles and news items appeared in movement periodicals across the country, distributed without the benefit of a feminist wire service. Carden cites the instance of the October 1972 newsletter from the North Shore Massachusetts Feminists, which reported that in September some women from the Los Angeles Women's Liberation Self-Help Clinic had been arrested for practicing medicine without a license (69). The same news item appeared, with follow-up stories, in Denver's *Big Mama Rag* and Iowa City's *Ain't I a Woman.* By connecting women across geographic boundaries, movement periodicals showed that what happened to women in one part of the country could happen anywhere in the country, that women were connected by virtue of gender (and as periodicals looked globally, it was possible to see global patterns of sexism). Acts of repression or discrimination were thus treated not as isolated instances of individual or local error but as part of a system that needed to be changed and was being changed in part by spreading the word in print.

11. Adrienne Rich references *For Her Own Good: 150 Years of the Experts' Advice to Women,* Ehrenreich and English's extension of their pamphlets, in her influential essay "Compulsory Heterosexuality." While Rich praises the book as "devastatingly informative" and "written with such lucid feminist wit," she also expresses deep disappointment that the authors never address "basic proscriptions against lesbianism" (29).

12. Most periodicals devoted sections to the recuperation of women's history. *Big Mama Rag* was fairly typical in running "Write Women Back into History," a column that appeared from the inaugural edition through much of the paper's existence. Periodicals included stories about individual women, such as Emma Goldman, or about specific eras, such as the Industrial Revolution in nineteenth-century England, not only in forms addressed to adult readers but also in ones intended for children, such as the multipart pull-out book on the life of Elizabeth Blackwell, the "first woman in modern times" to get her medical diploma (Heyn 33). The editorial groups understood their role in helping not only to re-create a forgotten past but also to create a record of history in the making, a record of women's revolutionary efforts in the present, so that women would not forget, would not in the future have to start again from scratch (as midcentury women felt they had to do). The *Notes from the Second Year* editors predict that their journal will itself become part of the historical record, "functioning politically much as did [Elizabeth Cady] Stanton and [Susan B.] Anthony's *Revolution* exactly a century ago" (Firestone and Koedt 2).

13. As chapter 3 will show, feminist poetry was not confined in subject matter or

orm to what might have been considered traditionally poetic. The special issue of *Moving Out* on health care includes several poems dealing in some way with women's health. Marian Alvin's "Fertility Man" is a narrative about a Dr. Trythall, who "loved" his patients, whom he called "My girls!" so much that he "sometimes, often, got them pregnant— / with the help of certain interested parties" (26). In Mary Jo Oleszek's lyric "The Science in Me," the speaker imagines herself first a molecule within a cluster of molecules, then a splitting atom, and then a paramecium to reflect on the random interconnectedness of existence.

14. Because the newsprint booklet sold so well—and as a way to keep the successful product out of the hands of a "capitalist publisher"—the New England Free Press reduced the price from thirty-five to thirty cents and expected to reduce it further (undated New England Free Press flyer). In May 1973 *oob* reviewed the first commercially published edition of *Our Bodies, Ourselves,* reporting that the new edition had sold 75,000 copies in the first three weeks (Hobbs 29). The *New York Times* recently reported that by 1997 *Our Bodies, Ourselves* had sold more than 4 million copies in fifteen languages (Rimer 27). The title changed slightly, from *Our Bodies Ourselves,* with no punctuation, to the title with a comma added.

15. In the *oob* review of the commercially published edition of *Our Bodies, Ourselves,* Chris Hobbs criticizes the Boston Women's Health Collective's decision to choose Simon and Schuster over the New England Free Press, which had published the earlier editions. While Hobbs can appreciate the desire for wider distribution, she argues that had they stayed with the New England Free Press, "a women's distribution system would have been developed, a resource would have been created that other women's publications could and would have used" (29). Hobbs is also less enthusiastic about editorial changes in terms of language and political analysis: "The new edition is less angry and contains fewer mentions of 'capitalism,' 'imperialism,' 'revolution,' and 'male chauvinism.'" The text was made more polite by changing *pee* to *urinate* and *communal fucking* to *communal lovemaking* (29). The strong heterosexist bias is also noted, with the exception of one chapter, "In AmeriKa they Call Us Dykes," written by the Boston Gay Collective (29).

16. Feminist periodicals reproduced information and images from a number of health guides. The spring 1972 issue of *Mother Lode,* for example, cites a Berkeley Women's Health Collective "fact sheet" and informational materials from the Los Angeles Self-Help Clinic for features on women's care. In 1975 *Big Mama Rag* praised *Circle One: A Woman's Beginning Guide to Self Health and Sexuality* as "44 pages of feeling and fact," noting that the guide extended *Our Bodies Our Selves* ("Circle One" 10).

17. A feminist paper published by "women in San Francisco's Women's Liberation," *Mother Lode* first appeared in January 1971 as a single sheet with the motto "We are sisters in experience." Produced by the Mother Lode Collective and typeset by Amazon Graphics, the paper draws explicitly on the experiences of the members of the collective.

18. Kathleen Jones offers a useful contemporary gloss on the question Kearon raised some thirty years earlier: "The standard analysis of authority in modern Western political theory begins with its definition as a set of rules," and these rules "generally have excluded females and values associated with the feminine. This seems to be an unexceptional observation.... But what if we argue that the very definition of authority as a set of practices designed to institutionalize social hierarchies lies at the root of the separation of women qua women from the process of 'authorizing'?" (119–20).

19. Newsletters were more likely to be produced by a single member of a local women's liberation group (or other local organization, such as a clinic) on behalf of the group and yet represented or sought to represent a collective perspective.

Chapter 2. Virtue Sallies Forth and Sees Her Adversary

The chapter title is a play on Milton's assertion from *Areopagitica* that he "cannot praise a fugitive and cloistered virtue, unexercised and unbreathed, that never sallies out and sees her adversary, but slinks out of the race where that immortal garland is to be run for, not without dust and heat" (728).

1. For a helpful introduction to the idea of ethos as positionality or location, see Nedra Reynolds's "Ethos as Location." See also Michelle Baillif's critical reading of the emphasis on this notion of ethos in writing pedagogy.

2. In a similar characterization, LaCapra suggests that historians have neglected rhetorical readings in part because of what he calls "one of the most fateful turns in the teaching of rhetoric," the move from a "pedagogy of emulation of exempla (poems, parodies, satires, and so forth) to a codification of terminology and principles" (42).

3. I read Sheila Tobias's *Faces of Feminism* as such a defense. Tobias argues that "feminist theory provided the energy, vision and rationale for feminist politics and was in turn deepened, elaborated, and sometimes complicated by the new scholarship on women" (203). I am less convinced that either theory or scholarship drove the movement. It might be more useful to think in terms of a reciprocating process between women's lived, material experiences and the articulation of systems of explanation, something akin to what historians of science have argued to be the relationship between scientific theory and invention, for example.

4. Whitacre points out how in the early Christian church, *polemic* referred to texts that addressed conflicts within a relatively small group. The writer of the Gospel attributed to John, for example, addressed Christianized Jews who had not yet been expelled from the Temple rather than people who had no association with Christianity. Similarly, post-Reformation controversialist writers for the most part were taking on fellow Protestants who differed over points of practice and discipline within a broad Calvinist consensus, and they concerned themselves with Catholics primarily as a way to name-call, to charge other Protestants with looking suspiciously like Papists.

5. In her cogent analysis, hooks observes that too often those in the women's movement "assumed that identifying oneself as oppressed freed one from being an oppressor" and that to a "very great extent such thinking prevented white feminists from understanding and overcoming their own sexist-racist attitudes toward black women" (*Ain't I a Woman* 9). Further, she argues: "Had feminists chosen to make explicit comparisons between the status of white women and that of black people, or more specifically the status of black women and white women, it would have been more than obvious that the two groups do not share an identical oppression. It would have been obvious that similarities between the status of women under patriarchy and that of any slave or colonized person do not necessarily exist in a society that is both racially and sexually imperialistic" (140–41). Contemporary criticism of the comparison is evident in Linda La Rue's 1970 essay "The Black Movement and Women's Liberation," originally published in the *Black Scholar* (repr. in Guy-Sheftall, *Words of Fire* 164–73). Florynce Kennedy had earlier made the case for understanding racism and sexism as linked, using language that seems to anticipate that of white feminists (see "A Comparative Study: Accentuating the Similarities of the Societal Position of Women and Negroes"). Kennedy's argument suggests that the comparison did not have to hinge on reductiveness.

6. In "Lesbianism and Feminism," a 1971 essay reprinted in *Notes from the Third Year,* Anne Koedt cautions against too utopian a view of same-sex relationships when she argues that there is nothing necessarily radical about homosexuality if the relationship simply parrots oppressive heterosexual relationships (85).

7. Alice Echols acknowledges that "from the early days of the movement there were black women like Florynce Kennedy, Frances Beale [*sic*], Cellestine Ware, and Patricia Robinson who tried to show the connections between racism and male dominance." But she stresses that "most politically active black women, even if they criticized the black movement for sexism, chose not to become involved in the feminist struggle." She dates "efforts to generate a black feminist movement" to 1973 with the founding of the short-lived National Black Feminist Organization," an effort she calls "less than successful" (*Daring* 291). Toni Cade Bambara's anthology alone would serve to put pressure on Echols's assumptions. See also Kristin Anderson-Bricker's and Benita Roth's important essays in Kimberly Springer's edited collection *Still Lifting, Still Climbing.*

8. For a more recent critique of this thesis, see Angela Davis's "Facing Our Common Foe" (26).

9. In fact, criticism of the report came from men prominent in the civil rights movement, including Floyd McKissick, director of the Congress on Racial Equality, who argued that Moynihan was imposing his sense of middle-class values on everyone in America (Sandel 325).

10. The anthology had begun as a special, enormously popular March–April 1969 issue of *MOTIVE,* a magazine published by the Board of Education of the United Methodist Church. The magazine issue, however, included no articles by black women, so to "fill in the gap," the editors asked Frances Beal to submit an essay.

11. In reading Ware's comment, I am reminded of Angela Davis's observation that "all too often—historically as well as at present—white leaders of the women's movement presume that when Black women raise our voices about the triple oppression we suffer, our message is at best of marginal relevance to their experience" (17).

12. Beal cites statistics from the Women's Bureau of the U.S. Department of Labor for 1967 showing a comparative wage scale (in median annual wages): "White Males: $6, 704; Non-White Males: 4, 277; White Females 3, 991; Non-White Females 2, 861" (50). These data, however, omit employment rates. Median annual wage rates are based on census data for those who are employed year-round, full-time. The wage inequities are significant, of course, but do not by themselves speak to an economic system that works to keep a greater proportion of black women and children in poverty. Marlene Dixon cites a similar set of wage data from 1960 in the pamphlet "Why Women's Liberation," but she adds to this information data showing how a higher percentage of black women were in the workforce. For example, "in 1960, 44 per cent of black married women with children under six years were in the labor force, in contrast to 29 per cent of white women" (62). Not only were black women paid less than their male counterparts in the workforce, but they did not have the luxury of staying home to raise their children. Unfortunately, neither Beal nor Dixon discusses unemployment rates among black men, information necessary if one is to get a purchase on the economic circumstances of the black family. These rates of employment in relation to median wage might also cast critical light on the controversy over the notion of a "black matriarchy" discussed earlier.

13. In an interview first published in *The Black Scholar* and later reprinted in *Woman's World,* Kathleen Cleaver identified one of the basic problems of the women's liberation movement as its dependence on other movements, "controlled and directed by men," to provide ideological direction (20).

14. Benita Roth raises an important issue about the "numbers game." She argues that the question of when black feminism emerged is conflated with how many black feminists were participating in white women's organizations (72). If the midcentury resurgence of feminist activism is in fact the "story of feminisms," Roth argues, then we should not be hunting for the presence of black women in white women's organizations but looking for how different groups of women articulated differing conceptions of feminism (70). bell hooks cites a 1972 Louis Harris–Virginia Slims poll revealing that "sixty-two percent of black women supported efforts to change woman's status in society as compared to forty-five percent of white women, and that sixty-seven percent of black women were sympathetic to women's liberation groups compared with only thirty-five percent of white women" (*Ain't I a Woman* 148). This sort of statistic supports Roth's sense that accounts of midcentury feminism have been looking too narrowly and that they necessarily find a white women's movement because they are attending only to white women's writing.

15. One might hear echoes of Abraham Maslow's theory of self-actualization in this. The intersection of humanistic psychology and the more inward-directed expressions of women's liberation is worth noting.

16. David Colburn and George E. Pozzetta suggest that Fanon and Malcolm X were especially important in the development of SNCC workers' thinking in the midsixties (122). Kenneth Cmiel traces the rhetoric of violence among some black activists to Fanon's *Wretched of the Earth* (273).

Chapter 3. That Train Full of Poetry

1. Beverly Tanenhaus quotes Lorde's poem in *To Know Each Other and Be Known* (31–32), an account of the women's writing workshops she organized at Hartwick College in Oneonta, New York, that I will discuss more fully in chapter 5. Lorde had been a guest speaker at the workshop in 1976 and 1977. The poem, "Power," was published in *Between Our Selves* (1975). Tanenhaus recalls that although workshop participants "gloried in [their] insight, [they] also discussed the difference between propaganda and art in order to avoid the forced ideology that can swamp the best-intentioned efforts." They were thus "unwilling to confuse politically correct rhetoric with eloquence or to record as awesome events mere bandwagon miracles" (30).

2. Sullivan borrows from Michel de Certeau when he reflects on the functioning of poetry outside "the hierarchy of proper access": "those who have acquired a competency in the approved interpretive practices (literature professors, scriptural exegetes, attorneys, and so on) have access to the form of that information considered most legitimate, while there is a danger that the untrained reader may draw extravagant inferences. Those extravagant inferences (misreadings, readings against the grain), constructed outside the structures of institutional control, ordinarily lie outside the realm of institutional notice, other than to be excluded or corrected. But undertrained, heresy-prone readers are constantly constructing their own readings out of . . . texts . . . by using their own, uncertified frames of reference" (3–4). While Certeau is interested in how audiences work against the grain to make unauthorized, creative use of texts, working against established institutions and practices through what he calls "poaching," Sullivan wants to extend the idea to consider what happens when readers are *invited* to make free, unfettered use of a text in the sense that he understands poetry broadsides to function. See also Robert McLaughlin's overview of alternative publishing in the United States, "Oppositional Aesthetics/Oppositional Ideologies."

3. The Redstockings Women's Liberation Archives for Action catalogue gives the date for this untitled folio pamphlet as October 1968 (see "Redstockings Classics of 1968" at <www.afn.org/~redstock/classics.html>).

4. Sor Juana Inés de la Cruz's poem was reprinted from a special Chicana issue of *Regeneración.*

5. Sullivan's is an especially useful study of the material workings of poetry broadsides in the sixties, but given its focus, it includes relatively little feminist poetry.

6. At the heart of Whitehead's very useful study are six poets—Judy Grahn, June Jordan, Gloria Anzaldúa, Irena Klepfisz, Joy Harjo, and Minnie Bruce Pratt—for

whom there exists not only an identifiable corpus of poetry but also prose reflections by the poets on the purpose and craft of poetry. As Cary Nelson has argued, such attention to the work of particular poets is necessary and important, but we also need to attend to the "collective enterprise of progressive poetry," and that can mean working without much knowledge of the writers, without either biography or a body of work from which to discern patterns, purposes or influences (*Revolutionary Memory* 6).

7. For recent and useful studies of a longer history of poet-activists, see Rachel Blau DuPlessis's *Genders, Races, and Religious Cultures in Modern American Poetry, 1908–1934* and Cary Nelson's *Revolutionary Memory.* In discussing the history of poets' participation in twentieth-century American social-political movements, Clausen mentions the Harlem Renaissance; Muriel Rukeyser's involvement in left movements from the thirties; Gwendolyn Brooks, Nikki Giovanni, and Sonia Sanchez within the Black Power movement; Denise Levertov's antiwar activism; Alice Walker's civil rights activism; and Robin Morgan and Marge Piercy's "roots in and disillusionment with the New Left" (9).

8. Kim Whitehead offers a very useful discussion of "antiestablishment movements of the 1950s—the Black Mountain poets, the Beats, the San Francisco Renaissance, and the New York School—all of which had their roots in the post-World War II trend away from formalism and the attendant conviction that the poet should speak only through a mask" (4). She traces the emphasis among these various groups on "open form, the banishment of persona, and a new emphasis on poetry performance" and asserts that "women throughout the movement—some who had substantial training, many who had none—found this emphasis on open form exhilarating" (4, 8). While there is some evidence that the poets appearing in the feminist periodicals had some familiarity with some aspects of these movements—the poem "later, ferlinghetti" is the most obvious and literal evidence, but one can see "open form" enacted in myriad ways—my sense is that the influence of the literary avant-garde, at least early on in the movement, tended to be more indirect, filtered through particular poems rather than through a conscious embrace of a well-articulated aesthetic. For a useful review of the literature on the difficulties in using the term *avant-garde* as distinct from modernism more generally, see Patricia Sullivan.

9. Organic form was not, of course, a new idea or one unique to feminist poetry. Rather, Levertov and Rukeyser were contributing to a larger modernist rethinking of the concept, carrying forward from romanticism an emphasis on dynamic processes rather than a reified object and on the interconnectedness of elements rather than the isolation of disconnected parts.

10. Jan Clausen has identified Fran Winant's *We Are All Lesbians* (Violet Press, 1973) as the first lesbian poetry anthology (15). What constitutes the "first" of anything is of course difficult to determine—much depends on how one defines the terms—but *Dykes for an Amerikan Revolution* seems to have proceeded Winant's collection by two years. I have found no copy of *Dykes for an Amerikan Revolution,* however.

11. This poem appears in Lonidier's small (six-by-six-inch) pamphlet of poems *The Female Freeway,* published by the Tenth Muse Press in 1970. Although she does not specify which poems, she notes on the verso to the title page that several appeared in *Artesian, Cohosh Dance, The Ladder, Make Love Not War,* and Hugh Fox's *Anthology of Contemporary American Poetry.* This is a wonderfully startling collection of poems and an especially good example of the small-press, inexpensive pamphlets that made feminist poetry available to a wide readership. See the posthumous collection *The Rhyme of the Ag-ed Mariness* for biographical background on Lonidier.

12. Summerhill was founded in 1923 in England by A. S. Neill, who believed children should be allowed time to grow emotionally without fear or coercion from adults. The school, which still exists, was intended to give children the tools to gain power over their own lives and "to develop naturally" (see "Brief History of Summerhill"). Neill's writings circulated widely, inspiring the creation of alternative and open schools in the United States.

13. The same image, without attribution, appears in the August 1971 issue of *Woman's World,* accompanying an article entitled "Women Take Catholic Church to Court" (Lawrence 4). Lorraine Oller's print *Variation on a Theme* offers another version of female crucifixion, this time with two nude women hanging from crosses (58).

14. "I Am Waiting" was published in *A Coney Island of the Mind* (1958), a collection that went through seventeen printings by the early seventies. Ferlinghetti continued to revise the work through performances of the poem to jazz accompaniment (48).

15. In the one entry in Harvard's *Guide to Contemporary American Literature* that references Millay, Elizabeth Janeway characterizes her poetry in terms of its "emphasis on romantic love in a fairly familiar mode, which [in Millay's era] had [been] taken as prototypically feminine" (356). Janeway does not present this as the definitive word on Millay but offers it as a way to suggest what the next generation of women poets—specifically, Marianne Moore, Elizabeth Bishop, and Babette Deutsch—might have been reacting against. A college anthology circulating widely in the sixties includes quite a few of Millay's poems or excerpts from longer poems, but the selection would do little to put pressure on Janeway's characterization of Millay as rather old-fashioned and safely feminine (Sanders et al. pt. 2, pp. 297–305). The editor includes primarily what Nelson calls the "rhapsodically romantic Millay," poetry that does not seem to be in dialogue with the "antiromantic" ("Fate of Gender" 348). Nelson cites "I, Being Born a Woman and Distressed," "Oh, Oh, You Will be Sorry for that Word," and the sequence "Sonnets from an Ungrafted Tree" as examples of the antiromantic. In contrast to the mainline remembering and belittling of the romantic work (as Nelson puts it), Walter Lowenfels includes Millay's "Justice Denied in Massachusetts" in his 1969 anthology *The Writing on the Wall: 108 American Poems of Protest* as part of a collection of poems that serve as "evidence that we know how to be more than rocks" ("What Time Is It?" n.p.).

16. As Lisa Maria Hogeland points out, "Plath was invoked as the archetypal victim of patriarchy" and became a "staple of emergent feminist literary criticism" (15).

17. James Sullivan notes that when the work of a major writer with a well-known name appears on a broadside, the name can "become nearly as important as anything the actual text has to say" (22). There is something of that going on here, where it is assumed that Plath would be an ally, however much the words might complicate the particular deployment.

18. The poem first appeared in 1970 and was later reprinted in the Dayton Women's Liberation newsletter in 1974.

Chapter 4. Locusts in the Nation's Cornfields

1. Charlotte Canning offers a particularly useful reading of how theater groups attempted to achieve integration without sacrificing attention to real differences. Additionally, she makes clear that women of color were not standing around waiting for white women to figure out how to integrate but founded their own theater groups or created one-woman shows. Onyx Women's Theater in New York City, founded in 1973, and Las Cucurachas in San Francisco, formed in 1974 as a project of the Concilo de Mujeres, which organized "Raza women's activities," are two early groups (Canning 121). Lesbian theater groups also arose partly in reaction to what was perceived as the ongoing homophobia of straight theater groups. Some lesbian groups wanted the freedom to produce theater to entertain other lesbians rather than to forever carry the burden of educating straight audiences about lesbian and gay concerns (see Canning 116–20).

2. Participants used the term *research* to refer both to reading and to interviewing women, and in general the term connoted uncovering hitherto neglected sources of knowledge.

3. Some herstory plays emphasized acts of recovery and celebration, representing such women as Sojourner Truth, who had been absented from the cultural-historical stage (Leavitt 46). Other performances engaged in what Helene Keyssar calls "doing dangerous history": instead of simply recuperating women's history, such theater aimed at examining "the conditions under which gender conflicts have repeatedly arisen and repeatedly been resolved such that women have remained subordinate to men" and confronting "the illusions of the past, including those that conceal women's complicity in the recurrent subjugation of women to men" (Breslauer and Keyssar 173).

4. Rosemary Curb and her colleagues surveyed feminist theater groups for a 1979 issue of *Chrysalis.* While some of the earlier groups were no longer performing, the survey is nonetheless suggestive in showing that over half the groups operated as collectives and that two-thirds worked through collective improvisation ("Catalog Part II" 64).

5. Yolanda Broyles González, in tracing a history of Chicano theater, has shown that "intense audience participation is . . . a hallmark" of a form of Mexican popular theater—the *carpa,* or itinerant tent-show tradition—that carried over into the practices of El Teatro Campesino, which was affiliated with the farmworkers movement (210).

6. Alan Read offers a useful caution in his discussion of improvisation in lay theater. He found that "improvisation was challenging not only because it was not fixed and demanded an ability to listen and respond[;] it was also deemed to be something, ironically, that was institutionally sanctioned and often thought to be fey" (33–34). He suggests, however, that rapping and sampling demonstrate a "sophistication born from knowing that appropriation and repetition was not just the darling of the avant-garde" (33).

7. The Stanislavski approach to theater training "sought to replace a conscious, mechanical, and long-established tradition with a creative process in which conscious and subconscious absorption and sincerity blended to produce inspiration" (O'Neill 9). Improvisation was key to helping actors make greater use of their powers of observation and imagination, their ability to draw on sensory memory, and their adaptability.

8. *Notes from the Third Year* printed Joan Holden's *Independent Female,* identifying the San Francisco Mime Troupe as a "self-supporting collectively run theatre company whose aim is to make art serve the people." *The Independent Female* was the company's "first production to be written, directed, and designed by women. They toured the Midwest with the play in the winter of 1970–71" (Holden 120).

9. Susan Glaspell (1876–1948) is perhaps best known as the cofounder of the Provincetown Players and for her play *Trifles* (see Barbara Ozieblo's critical biography, *Susan Glaspell*). See also a review of a WAFT performance of Crothers's 1912 play *He and She* in the December 1973 issue of *off our backs.*

10. Dell'Olio makes a point of the long title to emphasize the importance of a feminist renaissance. At the same time she appreciates the way "Feminist Repertory and Experimental Theatre" forms the acronym "free," as she puts it (101). Most theater historians, however, refer to the group as the New Feminist Theatre (see, for example, Curb).

11. Other groups offered dramatic presentations of women's history, of course, though not always with a satiric edge. Jane Buchanan and Marisa Jeffrey, who had performed with Circle in the Square Theatre, for example, advertised a national theatrical tour of *Dawn of Freedom,* an enactment of women's struggle for equality "including moments in the life of Susan B. Anthony, the Grimke sisters, Sojourner Truth and many others" (33).

12. *PM3* lists the pamphlet's title as *Sweet 16 to Soggy 36,* but the hand-lettered cover leaves room for another interpretation. Is this "soggy 36" or "saggy 36"? The latter might better reflect youth-culture attitudes.

13. On the booklet's inside cover the group names the "MDS forum" as the gathering but offers no explanation of MDS (Bunch et al.). Susan Brownmiller recalls that Charlotte Bunch had moved to Cleveland in 1969 and had helped to create the Cleveland group. She did not remain long in Cleveland, however, but returned to Washington, D.C., where she helped found *The Furies,* a lesbian-feminist newspaper (174–75).

14. A 1970 *Ain't I a Woman* review describes a somewhat more elaborate skit put on by the Chicago Women's Liberation Union: "9 skits strung loosely together and

interspersed with three songs (by a small rock band), very sober walk-ons giving grim statistics, and three witches who would come in at the end of each skit something like a Greek chorus and give a curse or warning." The reviewer found the witches' lines to be a powerful element in the performance because they served as a kind of contract with the women characters who "were usually getting fucked over" ("Witching the A.M.A." 4).

15. This quotation from Aristotle appears in other movement publications, including an article written in 1969 and reprinted in *Notes from the Second Year* (1970). Bonnie Kreps cites the same passage as summing up "the traditional view of women" (98).

16. The Student Nonviolent Coordinating Committee (SNCC) was founded in 1960 by black students who had participated in the lunch-counter sit-ins across the South. They organized voter registration drives. In 1964 northern white students were brought down south as part of "Freedom Summer." Many of the women who participated in the Freedom Rides later went on to organize woman's liberation groups. Alice Echols offers a context for understanding Carmichael's comment; although his remark "came to symbolize Movement men's hostility to women's liberation," and although he "betrayed a terrible insensitivity to women's situation," Echols reports that at least some women who were present when he made the remark understood it as a "self-parodic joke that referred to the days of Freedom Summer when sexuality seemed irrepressible" (*Daring* 31). See also David Chalmers discussion of SNCC in *And the Crooked Places Made Straight.*

17. WITCH was founded in 1968 by Robin Morgan and Florika, who appreciated the Yippie (Youth International Party) approach to cultural confrontation. In that sense, WITCH was from the outset performance oriented as it planned "zap actions," which were designed primarily to attract attention. The outrageousness of the public demonstrations was understood as proportional to the outrageousness of the cultural practices they were intended to attack (Echols, *Daring* 76).

18. It has become commonplace to consider reading as itself a performance of a text in the sense that the reader enacts a reading that is other than a simple reproduction or resaying of the words on the page. While this idea is a useful corrective to the dominance of text-centered notions of meaning making, it does not sufficiently register the importance of the simultaneity of bodies in space that distinguishes live performance—even the relatively text-bound form of performance found in reader's theater—from the performance of a text in one's head as an individual reader.

19. Charlotte Bunch had contributed to *MOTIVE*'s special issue on women. See chapter 2 for more on the magazine and the issue.

20. I took part in the Pullman service, and the typescript copy of the plan of service is from my files.

Chapter 5. The Do-It-Yourself Classroom

1. In 1971 the U.S. Department of Health, Education, and Welfare issued a report on higher education that urged universities and colleges not only to offer courses

in female studies but to evaluate the overall curriculum in terms of its relevance to women (University of Maryland 187). The American Association of University Women argued for similar reform in 1973 (ibid. 187–88). The New University Conference was "an organization of radicals who work[ed] in, around, or in spite of colleges and universities" and were "committed to struggle politically to create a new, American form of socialism and to replace an educational and social system that is an instrument of class, sexual, and racial oppression with one that belongs to the people" (Howe and Lauter 49).

2. The Columbia Women's Liberation Group included Rachel DuPlessis, Linda Edwards, Ann Harris, Kate Millett, and Harriet Zellner. In addition to offering data detailing the ratio of women to men across academic ranks and in various academic units, the report reflects on the training of future teachers, in particular the willingness of graduate faculty to teach women but not to hire them.

3. Some women's liberation schools, such as Breakaway, a free school for women in the San Francisco area, quite explicitly defined themselves in opposition to traditional educational institutions, and some expressed their intentions to avoid entanglement with women's studies programs in conventional university settings. But some of the women who helped create the schools had left the academy, some women reentered the academy after working in these alternate spaces, and so the existence of such schools can be usefully read as helping to demarcate the distance between the academy and the "outside." The *New Woman's Survival Catalog* published in 1973 lists some fifteen different women's liberation schools that varied in purpose and relative proximity to the academy (Grimstad and Rennie 123–28). These schools deserve greater attention than I can give them here.

4. Marilyn Boxer has argued that "while practitioners of feminist pedagogy share no singular method of teaching, they do often focus on such themes as the role of the teacher as nurturer, the problem of exercising authority, and the importance of classroom dynamics, all reflecting the experience of consciousness raising, all germane to student 'empowerment'" (80). But even this formulation gives greater emphasis to the originary role of consciousness raising than I am inclined to do. The difficulty seems to be in reading back onto the early courses a consolidation of practices (and a narrative for accounting for or justifying those practices) that came later.

5. See Judith Sealander and Dorothy Smith's article "The Rise and Fall of Feminist Organizations in the 1970s: Dayton as a Case Study," in which they argue that although Dayton Women's Liberation and the Women's Center had disappeared by the eighties, the work begun in such organizations was continued through such mainstream organizations as the YWCA.

6. Jane Kenway and Helen Modra cite Catherine MacKinnon's formulation that "feminism . . . is the theory of women's point of view [and] consciousness raising is its quintessential expression" (156). In the last fifteen years a number of articles have appeared offering consciousness raising as a model for classroom practice. In collections such as Gabriel and Smithson's *Gender in the Classroom,* Morton and Zavarzadeh's *Texts for Change,* and Caywood and Overing's *Teaching Writing,* and in

journals such as *Feminist Teacher, College English,* and *College Composition and Communication,* various writers have defined feminist pedagogy in terms of collaboration, process, democracy, and empowerment, and they see consciousness raising as the distinctive educational invention forged out of the developing woman's movement of the late sixties and early seventies, particularly suitable for the classroom today.

7. Accounts of the origins of consciousness raising bear some resemblance to folk etymologies. I cannot trace the "origin" of the accounts of origins, but something like word of mouth seems to have been operating, so that at least one of these various origins is offered in most contemporary accounts without attribution, and most accounts make a point to disavow any connection to therapeutic strategies—the talking cure, encounter groups, sensitivity or theater gaming, and the like—that might smack of the self-indulgent, the scientific, or the government sponsored. Maren Carden says, for example, that one cannot date consciousness raising because the transition from political discussions to "bitch sessions" is not so clear-cut (64). She explains that "the consciousness raising group probably derived from the New Left's discussions of Chinese Communists' group criticisms and from the young radicals' encouragement of open, democratic, and non-hypocritical expression of feelings" (34). Jo Freeman offers a slight variation when she notes that the "technique evolved independently of, but is similar to, the Chinese revolutionary practice of "speaking bitterness" (*Politics* 166n24). "Speaking bitterness" is a process described by the anthropologist William Hinton in *Fanshen,* his 1966 study of a Chinese village (Polletta 161). As Collette Price puts it, consciousness raising was "not therapy, self-help, [or] a Dale Carnegie primer course" (11). But the similarity between consciousness raising and other influential approaches to group dynamics is worth noting. According to Martin Lakin, sensitivity training had its roots in an American faith in scientific (rational) solutions, a commitment to democratic processes, "a concern for developing good helping relationships," and a belief in the "perfectibility of... society." The procedure has been traced to Kurt Lewin's work with gestalt psychology, John Dewey's pragmatist philosophy, and Martin Buber's existentialist philosophy. Lewin influenced a group of American researchers interested in developing leadership capabilities among people participating in government-sponsored programs. Training workshops and labs were held in the late forties to both observe group interaction and create "change agents," exemplary individuals who recognized "the need for change, [and were] able to diagnose the problems involved,... could plan for change, implement... plans, and evaluate the results." Such change agents were thought to require an understanding of group dynamics. As sensitivity training developed, it adopted Dewey's "linking of thought with action, meaning with cooperation, and theory with practice." Dewey's faith in the capacity of the ordinary person to change his or her circumstances and his emphasis on the centrality of interpersonal relationships to a democracy were seen as compatible with the sensitivity-training movement. Similarly, Buber's emphasis on dialogue and interaction as defining of the human gave further credence to sensitivity-training practices (Lakin 7–11).

8. My interest here is in finding some critical and historically complex space be-

tween the two poles in contemporary discussions of consciousness raising: a reverential view on the one hand and a kind of shorthand caricature on the other. Eichhorn and her colleagues, for example, find it necessary to distinguish their practice as feminist teachers from "consciousness-raising groups of the women's movement in the early seventies"; that is, they are doing something other than "sharing for sharing's sake,...confessional,...[or] celebration of any and all narratives" (297). While no doubt many women can recall such experiences with consciousness raising, the practice was more complex than that, and theories of consciousness raising from the beginning resisted the seductive pull toward confessional modes.

9. Jo Freeman asserts that many activist women thought consciousness raising to be a "'crutch' that young women who did not know their own minds needed before they 'progressed' to political action." The fear was that many would never get beyond examination of their own minds and feelings in order to begin to address pressing public issues (*Politics* 85). Such fears were reinforced when consciousness raising was appropriated in ways similar to Kenneth Bruffee's reading in the epigraph to this subsection. Writing in 1973, Bruffee overlooks collectivist or disruptive aspects of consciousness raising by referring to it as a process of self-development. It is not sufficient to dismiss such appropriations, however, simply as misreadings. In theory the purpose of the technique was to teach political activism by first changing the participants' perceptions of themselves and the larger society (Freeman, *Politics* 116). But the seductiveness of testimonial (and the immediacy of personal lives) made it likely that many groups never moved beyond the individual or began to see the individual as part of and shaped by a collectivity.

10. The New York–based Sappho Collective notes that some groups "find it of great value to write down the *generalizations* (not testimony) that emerge from each meeting so that they might refer to them in the event they want to write group papers, do actions, and so on in relation to consciousness raising" (49).

11. Although Allen does not say this, one can imagine that bringing readings to the small group could be a way to address criticisms of the quality of analysis generated through consciousness raising. Colette Price complains, for example, about the "problem with the analysis stage," specifically with her sense that the analyses were "inaccurate," by which she seems to mean politically inconsistent with radical feminism (11). The New York Radical Feminists, with whom Allen had been affiliated, offered as part of their founding statement on "organizing principles" three stages that any group would need to go through in order to join as a "full brigade." In the first stage, after a minimum of three months of consciousness raising, each group would spend at least three months of reading and discussion in order to educate themselves about the "broad spectrum of politics already apparent in the women's liberation movement." They would then spend six weeks reading and discussing feminist history and theory to develop a sense of continuity with the feminist political tradition and to provide a strong foundation on which to build further analysis ("Organizing Principles" 120).

12. One could track this idea as it is elaborated later in feminist theory in notions of locatedness or positionality. For a specifically pedagogical turn, see Kathleen Weiler's *Women Teaching for Change.*

13. In Kathie Sarachild's formulation, for example, participants were expected to plan "zap actions" (forms of fundraising), "consciousness programs" (publications), and media events, but she does not say how women were to go about doing so, how they would move from talk to action ("A Program" 79). While women in the movement emphasized again and again the importance of a feminist political agenda, the challenge seems to have been to develop strategies for moving from the personal, from testifying, to action. The enormity of this challenge seems to have led many to stay at the level of the personal, as some seasoned activists had feared. Carol Williams Payne observed that consciousness raising was a good way to reach large numbers of women and to build their self-confidence, but it was useless without an action component (100). More recently, Kathleen Weiler found among teachers that change in ideology was not as powerfully transformative as "direct personal involvement in attempts to change society" (95).

14. In some groups, for example, each participant would receive tokens. Each token represented one opportunity to contribute to the conversation. When a participant ran out of tokens, she also ran out of opportunities to talk and thus had to fall silent.

15. While Lester Faigley cites Kenneth Bruffee to trace the connection between contemporary composition and feminism in terms of collaboration, it might be useful to consider how the kinds of strategies for teaching writing that Tanenhaus describes were shared by teachers of composition. One might see similar kinds of concerns in the work of Cy Knoblauch and Lil Brannon, for example.

16. Women's studies courses and programs developed rapidly in the early seventies. A ten-course women's studies program began at San Diego State College in the spring of 1970 (receiving final authorization the following spring). Cornell instituted a female studies program in the same year. In the following year a dozen more women's studies programs were organized. During the 1970–71 academic year, some one hundred or more colleges and universities offered at least one course about women (University of Maryland 185–86). For a useful overview of the development of women's studies "content," see Marilyn Jacoby Boxer's *When Women Ask the Questions.*

17. The Feminist Press also published a series called *Female Studies* that included course plans and materials.

18. Edi Bjorkland identifies three publications that came out of the Wisconsin project: Elsie Adams and Mary Louise Briscoe's anthology *Up Against the Wall, Mother,* Myra Sadkar and Nancy Frazier's *Sexism in School and Society,* and Peggy Silvestrini and Margaret Anderson's children's book *A Pirate I Be* (produced by Babylon Printing Cooperative, identified by Bjorkland as an underground people's press) (182).

19. Nascent women's studies courses were not alone in bringing together traditional academic sources with materials from the larger culture. While the New University Conference publication *The Radical Teacher* provides examples of relatively familiar

reading lists, the journal also includes a number of examples of courses that treat a broader range of cultural materials than would have been thought of as appropriate for the classroom. In "Some Notes Toward a Radical Course in Black Literature," for example, Michele Russell argues that to understand black writing "on its own merits," it has to be read as part of living culture: "Writing on the Wall. Our walls/temples of the people: johns, bus stations, prisons, projects. Graffitti. Where context is everything and the 'writer' is just someone who happens to write/right something. Cutting sides. Recording. Our presence here" (2). Robert Meredith describes a sophomore American studies course in which students were asked to compose cultural critiques "ostensibly about a common subject (contemporary religious belief, Norman Mailer, records and paintings, the new left, technological systems, diaries—any of these or any materials like them arranged in some meaningful order will do), but in fact, no matter what the subject, always about 'culture'" (6).

20. At the national level, New University Conference publications did consider feminist issues (see *Radical Teacher*).

21. Valerie Saiving identifies "feminist appropriation" as characteristic of feminist process. Borrowing from Alfred North Whitehead, she is interested in the "active, critical, and imaginative" process by which feminists respond to and use ideas circulating in the culture (14).

22. Edi Bjorkland quotes Mary Louise Briscoe on the difficulty of "achieving credibility in the academy" for women's studies courses and programs: "It doesn't take long to discover that the majority of your colleagues and administrators expect Women Studies to be short-lived; that many view it as the kind of artificial structure that destroys the traditions they thrive on; and that they view you, regardless of your qualifications, with a wry amusement for taking your 'professional' life out on so weak a limb. In short, they're afraid of what it might do to their vested interests so they minimize and ridicule its importance. If this description strikes you as cynical, try talking with a student, a faculty member, or an administrator at random about the seriousness of your intent, and see what happens. Nonetheless, we have, at least for a moment in history, a chance to make a difference" (178).

23. Much exciting work has been produced in the last several years that makes visible the ways women found to educate themselves outside established institutions, including Lilian Faderman's *To Believe in Women,* Anne Gere's *Intimate Practices,* Nan Johnson's *Gender and Rhetorical Space in American Life, 1866–1910,* Carol Mattingly's *Well-Tempered Women,* and Jacqueline Jones Royster's *Traces of the Stream.*

24. As the American Council on Education annual report on attitudes among American freshmen makes clear, these attitudes toward education were not unique to women but distinguish a greater portion of a generation of students than is evident now. Changes in the economy, the increased cost of higher education, and increasing political conservatism in the general population all affect student attitudes and expectations. But clearly part of the context that made it possible to offer such courses as Jaggar's was the investment students had in courses that spoke more directly to their political concerns. See Alexander Astin et al., *The American Freshman.*

Works Cited

Alexander, Sally. *Becoming a Woman: And Other Essays in 19th and 20th Century Feminist History.* New York: New York University Press, 1995.

Allen, Pamela. *Free Space: A Perspective on the Small Group in Women's Liberation.* New York: Times Change, 1970.

Alvin, Marian. "Fertility Man." *Moving Out* 2, no. 1 (1972): 26.

Anderson, Terry. "The New American Revolution: The Movement and Business." In *The Sixties: From Memory to History,* edited by David Farber, 175–205. Chapel Hill: University of North Carolina Press, 1994.

———. *The Sixties.* New York: Longman, 1999.

Anderson-Bricker, Kristen. " 'Triple Jeopardy': Black Women and the Growth of Feminist Consciousness in SNCC, 1964–1975." In *Still Lifting, Still Climbing: Contemporary African American Women's Activism,* edited by Kimberly Springer, 49–69. New York: New York University Press, 1999.

The 'Anti-Riot' Act. Chicago: Chicago Defense Fund, n.d.

Arditi, Benjamin, and Jeremy Valentine. *Polemicization: The Contingency of the Commonplace.* New York: New York University Press, 1999.

Astin, Alexander, et al. *The American Freshman: National Norms for Fall 1988.* Los Angeles: Higher Education Research Institute, 1988.

Atwood, Margaret. "Power Politics." *Dayton Women's Liberation* (Oct. 1974): 2.

Auleta, Betsy, and Bobbie Goldstone. "History—Heaven or Hell?" *off our backs* 1, no. 8 (July 10, 1970): 4.

Bailey, Beth. "Sexual Revolution(s)." In *The Sixties,* edited by David Farber, 235–62. Chapel Hill: University of North Carolina Press, 1994.

Baillif, Michelle. "Seducing Composition: A Challenge to Identity-Disclosing Pedagogies." *Rhetoric Review* 16 (1997): 76–91.

Baker, Houston, Jr. *Black Public Sphere.* Chicago: University of Chicago Press, 1995.

Bambara, Toni Cade, ed. *The Black Woman: An Anthology.* New York: Signet, 1970.

Bartkowski, Frances. "Epistemic Drift in Foucault." In *Feminism and Foucault: Reflections on Resistance,* edited by Irene Diamond and Lee Quinby, 43–58. Boston: Northeastern University Press, 1988.

Bateson, Mary Catherine. *Composing a Life.* New York: Plume, 1990.

Beal, Frances M. "Double Jeopardy: To Be Black and Female." *The New Woman: A MOTIVE Anthology,* edited by Joanne Cooke, Charlotte Bunch, and Robin Morgan, 44–57. New York: Bobbs-Merrill, 1970.

Belgrade, Sandy. "Woman in the Purple Shirt." *Big Mama Rag* 3, no. 2 (Aug. 1974): 4.

Berger, John. *Another Way of Telling.* New York: Vintage, 1995.

Bernard, Jessie. Foreword. Maren Lockwood Carden, *The New Feminist Movement,* ix-xv. New York: Sage, 1974.

Bissell, Judy. "Looking at Racism . . ." *Lilith: Women's Majority Union or the Order of the Lead Balloon.* 1 (Fall 1968): 1.

Bjorkland, Edi. "Report on Women's Studies in the University of Wisconsin System." In *Female Studies VIII,* edited by Sarah Schramm, 178–83. Pittsburgh, Pa.: KNOW, 1975.

Black Women's Liberation Group. "Dear Brothers." In *Sisterhood is Powerful,* edited by Robin Morgan, 360–61. New York: Vintage, 1970.

Blair, Hugh. *Lectures on Rhetoric and Belles Lettres.* Philadelphia: Hayes and Zell, 1854.

Blight, David. "Introduction: A Psalm of Freedom." Frederick Douglass, *Narrative of the Life of Frederick Douglass: An American Slave, Written by Himself,* 1–23. Boston: Bedford, 1993.

Bond, Jean Carey, and Patricia Peery. "Is the Black Male Castrated?" In *The Black Woman,* edited by Toni Cade Bambara, 113–18. New York: New American Library, 1970.

Bordo, Susan. "Feminism, Postmodernism, and Gender-Scepticism." In *Feminism/Postmodernism,* edited by Linda Nicholson, 133–56. New York: Routledge, 1990.

Boston Women's Health Book Collective. *The New Our Bodies, Ourselves: A Book by and for Women.* New York: Simon and Schuster, 1984.

———. *The New Our Bodies, Ourselves: A Book by and for Women.* 25th anniversary ed. New York: Simon and Schuster, 1992.

Boston Women's Health Course Collective. *Our Bodies Our Selves: A Course by and for Women.* Boston: New England Free Press, 1971.

Boxer, Marilyn Jacoby. *When Women Ask the Questions: Creating Women's Studies in America.* Baltimore, Md.: Johns Hopkins University Press, 1998.

Brauer, Liz. "Letters from Mother." *Ain't I a Woman* 1, no. 2 (July 10, 1970): 9.

Breslauer, Jan, and Helene Keyssar. "Making Magic Public: Megan Terry's Traveling Family Circus." In *Making a Spectacle,* edited by Lynda Hart, 169–80. Ann Arbor: University of Michigan Press, 1989.

"A Brief History of Summerhill." <http://www.s-hill.demon.co.uk/history.htem#summerhill>. Accessed June 6, 2003.

Brody, Michal, ed. *Are We There Yet? A Continuing History of Lavender Woman.* Iowa City: Aunt Lute, 1985.

Brodkey, Linda. Introduction to Part I. *Writing Permitted in Designated Areas Only,* 27–29. Minneapolis: University of Minnesota Press, 1996.

———, and Michelle Fine. "Presence of Mind in the Absence of Body." *Writing Permitted in Designated Areas Only,* 114–29. Minneapolis: University of Minnesota Press, 1996.

Bronstein, Lynn. "Cinemasculinity." *Women: Journal of Liberation* 2, no. 1 (Fall 1970): 27–30.

Brooks, Cleanth. *Modern Poetry and the Tradition.* Chapel Hill: University of North Carolina Press, 1939.

Brown, Connie, and Jane Seitz. "'You've Come a Long Way, Baby': Historical Perspectives." In *Sisterhood is Powerful,* edited by Robyn Morgan, 3–28. New York: Vintage, 1970.

Brown, Rita Mae. "Sappho's Reply (1970)." *Dayton Women's Liberation* (Oct. 1974): 2.

Brownmiller, Susan. *In Our Time: Memoir of a Revolution.* New York: Delta, 2000.

Bruffee, Kenneth. "Collaborative Learning: Some Practical Models." *College English* 34 (1972–3): 634–43.

Buchanan, Jane, and Marisa Jeffrey. "On Tour." *off our backs* 2, no. 2 (Oct. 1971): 33.

Bunch, Charlotte. "Feminism and Education: Not by Degrees." *Quest: A Feminist Quarterly* 5, no. 1 (1979): 7–18.

———, Barbara Toeppen, Julie Reinstein, Jane Adams, Carol McEldowney, and Sue Streeter. *Sweet 16 to Soggy 36: Saga of American Womanhood.* Cleveland, Ohio: Cleveland Radical Women's Group, 1969.

———, and Frances Doughty. "Charlotte Bunch on Women's Publishing." *Sinister Wisdom* 13 (1980): 71–77.

Bunnell, Rhoda, et al. "A Proposal for a Women's Studies Program: Indiana University-Bloomington." In *Female Studies VIII,* edited by Sarah Schramm, 195–203. Pittsburgh, Pa.: KNOW, 1975.

Burris, Barbara. "The Fourth World Manifesto." In *Notes from the Third Year: Women's Liberation,* edited by Shulamith Firestone and Anne Koedt, 102–19. New York: Notes, 1971.

Burton, Gabrielle. "People Who Listen to Voices End Up in the Loony Bin (Written before WL)." *Women: A Journal of Liberation* 2 (1971): 48.

"Butter Balls." *off our backs.* 1, no. 13 (Nov. 8, 1970): 8–9.

CWLU Herstory. Official Web site. <http://www.cwluherstory.com>. Accessed June 8, 2003.

Callaghan, Dympna. "The Aesthetics of Marginality: The Theatre of Joan Littlewood and Buzz Goodbody." In *Theatre and Feminist Aesthetics,* edited by Karen

Laughlin and Catherine Schuler, 258–85. Madison, Wisc.: Fairleigh Dickinson University Press, 1995.

Canning, Charlotte. *Feminist Theaters in the U.S.A.: Staging Women's Experience.* New York: Routledge, 1996.

Carden, Maren Lockwood. *The New Feminist Movement.* New York: Sage, 1974.

Caywood, Cynthia, and Gillian Overing. *Teaching Writing: Pedagogy, Gender, and Equity.* Albany: State University of New York Press, 1987.

Cenker. "She's Young but She Has the Makings of a Good Box." *Women: A Journal of Liberation* 2, no. 1 (Fall 1970): 24.

Certeau, Michel de. *The Practice of Everyday Life.* Trans. Steven Rendall. Berkeley: University of California Press, 1984.

Chalmers, David. *And the Crooked Places Made Straight: The Struggle for Social Change in the 1960s.* Baltimore, Md.: Johns Hopkins University Press, 1991.

Chapman, Frances. Review of *Dykes for an Amerikan Revolution. off our backs* 2, no. 2 (Oct. 1971): 35.

Chartier, Roger. *On the Edge of the Cliff: History, Language, and Practices.* Trans. Lydia G. Cochrane. Baltimore, Md.: Johns Hopkins University Press, 1997.

———. *The Order of Books.* Stanford, Calif.: Stanford University Press, 1994.

———. *Publishing Drama in Early Modern Europe.* London: British Library, 1999.

"Chicago Liberation School for Women."In *The New Woman's Survival Catalog: A Woman-Made Book,* edited by Kirsten Grimstad and Susan Rennie, 124. New York: Coward, McCann, and Geoghegan, 1973.

Chmaj, Betty. "American Women and American Studies."In *The New Woman's Survival Catalog: A Woman-Made Book,* edited by Kirsten Grimstad and Susan Rennie, 136. New York: Coward, McCann, and Geoghegan, 1973.

"Circle One." *Big Mama Rag* 3-A, no. 4 (May 1975): 10.

Clark, Kenneth B. *Dark Ghetto: Dilemmas of Social Power.* New York: Harper and Row, 1965.

Clark, Michele. "Concerning Certain Sentiments." *off our backs* 1, no. 3 (Apr. 11, 1970): 13.

Clausen, Jan. *A Movement of Poets: Thoughts on Poetry and Feminism.* Brooklyn: Long Haul, 1982.

Cleaver, Kathleen. Interview. *Woman's World* 4 (Mar.–May 1972): 20–21.

Cmiel, Kenneth. "The Politics of Civility." In *The Sixties,* edited by David Farber, 263–90. Chapel Hill: University of North Carolina Press, 1994.

Code, Lorraine. *Rhetorical Spaces: Essays on Gendered Locations.* New York: Routledge, 1995.

Codrescu, Andrei. "Newspapers and Poetry." *All Things Considered.* Radio Broadcast. National Public Radio, July 24, 2001.

Coider, Brenda. Untitled. *Women: A Journal of Liberation* 2, no. 2 (1971): 32.

Colburn, David, and George Pozzetta. "Race, Ethnicity, and the Evolution of Political Legitimacy." In *The Sixties,* edited by David Farber, 119–48. Chapel Hill: University of North Carolina Press, 1994.

"Comments on Elitism." *Ain't I a Woman* 1, no. 2 (July 10, 1970): 10.

Cooke, Joanne, Charlotte Bunch, and Robin Morgan, eds. *The New Women: A MOTIVE Anthology on Women's Liberation.* Indianapolis: Bobbs-Merrill, 1970.

Corbett, Edward. *Classical Rhetoric for the Modern Student.* 3d. ed. New York: Oxford University Press, 1990.

Covintree, Winifred. "you sing a song to yourself." *Moving Out* 2, no. 1 (1972): 93.

Cruz, Sor Juana Inés de la. "Roundelays." *Woman's World* 4, no. 1 (Mar.–May 1972): 15.

Curb, Rosemary, Phyllis Mael, and Beverley Byers Pevitts. "Catalog of Feminist Theater—Part II." *Chrysalis* 10 (1979): 63–75.

Damon, Gene. "The Least of These." In *Sisterhood is Powerful,* edited by Robin Morgan, 297–306. New York: Vintage, 1970.

Davis, Angela. "Facing Our Common Foe: Women and the Struggle against Racism." *Women, Culture, and Politics,* 16–34. New York: Vintage, 1990.

"Dear Sisters." *off our backs* 1, no. 1 (Feb. 1970): 2.

"A Decade of Publishing—with a Difference." *NewsNotes for the Feminist Press* 9 (Fall 1980): 1.

"Dedication." *Big Mama Rag* 1, no. 1 (n.d. [Oct. 1972]): 1.

Dell'Olio, Anselma. "The Founding of the New Feminist Theatre." In *Notes from the Second Year: Women's Liberation,* edited by Shulamith Firestone and Anne Koedt, 101–2. New York: Notes, 1970.

———. "*In the Shadow of the Crematoria:* An Introduction." In *Women's Liberation: A Blueprint for the Future,* edited by Sookie Stambler, 240–43. New York: Ace, 1970.

"Denver Women's Theatre." Advertisement. *Big Mama Rag* 1, no. 2 (n.d.): 1.

Diamond, Elin. "(In)Visible Bodies in Churchill's Theater." In *Making a Spectacle,* edited by Lynda Hart, 259–81. Ann Arbor: University of Michigan Press, 1989.

Dixon, Marlene. *Why Women's Liberation?* Ithaca, N.Y.: Glad Day, n.d.

Dolega, Chris Lahey. "When My Dude Walked Out the Door." *Moving Out* 2, no. 1 (1972): 82.

Douglass, Frederick. *Narrative of the Life of Frederick Douglass: An American Slave, Written by Himself.* Edited by David Blight. Boston: Bedford, 1993.

DuPlessis, Rachel Blau. *Genders, Races, and Religious Cultures in Modern American Poetry, 1908–1934.* Cambridge, Mass.: Cambridge University Press, 2001.

———, Linda Edwards, Ann Harris, Kate Millett, and Harriet Zellner. "Columbia Women's Liberation." *The Radical Teacher* 2 (Dec. 30, 1969): 29–35.

———, and Ann Snitow. *The Feminist Memoir Project: Voices from Women's Liberation.* New York: Three Rivers, 1998.

"Earth Onion Theatre Group Scrapbook." *off our backs* 2, no. 2 (Oct. 1971): 1–5.

"Earth Onion, a Woman's Improvisational Theatre Group." *off our backs* 1, no. 22 (May 27, 1971): 19.

Echols, Alice. *Daring to Be Bad: Radical Feminism in America, 1967–1975.* Minneapolis: University of Minnesota Press, 1989.

———. "Nothing Distant about It: Women's Liberation and Sixties Radicalism." In *The Sixties: From Memory to History,* edited by David Farber, 149–74. Chapel Hill: University of North Carolina Press, 1994.

———. "The Radical Feminist Movement in the United States, 1967–75." Ph.D. diss., University of Michigan, 1986.

———. *Shaky Ground: The '60s and Its Aftershocks.* New York: Columbia University Press, 2002.

Editorial. *Ain't I a Woman* 1, no. 1 (June 26, 1970): 2.

Editorial. *Ain't I a Woman* 1, no. 3 (July 1970): 2.

Editorial. *Big Mama Rag* 1, no. 3 (n.d. [1973?]): 2.

Editorial. *Mother Lode* 4 (Spring 1972): 1.

Editorial. *Women: A Journal of Liberation* 2, no. 2 (Winter 1971): 1, 65.

Ehrenreich, Barbara, and Deirdre English. *Complaints and Disorders: The Sexual Politics of Sickness.* Glass Mountain Pamphlet no. 2. Old Westbury, N.Y.: Feminist Press, n.d.

———. *Witches, Midwives, and Nurses: A History of Women Healers.* Glass Mountain Pamphlet no. 1. Old Westbury, N.Y.: Feminist Press, 1973.

Eichhorn, Jill, et al. "A Symposium on Feminist Experiences in the Composition Classroom." *College Composition and Communication* 43 (1992): 297–322.

EnDean-Conner, Cynthia. "Filing Clerk." *Woman Becoming* 2, no. 1 (Feb. 1974): 14.

Epstein, Barbara. "Ambivalence about Feminism." In *The Feminist Memoir Project: Voices from Women's Liberation,* edited by Rachel Blau DuPlessis and Ann Snitow, 124–48. New York: Three Rivers, 1998.

Estellachild, Vivian. "Hippie Communes." *Women: A Journal of Liberation* 2, no. 2 (Winter 1971): 40–43.

Evans, Sara. *Personal Politics: The Roots of Women's Liberation in the Civil Rights Movement and the New Left.* New York: Knopf, 1979.

———. "Women's History and Political Theory: Toward a Feminist Approach to Public Life." In *Visible Women: New Essays on American Activism,* edited by Nancy A. Hewitt and Suzanne Lebsock, 119–39. Urbana: University of Illinois Press, 1993.

Faderman, Lillian. *To Believe in Women: What Lesbians Have Done for America.* New York: Houghton Mifflin, 1999.

Faigley, Lester. *Fragments of Rationality: Postmodernity and the Subject of Composition.* Pittsburgh, Pa.: University of Pittsburgh Press, 1992.

Farber, David. *The Age of Great Dreams: America in the 1960s.* New York: Hill and Wang, 1994.

———, and Beth Bailey. *The Columbia Guide to America in the 1960s.* New York: Columbia, 2001.

Feminist Press. *NewsNotes* 2 (June 1972): n.p.

"Feminist Women's Health Centers." In *The New Woman's Survival Catalog: A Woman-Made Book,* edited by Kirsten Grimstad and Susan Rennie, 71–73. New York: Coward, McCann, and Geoghegan, 1973.

Ferlinghetti, Lawrence. "I Am Waiting." *A Coney Island of the Mind*, 48–53. New York: New Directions, 1958.

Firestone, Shulamith, and Anne Koedt. Editorial. In *Notes from the Second Year: Women's Liberation*, edited by Firestone and Koedt, 2. New York: Notes, 1970.

———. Editorial. In *Notes from the Third Year: Women's Liberation*, edited by Firestone and Koedt, 2. New York: Notes, 1971.

Fitzsimmons, Linda. "Archiving, Documenting, and Teaching Women's Theatre Work." In *The Routledge Reader in Gender and Performance*, edited by Lizbeth Goodman, 113–17. New York: Routledge, 1998.

Flannery, Kathryn. "Performance and the Limits of Writing." *Journal of Teaching Writing* 16 (1998): 43–73.

Forte, Jeanie. "Women's Performance Art: Feminism and Postmodernism." In *Performing Feminisms: Feminist Critical Theory and Theatre*, edited by Sue-Ellen Case, 251–69. Baltimore, Md.: Johns Hopkins University Press, 1990.

Frazier, E. Franklin. *The Negro Family in the United States*. Chicago: University of Chicago Press, 1939.

"'Freedom' to Oppress?" *Ain't I a Woman* 1, no. 2 (July 10, 1970): 5.

Freeman, Jo [Joreen]. "The Bitch Manifesto." In *Notes from the Second Year: Women's Liberation*, edited by Shulamith Firestone and Anne Koedt, 5–9. New York: Notes, 1970.

———. *The Politics of Women's Liberation: A Case Study of an Emerging Social Movement and Its Relation to the Policy Process*. New York: David McKay, 1975.

———. *The Women's Liberation Movement: Its Origins, Structures, and Ideas*. Pittsburgh, Pa.: KNOW, 1971.

Friedman, Susan Stanford. "Making History: Reflections on Feminism, Narrative, and Desire." In *Feminism beside Itself*, edited by Diane Elam and Robyn Wiegman, 11–53. New York: Routledge, 1995.

Gabriel, Susan, and Isaiah Smithson. *Gender in the Classroom*. Urbana: University of Illinois Press, 1990.

Garver, Paul. "Who We Are." In *The Counter-Culture Joins the Faculty*, 22–28. Cambridge, Mass.: Church Society for College Work, 1971.

Geller, Ruth. Untitled sketch. *Women: A Journal of Liberation* 2, no. 2 (Winter 1971): 19.

Gender Issues Research Center. "Marriage, Divorce and Remarriage in the United States." <http://www.gendercenter.org>. Accessed April 29, 2003.

Gere, Anne. *Intimate Practices: Literacy and Cultural Work in U.S. Women's Clubs, 1880–1920*. Urbana: University of Illinois Press, 1997.

Gilmore, Leigh. *Autobiographics: A Feminist Theory of Women's Self-Representation*. Ithaca, N.Y.: Cornell University Press, 1994.

Glixon, Lynn. "To Earth Onion." *off our backs* 2, no. 2 (Oct. 1971): 25.

González, Yoland Broyles. "Toward a Re-Vision of Chicano Theatre History: The Women of El Teatro Campesino." In *Making a Spectacle*, edited by Lynda Hart, 209–38. Ann Arbor: University of Michigan Press, 1989.

Gore, Jennifer. *The Struggle for Pedagogies: Critical and Feminist Discourses as Regimes of Truth.* New York: Routledge, 1993.

———. "What we can do for you! What *can* 'we' do for 'you'?: Struggling over Empowerment in Critical and Feminist Pedagogy." In *Feminisms and Critical Pedagogy,* edited by Carmen Luke and Jennifer Gore, 54–73. New York: Routledge, 1992.

Graff, Harvey. "Literacy, Jobs, and Industrialization: The Nineteenth Century." In *Literacy and Social Development in the West: A Reader,* edited by Graff, 232–60. Cambridge: Cambridge University Press, 1981.

Graham, Kenneth. *The Performance of Conviction: Plainness and Rhetoric in the Early English Renaissance.* Ithaca, N.Y.: Cornell University Press, 1994.

Grahn, Judy. "Carol, in the park, chewing on straws." *off our backs* 1, no. 11 (Sept. 30, 1970): 7.

Gramsci, Antonio. *Selections from the Prison Notebooks.* Edited by Quintin Hoare and Geoffrey Nowell Smith. New York: International, 1971.

Gray, Vernita M. "prose poem, a christmas card." In *Are We There Yet?* edited by Michal Brody, 74–75. Iowa City: Aunt Lute, 1985.

Grimstad, Kirsten, and Susan Rennie, eds. *The New Woman's Survival Catalog: A Woman-Made Book.* New York: Coward, McCann, and Geoghegan, 1973.

Grotowski, Jerzy. *Towards a Poor Theatre.* New York: Simon and Schuster, 1968.

Guillory, John. *Cultural Capital: The Problem of Literary Canon Formation.* Chicago: University of Chicago Press, 1993.

Guy-Sheftall, Beverly. *Words of Fire: An Anthology of African-American Feminist Thought.* New York: New Press, 1995.

———. "Sisters in Struggle: A Belated Response." In *The Feminist Memoir Project: Voices from Women's Liberation,* edited by Rachel Blau DuPlessis and Ann Snitow, 485–92. New York: Three Rivers.

Hall, Anne Drury. *Ceremony and Civility in English Renaissance Prose.* University Park: Pennsylvania State University Press, 1991.

Hamann, Sally. "poem." *Ain't I a Woman* 1, no. 2 (July 10, 1970): 5.

"Hang Up." *Ain't I a Woman* 1, no. 1 (June 26, 1970): 2.

Hanisch, Carol. "The Personal Is Political." In *Notes from the Second Year: Women's Liberation,* edited by Shulamith Firestone and Anne Koedt, 76–77. New York: Notes, 1970.

Haraway, Donna. "A Manifesto for Cyborgs." In *Feminism/Postmodernism,* edited by Linda Nicholson, 190–233. New York: Routledge, 1990.

Review of *Harper's Bizarre. Big Mama Rag* 2, no. 7 (May 1974): 8.

Harrington, Michael. *The Long-Distance Runner: An Autobiography.* New York: Henry Holt, 1988.

Hart, Lynda. "Performing Feminism." In *Making a Spectacle: Feminist Essays on Contemporary Women's Theatre,* edited by Hart, 1–21. Ann Arbor: University of Michigan Press, 1989.

Heath, Shirley Brice. "Protean Shapes in Literacy Events: Ever-Shifting Oral and Literate Traditions." In *Perspectives on Literacy,* edited by Eugene Kintgen, Barry Kroll, and Mike Rose, 348–70. Carbondale: Southern Illinois University Press, 1988.

Heilbrun, Carolyn G. *The Education of a Woman: The Life of Gloria Steinem.* New York: Dial, 1995.

Heyn, Leah. "Challenging to Become a Doctor: The Story of Elizabeth Blackwell." Part 4. *Women: A Journal of Liberation* 2, no. 2 (Winter 1971): center insert.

"High School Women and Health." *Mother Lode* 4 (Spring 1972): 10.

Hobbs, Chris. Review of *Our Bodies Ourselves. off our backs* 3, no. 8 (May 1973): 29.

Hogeland, Lisa Maria. *Feminism and Its Fictions: The Consciousness-Raising Novel and the Women's Liberation Movement.* Philadelphia: University of Pennsylvania Press, 1998.

Holden, Joan. "The Independent Female (or, A Man Has His Pride)." In *Notes from the Third Year: Women's Liberation,* edited by Shulamith Firestone and Anne Koedt, 120–31. New York: Notes, 1971.

Hole, Judith, and Ellen Levine. *Rebirth of Feminism.* New York: Quadrangle, 1971.

hooks, bell. *Ain't I a Woman: Black Women and Feminism.* Boston: South End, 1981.

———. "Black Women: Shaping Feminist Theory." *Feminist Theory: From Margin to Center,* 1–15. Boston: South End, 1984.

———. "Educating Women: A Feminist Agenda." *Feminist Theory: From Margin to Center,* 107–15. Boston: South End, 1984.

House, Gloria Larry. "Woman." *Moving Out* 2, no. 1 (1972):60.

"How to Get Hooked: Your Family Doctor as Pusher." *Mother Lode* 4 (Spring 1972): 12.

Howe, Florence, and Carol Ahlum. "Women's Studies and Social Change." In *Academic Women on the Move,* edited by Alice Rossi and Ann Calderwood, 393–423. New York: Sage, 1973.

Howe, Florence, and Paul Lauter. "From the Editors." *The Radical Teacher* (Dec. 30, 1969): n.p.

Hunter, Mary Ann. "No Safety Gear: Skate Girl Space and the Regeneration of Australian Community-Based Performance." In *Performing Democracy: International Perspectives on Urban Community-Based Performance,* edited by Susan C. Haedicke and Tobin Nellhaus, 326–40. Ann Arbor: University of Michigan Press, 2001.

Huse, Donna. "Women's Liberation and the Politics of Evolution." In *The Counter-Culture Joins the Faculty,* 44–53. Cambridge, Mass.: Church Society for College Work, 1971.

Ikeler, Ruth. "A Note to William Wordsworth." *Women: A Journal of Liberation* 2, no. 1 (Fall 1970): 17.

Index for the First Five Years, 1970–1974. *off our backs.*

Jaggar, Alison, ed. *Living with Contradictions: Controversies in Feminist Ethics.* Boulder, Colo.: Westview, 1994.

———, and Susan Bordo, eds. *Gender/Body/Knowledge: Feminist Reconstructions of Being and Knowing.* New Brunswick, N.J.: Rutgers University Press, 1992.

Janeway, Elizabeth. “Women’s Literature.” In *Harvard Guide to Contemporary American Writing,* edited by Daniel Hoffman, 342–95. Cambridge, Mass.: Harvard University Press, 1979.

Johnson, Nan. *Gender and Rhetorical Space in American Life, 1866–1910.* Carbondale: Southern Illinois University Press, 2002.

Johnston, Jill. “Priorities*.” *off our backs* 2, no. 2 (Oct. 1971): 25.

Jones, Beverly, and Judith Brown. *Toward a Female Liberation Movement.* Boston: New England Free Press, 1968.

Jones, Kathleen B. “On Authority: or, Why Women are not Entitled to Speak.” In *Feminism and Foucault: Reflections on Resistance,* edited by Irene Diamond and Lee Quinby, 119–33. Boston: Northeastern University Press, 1988.

Kaplan, Laura. *The Story of Jane: The Legendary Underground Feminist Abortion Service.* Chicago: University of Chicago Press, 1995.

Kates, Susan. *Activist Rhetorics and American Higher Education, 1885–1937.* Carbondale: Southern Illinois University Press, 2001.

Kearon, Pamela. “Power as a Function of the Group.” In *Notes from the Second Year: Women’s Liberation,* edited by Shulamith Firestone and Anne Koedt, 108–10. New York: Notes, 1970.

Kennedy, Florynce. “A Comparative Study: Accentuating the Similarities of the Societal Position of Women and Negroes.” In *Words of Fire: An Anthology of African American Feminist Thought,* edited by Beverly Guy-Sheftall, 102–6. New York: New Press, 1995.

Kenway, Jane, and Helen Modra. “Feminist Pedagogy and Emancipatory Possibilities.” In *Feminisms and Critical Pedagogy,* edited by Carmen Luke and Jennifer Gore, 138–66. New York: Routledge, 1992.

Kessler, Lauren. *The Dissident Press: Alternative Journalism in American History.* Beverly Hills, Calif.: Sage, 1984.

Keyssar, Helene. *Feminist Theatre: An Introduction to Plays of Contemporary British and American Women.* New York: Grove, 1985.

Knoblauch, C. H., and Lil Brannon. *Critical Teaching and the Idea of Literacy.* Portsmouth, N.H.: Boynton/Cook, 1993.

Koedt, Anne. “Lesbianism and Feminism.” In *Notes from the Third Year: Women’s Liberation,* edited by Shulamith Firestone and Anne Koedt, 84–89. New York: Notes, 1971.

Kreps, Bonnie. “The ‘New Feminist’ Analysis.” In *Notes from the Second Year: Women’s Liberation,* edited by Shulamith Firestone and Anne Koedt, 98–100. New York: Notes, 1970.

Kuumba, M. Bahati. *Gender and Social Movements.* Walnut Creek, Calif.: Altamira, 2001.

LaCapra, Dominick. *History and Criticism.* Ithaca, N.Y.: Cornell University Press, 1985.

Lakin, Martin. *Interpersonal Encounter: Theory and Practice of Sensitivity Training.* New York: McGraw-Hill, 1972.

Lamb, Myrna. *The Mod Donna and Scyklon Z: Plays of Women's Liberation.* New York: Merit, 1971.
La Rue, Linda. "The Black Movement and Women's Liberation." In *Words of Fire: An Anthology of African-American Feminist Thought,* edited by Beverly Guy-Sheftall, 164–73. New York: New Press, 1995.
Lawrence, Patricia. "Women Take Catholic Church to Court." *Woman's World* 1, no. 2 (July–Aug. 1971): 4–5.
Leavitt, Dinah Luise. *Feminist Theatre Groups.* Jefferson, N.C.: McFarland, 1980.
Leon, Barbara. "Let's Hear from the Quiet Women." *Woman's World* 1, no. 2 (July–Sept. 1972): 13.
"Letter to Dr. Phillip Goldstein." *Mother Lode* 4 (Spring 1972): 11.
"Letter to Our Contributors." *Women: A Journal of Liberation* 2, no. 1 (Fall 1970): inside back cover.
Levertov, Denise. *The Poet in the World.* New York: New Directions, 1973.
Lindsey, Kay. "Poem." In *Black Woman,* edited by Toni Cade Bambara, 17. New York: Signet, 1970.
"Living Stage." *off our backs* 1, no. 23 (June 24, 1971): 8–9.
Loesch, Juli. "Hitch." *Woman Becoming* 2, no. 1 (Feb. 1974): 67.
Lonidier, Lynn. *The Female Freeway.* San Francisco: Tenth Muse, 1970.
———. *The Rhyme of the Ag-ed Mariness: The Last Poems of Lynn Lonidier.* Edited by Janine Canan. Barrytown, N.Y.: Station Hill, 2001.
Lowell, Sondra. "Art Comes to the Elevator: Women's Guerrilla Theater." *Women: A Journal of Liberation* 2, no. 1 (Fall 1970): 50–51.
Lowenfels, Walter. "What Time Is It?" *The Writing on the Wall: 108 American Poems of Protest,* n.p. Garden City, N.Y.: Doubleday, 1969.
Luke, Carmen, ed. *Feminisms and Pedagogies of Everday Life.* Albany: State University of New York Press, 1996.
Lyon, Janet. *Manifestoes: Provocations of the Modern.* Ithaca, N.Y.: Cornell University Press, 1999.
Malnig, Julie, and Lisa Merrill. Preface. *Women and Performance: A Journal of Feminist Theory* 6, no. 1 (1993): 5–8.
Mansnerus, Laura. "More Research, More Profits, More Conflict." *New York Times* 22 June 1977, sec. 14.
Marsden, Karen. "plastic wrinkle war." *Woman Becoming.* 2, no. 1 (Feb. 1974): 11–12.
Martin, Jane Roland. *Coming of Age in Academe: Rekindling Women's Hopes and Reforming the Academy.* New York: Routledge, 2000.
Mather, Anne. "A History of Feminist Periodicals, Part I." *Journalism History* 1, no. 3 (1974): 82–88.
———. "A History of Feminist Periodicals, Part II." *Journalism History* 1, no. 4 (Winter 1974–75): 108–11.
———. "A History of Feminist Periodicals, Part III." *Journalism History* 2, no. 1 (1975): 19–23.

Mattingly, Carol. *Well-Tempered Women: Nineteenth-Century Temperance Rhetoric.* Carbondale: Southern Illinois University Press, 1998.
McAfee, Kathy, and Myrna Wood. *What Is the Revolutionary Potential of Women's Liberation?* Boston: New England Free Press, 1969.
McDermott, Patrice. *Politics and Scholarship: Feminist Academic Journals and the Production of Knowledge.* Urbana: University of Illinois Press, 1994.
McDonald, Christie. "Personal Criticism: Dialogue of Differences." In *Feminism beside Itself,* edited by Diane Elam and Robyn Wiegman, 237–59. New York: Routledge, 1995.
McLaughlin, Robert L. "Oppositional Aesthetics/Oppositional Ideologies: A Brief Cultural History of Alternative Publishing in the United States." *Critique: Studies in Contemporary Fiction* 37 (1996): 171–86.
McLuhan, Marshall, and Quentin Fiore. *The Medium Is the Massage: An Inventory of Effects.* San Francisco: Hardwired, 1967; repr, 1999.
Mazanka, Ann. "Genesis According to Womens Liberation." *Moving Out* 2, no. 1 (1972): 72.
Meir, Golda. "Once in cabinet . . ." In *Notes from the Third Year: Women's Liberation,* edited by Shulamith Firestone and Anne Koedt, 43. New York: Notes, 1971.
Meredith, Robert. "Subverting Culture." *The Radical Teacher* 2 (Dec. 30, 1969): 5–8.
"A Method for the Movement." *Ain't I a Woman* 1, no. 3 (July 1970): 9.
Meyer, Elissa. "Big Mama Rag Born Out of Frustration, Success." *Big Mama Rag* 2, no. 7 (May 1974): 5.
Milton, John. *Areopagitica. Complete Poems and Major Prose,* edited by Merrit Hughes, 716–49. Indianapolis: Odyssey, 1957.
Morgan, Robin, ed. Introduction. *Sisterhood is Powerful: An Anthology of Writings from the Women's Liberation Movement.* New York: Vintage, 1970.
Morlock, Laura. "Discipline Variation in the Status of Academic Women." In *Academic Women on the Move,* edited by Alice Rossi and Ann Calderwood, 255–303. New York: Sage, 1973.
Morton, Donald, and Ma'sud Zavarzadeh, eds. *Theory/Pedagogy/Politics: Texts for Change.* Urbana: University of Illinois Press, 1991.
Moynihan, Daniel P. *Maximum Feasible Misunderstanding: Community Action in the War on Poverty.* New York: Free Press, 1970.
M'Rabet, Fadela. *La Femme algerienne.* Paris: Maspero, 1965.
Munday, Mildred Brand. "Women, Literature, and the Dynamics of the Classroom." In *Female Studies VIII,* edited by Sarah Slavin Schramm, 68–85. Pittsburgh: KNOW, 1975.
"My Tour Notes." *off our backs* 2, no. 2 (Oct. 1971): 4–5.
Natalle, Elizabeth J. *Feminist Theatre: A Study of Persuasion.* Metuchen, N.J.: Scarecrow, 1985.
Nelson, Cary. "The Fate of Gender in Modern American Poetry." In *Marketing*

Modernisms: Self-Promotion, Canonization, Rereading, edited by Kevin J. H. Dettmar and Stephen Watt, 321–60. Ann Arbor: University of Michigan Press, 1996.

———. *Revolutionary Memory: Recovering the Poetry of the American Left.* New York: Routledge, 2001.

"Newswomen at Work." *off our backs* 1, no. 17 (Feb. 12, 1971): 13.

New University Conference, Miami University Chapter. *The Gentle Revolution: A Call for Radical Reform.* N.p.: n.p, n.d.

Nord, David. "Reading the Newspaper: Strategies and Politics of Reader Response, Chicago, 1912–1917." Unpublished paper. Indiana University, 1993.

———. "Religious Reading and Readers in Antebellum America." Unpublished paper. Indiana University, 1993.

O'Connor, Lynn. "Defining Reality." *Tooth and Nail* (Oct. 1, 1969). Repr. in *Redstockings: First Literature List,* 35–38. Gainesville, Fla.: Restockings Archives Distribution Project, 2002.

O'Donnell, Ellen. "The Sullen Cameo." Untitled [later, *No More Fun and Games: A Journal of Female Liberation*] [Oct. 1968]: n.p.

———. "there are five senses." Untitled [later, *No More Fun and Games: A Journal of Female Liberation*] [Oct. 1968]: n.p.

Oleszek, Mary Jo. "The Science in Me." *Moving Out* 2, no. 1 (1972): 35.

Oller, Lorraine. *Variation on a Theme.* Graphic image. *Women: A Journal of Liberation* 2, no. 1 (1970): 58.

"On-Going Events." *Moving Out* 2, no. 1 (1972): 2.

O'Neill, Cicely. *Drama Worlds: A Framework of Process Drama.* Portsmouth, N.H.: Heinemann, 1995.

"Organizing Principles of the New York Radical Feminists." In *Notes from the Second Year: Women's Liberation,* edited by Shulamith Firestone and Anne Koedt, 119–22. New York: Notes, 1970.

Ortho-McNeil Pharmaceutical. "Oral Contraceptives: From Historical Evolution to Modern Revolution." <http://www.orthotri-cyclen.com/answer/birth_answers/history.html>. Accessed 2002.

Otter, Kay. "Our Health Is Up to Us." *Moving Out* 2, no. 1 (1972): 28–32.

Ozieblo, Barbara. *Susan Glaspell: A Critical Biography.* Chapel Hill: University of North Carolina Press, 2000.

Patton, Gwen. "Black People and the Victorian Ethos." In *The Black Woman: An Anthology,* edited by Toni Cade Bambara, 143–48. New York: Signet, 1970.

Payne, Carol. "Consciousness Raising: A Dead End?" In *Notes from the Third Year: Women's Liberation,* edited by Shulamith Firestone and Anne Koedt, 99–100. New York: Notes, 1971.

Peck, Abe. *Uncovering the Sixties: The Life and Times of the Underground Press.* New York: Pantheon, 1985.

Perreault, Jeanne. *Writing Selves: Contemporary Feminist Autography.* Minneapolis: University of Minnesota Press, 1995.

Personal Narratives Group. *Interpreting Women's Lives: Feminist Theory and Personal Narratives.* Bloomington: Indiana University Press, 1989.

Peslikis, Irene. "Resistances to Consciousness." In *Notes from the Second Year: Women's Liberation,* edited by Shulamith Firestone and Anne Koedt, 81. New York: Notes, 1970.

Piercy, Marge. "Burying Blues for Janis." *off our backs* 2, no. 3 (Nov. 1971): centerfold.

———. *Early Grrl: The Early Poems.* Wellfleet, Mass.: Leapfrog, 1999.

———. "The Grand Coolie Damn." In *Sisterhood is Powerful,* edited by Robin Morgan, 421–38. New York: Vintage, 1970.

PM3: The Women's Movement, Where It's At. Tallahassee: Florida Free Press, 1971.

"Polemic." *American Heritage Dictionary.* 2d college ed. 1985.

"Polemic." *Oxford English Dictionary.* Compact ed. 1971.

Polletta, Francesca. *Freedom Is an Endless Meeting: Democracy in American Social Movements.* Chicago: University of Chicago Press, 2002.

Price, Colette. "Developing Feminist Theory: Consciousness-Raising." *Woman's World* 1, no. 2 (July–Sept. 1972): 10–12.

Probyn, Elspeth. "Travels in the Postmodern: Making Sense of the Local." In *Feminism/Postmodernism,* edited by Linda Nicholson, 176–89. New York: Routledge, 1990.

Radicalesbians. "The Woman Identified Woman." In *Notes from the Third Year: Women's Liberation,* edited by Shulamith Firestone and Anne Koedt, 81–84. New York: Notes, 1971.

Rea, Charlotte. "Women for Women." *Drama Review* 18, no. 4 (1974): 77–87.

———. "Women's Theatre Groups." *Drama Review* 16, no. 2 (1972): 79–89.

Read, Alan. *Theatre and Everyday Life: An Ethics of Performance.* New York: Routledge, 1993.

Reisig, Robin. "Holy Mother of Ireland! It's the Feminists!" In *Women's Liberation: Blueprint for the Future,* edited by Sookie Stambler, 227–30. New York: Ace, 1970.

Reynolds, Nedra. "Ethos as Location: New Sites for Understanding Discursive Authority." *Rhetoric Review* 11 (1993): 325–38.

Rich, Adrienne. "Blood, Bread, and Poetry: The Location of the Poet." *Blood, Bread, and Poetry: Selected Prose, 1979–1985,* 167–87. New York: Norton, 1986.

———. Foreword. *Blood, Bread, and Poetry,* vii–xiv. New York: Norton, 1986.

———. "Compulsory Heterosexuality and Lesbian Experience." *Blood, Bread, and Poetry,* 23–75. New York: Norton, 1986.

———. "Notes toward a Politics of Location." *Blood, Bread, and Poetry,* 210–31. New York: Norton, 1986.

———. "Power and Danger: Works of a Common Woman." *On Lies, Secrets, and Silence: Selected Prose 1966–1978,* 247–58. New York: Norton, 1979.

———. "Toward a More Feminist Criticism." *Blood, Bread, and Poetry: Selected Prose, 1979–1985,* 85–99. New York: Norton, 1986.

———. "Toward a Woman-Centered University." *On Lies, Secrets, and Silence: Selected Prose 1966–1978,* 125–55. New York: Norton, 1979.

Riley, Glenda. *Inventing the American Woman.* Arlington Heights, Ill.: Harlan Davidson, 1987.

Rimer, Sara. "They Talked and Talked, and Then Wrote a Classic." *New York Times* 22 June 1997, sec. 14, p. 27.

"Rising Up Together." *Ain't I a Woman* 1, no. 2 (July 10, 1970): 2.

Roberts, Joan I. "A Multi-faceted Approach to a Women's Studies Course: Using a Little to Accomplish a Lot." In *Female Studies VIII,* edited by Sarah Slavin Schramm, 86–106. Pittsburgh, Pa.: KNOW, 1975.

Robinson, Lora. *Women's Studies: Courses and Programs for Higher Education.* ERIC Higher Education Report 1. Washington, D.C.: American Association of Higher Education, 1973.

Robinson, Patricia. "Dear Brothers." *Lilith* (Fall 1968): 7–10.

———, and Group. "A Historical and Critical Essay for Black Women in the Cities, June 1969." In *The Black Woman: An Anthology,* edited by Toni Cade Bambara, 198–210. New York: Signet, 1970.

Roof, Judith, and Robyn Wiegman. *Who Can Speak? Authority and Critical Identity.* Urbana: University of Illinois Press, 1995.

Rosga, AnnJanette, and Meg Satterthwaite. "Notes from the Aftermath." In *The Feminist Memoir Project,* edited by Rachel Blau DuPlessis and Ann Snitow, 469–76. New York: Three Rivers, 1998.

Roth, Benita. "The Making of the Vanguard Center: Black Feminist Emergence in the 1960s and 1970s." In *Still Lifting, Still Climbing: African American Women's Contemporary Activism,* edited by Kimberly Springer, 70–90. New York: New York University Press, 1999.

Royster, Jacqueline Jones. *Traces of the Stream: Literacy and Social Change among African American Women.* Pittsburgh, Pa.: University of Pittsburgh Press, 2000.

Rukeyser, Muriel. *The Life of Poetry.* Edited by Jane Cooper. New York: Paris, 1996.

Russell, Michele. "Some Notes Toward a Radical Course in Black Literature." *The Radical Teacher* 2 (Dec. 30, 1960): 1–3.

Ryan, Maureen. "Classrooms and Contexts: The Challenge of Feminist Pedagogy." *Feminist Teacher.* 4, nos. 2–3 (1989): 39–42.

Saiving, Valerie C. "Androgynous Life: A Feminist Appropriation of Process Thought." In *Feminism and Process Thought,* edited by Sheila Greeve Davaney, 11–31. New York: Edwin Mellen, 1981.

Salvatori, Mariolina, ed. *Pedagogy: Disturbing History, 1819–1929.* Pittsburgh, Pa.: University of Pittsburgh Press, 1996.

Sandel, Michael J. *Democracy's Discontents: America in Search of a Public Philosophy.* Cambridge, Mass.: Harvard University Press, 1996.

Sanders, Gerald DeWitt, et al., eds. "Edna St. Vincent Millay." *Chief Modern Poets of Britain and America,* 5th ed., 297–305. London: Macmillan, 1970.

Sandie. "later, ferlinghetti." *off our backs* 1, no. 13 (Nov. 8, 1970): cover.

San Francisco Women's Street Theater. "This Is a Cranky." In *Guerilla Street Theater,* edited by Henry Lesnick, 317–55. New York: Bard, 1973.

Sappho Collective. "Rapping in Small Groups: Perspectives on Consciousness-Raising. *Women: A Journal of Liberation* 2, no. 2 (Winter 1971): 49–50.

Sarachild, Kathie. "Consciousness-Raising: A Radical Weapon." *Feminist Revolution.* New Paltz, N.Y.: Redstockings, 1975.

———. "A Program for Feminist 'Consciousness Raising.'" In *Notes from the Second Year: Women's Liberation,* edited by Shulamith Firestone and Anne Koedt, 78–80. New York: Notes, 1970.

———. "Women and the Elections." *Woman's World* 3 (Nov–Dec. 1971): 1, 11.

Schramm, Sarah Slavin. "Do-It-Yourself: Women's Studies." In *Female Studies VIII,* edited by Schramm, 1–6. Pittsburgh, Pa.: KNOW, 1975.

Sealander, Judith, and Dorothy Smith. "The Rise and Fall of Feminist Organizations in the 1970s: Dayton as a Case Study." *Feminist Studies* 12 (1986): 321–41.

Shank, Theodore. "Political Theatre as Popular Entertainment." *Drama Review* 18, no. 1 (1974): 110–17.

Shuger, Debra. *Habits of Thought in the English Renaissance.* Berkeley: University of California Press, 1990.

"Slavery." Untitled [later, *No More Fun and Games: A Journal of Female Liberation*] [Oct. 1968]: n.p.

Socialist-Feminist Consciousness Raising Group. "DWL: A Time for Change." *Dayton Women's Liberation Newsletter* (Sept. 1974): n.p.

Solomon, Barbara Miller. *In the Company of Educated Women.* New Haven, Conn.: Yale University Press, 1985.

Spolin, Viola. *Improvisation for the Theater: A Handbook of Teaching and Directing Techniques.* Evanston, Ill.: Northwestern University Press, 1963.

Stambler, Sookie. Introduction. In *Women's Liberation: Blueprint for the Future,* edited by Stambler, 9–12. New York: ACE, 1970.

Stone, Paula. "A Quarter Century Retrospect." *Moving Out* 2 (1972): 43.

Sugrue, Thomas J. *The Origins of the Urban Crisis: Race and Inequality in Postwar Detroit.* Princeton, N.J.: Princeton University Press, 1996.

Sullivan, James. *On the Walls and in the Streets: American Poetry Broadsides from the 1960s.* Urbana: University of Illinois Press, 1997.

Sweet, Jeffrey. *Something Wonderful Right Away.* New York: Discus, 1978.

Tanenhaus, Beverly. *To Know Each Other and Be Known: Women's Workshops.* Pittsburgh, Pa.: Motheroot, 1978; rept, 1982.

Tax, Meredith. "there was a young woman who swallowed a line." *off our backs* 1, no. 2 (Mar. 19, 1970): 10.

———. "Woman and Her Mind: The Story of Everyday Life." In *Notes from the Second Year: Women's Liberation,* edited by Shulamith Firestone and Anne Koedt, 10–16. New York: Notes, 1970.

Taylor, Verta, and Leila J. Rupp. "Lesbian Existence and the Women's Movement: Researching the 'Lavender Herring.'" In *Feminism and Social Change: Bridging Theory and Practice,* edited by Heidi Gottfried, 143–159. Urbana: University of Illinois Press, 1996.

Terr, Lyndia B. "Child in Pelvic Cup." *Moving Out* 2, no. 1 (1972): 33.

Tobias, Sheila. *Faces of Feminism: An Activist's Reflections on the Women's Movement.* Boulder, Colo.: Westview, 1997.

"Towards a Poor Theatre." *The Last Whole Earth Catalog: Access to Tools.* Menlo Park, Calif.: Portola Institute, 1971.

Tribble, Evelyn. "The Peopled Page: Polemic, Confutation, and Foxe's *Book of Martyrs.*" In *The Iconic Page in Manuscript, Print, and Digital Culture,* edited by George Bornstein and Theresa Tinkle, 109–22. Ann Arbor: University of Michigan Press, 1998.

Tripp, Maggie. "The Changing Consciousness and Conscience of Women—Liberation How?" In *Female Studies VIII,* edited by Sarah Slavin Schramm, 54–60. Pittsburgh, Pa.: KNOW, 1975.

United States Census Bureau. "Historical Income Tables—People." Table P-24. <http://www.census.gov/hhes/income/histinc/p40.html>.

United States Department of Education. "Title IX: 25 Years of Progress." <http://www.ed.gov/pubs/TitleIX/title.html>. Accessed June 9, 1997.

———. "Title IX and Sex Discrimination." <http://www.ed.gov/offices/OCR/docs/tix_dis.html>. Accessed Aug. 1998.

University of Maryland. "Women's Studies Proposal." In *Female Studies VIII,* edited by Sarah Slavin Schramm, 184–94. Pittsburgh: KNOW, 1975.

Vickers, Brian. *In Defence of Rhetoric.* Oxford: Clarendon, 1988.

Walsh, Joseph. "New Consciousness as New Blood: An Introduction and an Interpretation." In *The Counter-Culture Joins the Faculty,* 3–12. Cambridge, Mass.: Church Society for College Work, 1971.

"Wanted: Copy." *off our backs* 1, no. 2 (Mar. 19, 1970): 11.

Warren, Robert Penn. "Mortmain." In *Poet's Choice,* edited by Paul Engle and Joseph Landland, 72–79. New York: Time, 1966.

Ware, Cellestine. *Woman Power.* New York: Tower, 1970.

Watson, Steven. *The Birth of the Beat Generation: Visionaries, Rebels, and Hipsters, 1944–1960.* New York: Pantheon, 1995.

Weathers, Mary Ann. "An Argument for Black Women's Liberation as a Revolutionary Force." In *Women's Liberation: Blueprint for the Future,* edited by Sookie Stambler, 161–65. New York: Ace, 1970.

Webb, Marilyn. Untitled. *off our backs* 10, no. 2 (Feb. 1980): 5, 33.

Weiler, Kathleen. *Women Teaching for Change: Gender, Class, and Power.* Critical Studies in Education Series. South Hadley, Mass.: Bergin and Garvey, 1988.

"Where We're At." *Big Mama Rag* 2, no. 8 (June 1974): 9.

"Where We're At." *Big Mama Rag* 3, no. 3 (Sept. 1974): 16.

"Where We're At." *Big Mama Rag* 3-A:4 (June 1975): 4.

"Where We're At." *Big Mama Rag* 3-A:5 (July 1975): 4.
"Where We're At." *Big Mama Rag* 3-A:6 (July 1975): 2.
"Where We're At." *Big Mama Rag* 3-A:9 (Oct. 1975): 4.
Whitacre, Rodney. *Johannine Polemic: The Role of Tradition and Theology.* Chico, Calif.: Scholars, 1982.
Whitehead, Kim. *The Feminist Poetry Movement.* Jackson: University Press of Mississippi, 1996.
Williamson, Joseph. "Recruiting for Joshua." In *The Counter-Culture Joins the Faculty,* 39–43. Cambridge, Mass: Church Society for College Work, 1971.
"Witching the A.M.A." *Ain't I a Woman: A Midwest Newspaper of Women's Liberation* 1, no. 2 (July 10, 1970): 4.
"Womankind: Women for a Better Society." *Womankind: A Newspaper for Women* 1, no. 1: 1.
"A Woman's Reflections on Seeing Her Painted Sisters Hanging on a Museum Wall!" *Big Mama Rag* 1, no. 1: 6.
"Women Must Control Own Medical Destiny." *Big Mama Rag* 2, no. 7 (May 1974): 7, 11.
Women's Education Equity Association. "Title IX Before and After." *Resources to Infuse Equity.* WEEA Equity Resource Center. <http://www.edc.org/WomensEquity/resource/title9>. Accessed June 16, 2003.
"Women's History Research Center." In *Women's Survival Catalog,* edited by Kirsten Grimstad and Susan Rennie, 140–41. New York: Coward, 1973.
"Women's Political Caucus." *Big Mama Rag* 1, no. 3 (1973): 9.
Yates, Barbara. "Women and Health." In *We'll Do It Ourselves: Combatting Sexism in Education,* edited by Barbara Yates, Steve Werner, and David Rosen, 219–31. Lincoln: University of Nebraska, 1974.
Yosano Akiko. "The mountain-moving day is coming." *Woman's World* 1 (Apr. 15, 1971): n.p.
"Yurok Doctors." *Mother Lode* 4 (Spring 1972): 11.
Zinn, Howard. *A People's History of the United States.* New York: HarperCollins, 1990.

Index

KATHRYN T. FLANNERY is a professor of English and women's studies at the University of Pittsburgh, where she directs the Women's Studies Program. Professor Flannery is the author of *The Emperor's New Clothes: Literature, Literacy, and the Ideology of Style* (University of Pittsburgh Press, 1995), as well as articles about women's literacy practices from the early modern era to the present.

The University of Illinois Press
is a founding member of the
Association of American University Presses.

Composed in 10.5/13 Adobe Minion
at the University of Illinois Press
Designed by Dennis Roberts
Manufactured by Sheridan Books, Inc.

University of Illinois Press
1325 South Oak Street
Champaign, IL 61820-6903
www.press.uillinois.edu